Educational Transitions

Routledge Research in Education

Educational Transitions

Moving Stories from Around the World

Edited by Divya Jindal-Snape

Routledge
Taylor & Francis Group
New York   London

First published 2010
by Routledge
270 Madison Avenue, New York, NY 10016

Simultaneously published in the UK
by Routledge
2 Park Square, Milton Park, Abingdon, Oxon OX14 4RN

Routledge is an imprint of the Taylor & Francis Group, an informa business

© 2010 Taylor & Francis

Typeset in Sabon by IBT Global.
Printed and bound in the United States of America on acid-free paper by IBT Global.

Library of Congress Cataloging in Publication Data
Educational transitions : moving stories from around the world / edited by Divya Jindal-Snape.
    p. cm.—(Routledge research in education)
Includes bibliographical references and index.
1. Students, Transfer of.   2. Student adjustment.   I. Jindal-Snape, Divya.
LB3064.E38 2010
371.2'91—dc22
2009032282

ISBN10: 0-415-80591-0 (hbk)
ISBN10: 0-203-85912-X (eBk)

ISBN13: 978-0-415-80591-9 (hbk)
ISBN13: 978-0-203-85912-4 (eBk)

Contents

PART III
Transition from Primary to Secondary School

PART IV
Transition to Post-School

PART V
Conclusions

Figures

Tables

Acknowledgments

I would like to first of all thank all the contributors who have so willingly given their valuable scholarly work for inclusion in this book. I have learned a lot from you all.

My sincere thanks to Ben Holtzman (formerly Routledge) and Michael Watters (IBT Global). They have been invaluable members of the team despite knowing that their names might never be mentioned!

I would also like to extend my gratitude to my colleagues, friends, and family who have motivated me and with whom I have had very useful discussions about this book.

I would also like to say a special thank you to Professor Ashok Kumar Gupta, Professor Peter Pumfrey, and Professor Hideo Nakata for their constant support and encouragement.

Most of all I would like to thank Jonathan, Nik, and Anjini for their love and unfailing support especially during the writing and editing of this book.

1 Setting the Scene
Educational Transitions and Moving Stories

Divya Jindal-Snape

This chapter briefly reports on the concept of educational transition and sets the context for the concept of transition from the perspective of this book and the authors. This chapter makes connections between the five parts and previews all the chapters for the reader.

EDUCATIONAL TRANSITIONS

Transition involves moving from one context and set of interpersonal relationships to another. Newman and Blackburn (2002) have defined transition as any episode of potentially challenging change that a child might experience, such as progressing through developmental stages, bereavement, leaving care, etc. In today's changing world, individuals make several transitions at home, in an educational context and at work.

In an educational context, transition, also referred to as 'transfer' and 'moving on,' has been conceptualized in various ways. Some of the literature tends to focus on the skills of the children and young people, and how they deal with any change in the context and/or setting. Others have focused on the role of significant others, such as the professionals, family and the community (e.g., Jindal-Snape & Foggie, 2008). Some have conceptualized transition as a single event which marks the completion of one stage and signals the beginning of another stage in the educational journey. Others look at transition as an ongoing process that focuses on interactions between the child and peers, teachers, and families. They, therefore, emphasize that the experience of transition needs to be understood from these multiple perspectives and how the stakeholders in the process make sense of ongoing changes.

In this book the focus is on *educational transitions* that children and young people make from one educational context to another. In some cases this involves transition to a formal educational setting, moving across different stages of education, moving from one school to another, from educational context to employment, and moving from one country to another. Many of these children and young people make this transition successfully and for some it involves adaptation and adjustment over a longer time. It is important to note that transition is satisfying and fulfilling for some, and individuals yearn for this change and the opportunity to 'move on' and 'move up' with increased choices (Jindal-Snape & Foggie, 2008; Lucey & Reay, 2000). However, some find it challenging and stressful. This period is not challenging for children and young people alone. It can cause anxiety for parents/carers and family, with some finding it equally difficult to adapt to changing systems, 'unspoken rules' of institutions, expectations of them as parents/carers, as well as the additional responsibility of working through this with their child at home. Similarly, professionals working with these children, young people, and families have to learn to implement new strategies according to their varying needs and ways of dealing with transition.

In most countries, transition to school normally is in the age range of 5 to 7 years, and signals a transition from a play-based and informal curriculum to a more formal one (Fabian, 2002). This transition then carries on from local primary to a much bigger secondary school, followed by transition to tertiary education or employment. It seems that despite the variation of educational systems, pupil's age, or country, when they face these transitions the pedagogical, social, and emotional challenges which pupils, parents, and professionals undergo are quite similar (see, for example, Adeyemo, 2007; Akos, 2004; Dockett & Perry, 2001; Eccles, Wigfield, Midgley, Reuman, Mac Iver, & Feldlaufer, 1993; Jindal-Snape & Foggie, 2008). In other words, these various transitions in pupils' learning path significantly impact on their everyday life. Therefore, transitions are phases in which pupils, peer groups, and teachers have to constantly rebuild their learning environment in the educational context.

MOVING STORIES

As previously mentioned, the focus in this book is on transition or 'moving on.' This moving on or moving up is from one educational context to another— preschool to primary, primary to secondary, and secondary to post-school. The book has captured 'moving on' stories from different countries, theoretical perspectives and interventions, giving the reader a chance to see how these issues are similar or different and giving the feeling of moving around the world. Again, the book captures how the stories constantly change for the same child or young person as he/she works through the changes. Most importantly, these stories are not only about us writing them as objective researchers and professionals, these are stories that have moved us along with the children and young people directly affected by them, and moved us in our thinking about how to meet the challenges of transition.

INTRODUCTION TO THE CHAPTERS

As can be seen, educational transitions can be very complex for pupils at different stages of their educational progression. This book explores transition at various stages of educational progression, and in different contexts across several countries, theoretical perspectives, interventions, small/large schools, etc. This book encompasses contributions from experts from the field of transitions, who are well grounded in theory, practice, and research, and is a book which is truly internationally relevant and will lead to a more in-depth insight into this very important educational aspect.

This book addresses various stages of educational transition, that is, nursery to primary, primary to secondary, and secondary to post-school. Within these stages, literature review, research, interventions, and gaps in literature and research have been detailed within the context of different countries and learners with varied needs. There are four main parts: transitions and theoretical understanding of the processes, transition from pre-school to primary school, transition from primary to secondary school, and transition to post-school. The fifth part concludes the book.

Part I: Transitions and Theoretical Understanding of the Processes

Chapters 2 and 3 explore the theoretical dimensions of all stages of educational transitions and areas requiring further research and improvement in practice, with a focus on resilience, self-esteem, emotional intelligence, and self-efficacy. Chapter 2 focuses on the theoretical and empirical work in the area of resilience and self-esteem to help illuminate how processes of transition can impact upon children over this important period in their lives. Resilience has been chosen because it focuses on a range of factors (both within individuals and in their immediate environment) that influence whether and how these individuals are able to cope with a period of adversity or threat. As argued by Jindal-Snape and Miller in this chapter, for many children and young people transition does constitute such a period of potential threat. They have also used self-esteem theory, specifically, that which emphasizes the duality of self-esteem, to provide insights into the socio-emotional processes experienced by the children and young people. They detail how this two-dimensional theory of self-esteem rests upon the belief that an individual's self-esteem is dependent upon two types of judgment: the extent to which one feels *worthy* of respect from others, and *competent* to face the challenges which lie ahead. This theoretical perspective alerts us to a range of challenges to an individual's worth and competence which are likely to occur during this transition period. They discuss the nature and source of these messages and outline some implications for academics, researchers, practitioners, and policy makers.

In Chapter 3, Adeyemo employs theoretical perspectives from literature and research on emotional intelligence to examine the relationship between emotional intelligence and successful transition. He argues that emotions, though very important, have been somewhat overlooked in transition literature and research. In this chapter he explores the development of emotional intelligence intervention and its effect on adjustment of students during transition. This chapter presents an experimental application of emotional intelligence to enhancement of adjustment among university freshmen. Academic self-efficacy was used as the moderating variable. Participants were pre-tested and post-tested by using relevant and validated instruments. He employed appropriate statistical tools to determine intervention effectiveness in enhancing adjustment of students in transition.

Part II: Transition from Early Years Setting to Primary School

Chapters 4, 5, and 6 focus on literature and research regarding decisions and issues related to readiness for school and moving from preschool to primary school, with special focus on lessons to be learnt from the UK, New Zealand, and the US. In Chapter 4, Hannah, Gorton, and Jindal-Snape have considered the concept of school readiness in relation to the move to formal schooling. They explore how the outcomes of the research studies have shifted the debate from whether age is a useful or valid indicator of school readiness to looking at the range of definitions and models of school readiness that have been developed. They argue that an effective way to help children start school successfully is through ensuring that an effective transition process occurs. They present a Scottish case study on the perspectives of parents regarding their and their child's experience of moving to primary school, using an ecological systems framework. Implications for policy and practice, and possibilities for future research, have been highlighted.

In Chapter 5, Peters highlights the complexity of children's transition journeys, drawing on sociocultural and ecological perspectives, whilst acknowledging that notions of capital, drawing on sociology, and rites of passage, from anthropology, are also useful in coming to understand transition experiences. She presents this is in the context of New Zealand which has a new school curriculum, which, with its focus on key competencies takes a different approach to learning than the previous curriculum documents. She suggests that this theoretically offers the potential for teachers to connect more easily with children's learning in early childhood settings, and to enhance their early experiences of school. She supports and illustrates her arguments by findings from a number of projects with teachers including a three-year Teaching and Learning Research Initiative exploring learning dispositions and key competencies in early childhood and school settings, and a three-year Centre of Innovation project looking at transitions and 'border crossing.' She compares these with earlier data from her Ph.D. work to illustrate the potential of the 2007 curriculum, whilst considering the implications for children and teachers.

In Chapter 6, Mayer, Amendum, and Vernon-Feagans explore transitions from the perspective of children's successful literacy development and the concept of 'ready schools.' They report that children in the US enter primary school from a variety of early care settings and with differences in their early knowledge of, and experiences with, reading and writing. They suggest that children who experience similar environments and expectations in early care settings and school have less difficulty in the transition to school than children whose early care and school cultures differ. This chapter synthesizes existing research on the transition to school and the relationship with the characteristics of children, families, teachers, and schools and communities in order to identify implications for practitioners, as well as areas in need of further research.

Part III: Transition from Primary to Secondary School

Chapters 7, 8, and 9 explore primary to secondary school transition issues, literature review, research, and interventions in a variety of geographical contexts from the UK, the US, and Finland. In Chapter 7, Galton outlines the context of major school transitions for adolescents in England, reviews the literature/policy in that context, looks at existing theories, explores the identified issues, and presents some empirical findings related to the issues and interventions. Building on a recent review he suggests that the patterns of transfer (who is at risk and why such pupils are at risk, etc.) have shown little change over three decades. This chapter then explores data from his recent study regarding the reactions of pupils as they make the transition from primary to secondary school. Cases cover both pupils who settled easily into the new school and those who experienced difficulty. He makes suggestions for improving the transition process.

In Chapter 8, Akos outlines the context of major school transitions for early adolescents in the US. He highlights the outcomes and empirical research that document risk and opportunity in these transitions. He discusses the concurrent personal and contextual change in the transition from elementary to middle school, as well as the contemporary educational reform efforts (e.g., Smaller Learning Communities) to engage ninth grade students. Further, additional configurations (e.g., K–8 schools, elemiddle, K–12 schools) in the US and the related transitions are explored. He makes an argument for more intentional strengths building (e.g., coping skills) with students that engage personal agency in the transition process. This chapter advocates the creation of strengths-enhancing environments in schools.

In Chapter 9, Pietarinen, Soini, and Pyhältö provide an insight into the most recent national pedagogical school reform in Finland, that is, the undivided basic education (UBE). They describe the aim of this reform, which is to support pupils in their learning path through various transitions during their school career, ensuring a consistent, coherent, and understandable comprehensive school for each pupil, both in terms of learning different subjects in meaningful continuums, and in terms of safe and supportive everyday learning environment. They argue that in order to construct the UBE, the school's pedagogical processes should be evaluated and developed in both vertical and horizontal dimensions. They discuss how in a pupil's school career, the success or failure in transitions from, for instance, one class-level to another (vertical dimension) is based on his/her social and cognitive skills, attitudes and intentions to cope with the challenges, and also on the opportunities of participation manifested to her/him in schools' everyday life and culture (horizontal dimension). They present some empirical findings to suggest that pupils perceive that the processing of the social conflicts both in the pupil–teacher interaction and within the peer group is crucial for learning and well-being in school.

Part IV: Transition to Post-School

Chapters 10, 11, and 12 focus on the transition to post-school, exploring the literature and research, and then focusing on international transition and transition for young people with exceptional needs in the context of the UK, China, and Japan. In Chapter 10, Topping and Foggie firstly outline the context of post-school transitions for young people in the UK, and review the literature and policy in that context, exploring the identified issues. Secondly they present some empirical findings related to these issues. Their literature review focuses on the small number of studies that have some empirical foundation. They report data from a Scottish transitions project which deployed key workers to support young people who had recently left school and were at risk of social exclusion, aiming to enhance independence, self-sufficiency, and employability. The young people were exceptional and vulnerable in the sense that many had a variety of special needs, while others were involved with drugs or the criminal justice system.

In Chapter 11, Zhou, Todman, Topping, and Jindal-Snape have focused on the double transition that some students face when moving from undergraduate to postgraduate programs and from one country to another. As well as adapting to general cultural differences, international students coming to the UK also have to adapt to cultural differences in expectations about and experience of teaching and learning traditions and practices. This chapter reports on the findings of an investigation into the adaptation of Chinese postgraduate students studying in the UK and the differing patterns of adaptation over time with regard to general life, social life, and study life. They discuss the different patterns of adaptation of students who came in groups and those who came individually. This chapter considers the extent to which there is reciprocal adaptation by international students and UK staff, and the barriers to such reciprocal adaptation. Theoretical and practical implications for academics and professionals working with students making cross-cultural transitions are discussed.

In Chapter 12, Yaeda notes that despite the provision of a range of educational and vocational initiatives to facilitate school to work transition for students with disabilities in Japan, the employment rate remains low. He reports that one major problem is a definite lack of transition coordination which could connect schools and vocational rehabilitation agencies or welfare facilities. This chapter introduces recent professional development issues including collaboration between a special support education coordinator and vocational rehabilitation professionals. He introduces a cultural perspective, that is, the spirit of harmony, or the 'WA' spirit. He argues that a smooth transition from school to work is the most effective and efficient way forward in order to avoid unnecessary institutionalization, and also to improve the quality of life of students with disabilities and their family members. National data, public policies, and professional development issues are also covered.

Part V: Conclusions

Chapter 13 summarizes the ideas, research, and theoretical underpinnings from the preceding chapters. It looks at the emerging trends across various aspects of transition within educational stages and across the stages. It concludes this book by considering the way forward for academics, researchers, and practitioners.

Before you start your journey, it is important to highlight that although these chapters have been presented under parts and according to educational stages, each chapter can stand on its own. The reader can start his/her journey at any stage and move around in the way that is most relevant to his/her own context. Some readers might find it useful to read Chapter 13 first to get an overview of the trends that emerged from the various chapters and then go to the specific chapter they wish to read in detail. Others might want to focus on a particular part first. Or for that matter, you might want to start on the stories from a particular continent. Feel free to move around this book according to your own preferences—maybe your journey will take you to a different and unique place from other readers! We hope that either way your journey will result in better practice, research, and policy for these children and young people.

REFERENCES

Adeyemo, D. A. (2007). Moderating influence of emotional intelligence on the link between academic self-efficacy and achievement of university students. *Psychology and Developing Society, 19*(2), 199–213.

Akos, P. (2004). Advice and student agency in the transition to middle school. *Research in Middle Level Education, 27*, 1–11.

Dockett, S., & Perry, B. (2001). Starting school: Effective transitions. *Early Childhood Research and Practice, 3*(2). Retrieved September 16, 2008, from http://ecrp.uiuc.edu/v3n2/dockett.html

Eccles, J. S., Wigfield, A., Midgley, C., Reuman, D. A., Mac Iver, D. J., & Feldlaufer, H. (1993). Negative effects of traditional middle schools on students' motivation. *The Elementary School Journal, 93*, 1553–1574.

Fabian, H. (2002). *Children starting school*. London: David Fulton Publishers.

Jindal-Snape, D., & Foggie, J. (2008). A holistic approach to primary–secondary transitions. *Improving Schools, 11*, 5–18.

Lucey, H., & Reay, R. (2000). Identities in transition: Anxiety and excitement in the move to secondary school. *Oxford Review of Education, 26*, 191–205.

Newman, T., & Blackburn, S. (2002). *Transitions in the lives of children and young people: Resilience factors*. Edinburgh: Scottish Executive Education Department.

Part I

Transitions and Theoretical Understanding of the Processes

2 Understanding Transitions Through Self-Esteem and Resilience

Divya Jindal-Snape and David J. Miller

INTRODUCTION

The research on transition between nursery–primary, primary–secondary, and secondary to post-school shows that it is a period of anxiety for many children and young people (Adeyemo, 2007; Fabian, 2002; Galton & Morrison, 2000; Jindal-Snape & Foggie, 2008; Jindal-Snape & Miller, 2008; Yeboah, 2002), with substantial decline in self-esteem, academic motivation, and achievement (Eccles & Midgley, 1989; Wigfield, Eccles, Mac Iver, Reuman, & Midgley, 1991). For example, young children might find the transition from preschool to primary school difficult and confusing because they move out of an environment of autonomy into one that can be based on conformity to the school norm, with what might seem like lack of choice and lack of explanation regarding what is happening (Fabian & Dunlop, 2002, 2006; Fortune-Wood, 2002). That most children and young people navigate this process successfully can be attributed in part to raised awareness among professionals of the issues related to transition. Many schools now have formalized procedures related to transition; examples include a range of induction strategies to help with the settling-in period, coupled with improvements in the transfer of information from one setting to another (see Hargreaves & Galton, 2002; Jindal-Snape & Foggie, 2008). However, successful adaptation may equally be due to students remaining resilient and coping with change and/or receiving support from external networks that may serve as a protective factor (Akos, 2004; Jindal-Snape & Miller, 2008).

In this chapter, we focus on theoretical and empirical work in the area of self-esteem and resilience to help illuminate how processes of transition can impact upon children and young people over these important periods in their lives. Self-esteem theory, specifically that which emphasizes the duality of self-esteem, has insights to offer. This theory is described in some detail in this chapter, but in essence it rests upon the belief that an individual's self-esteem is dependent upon two types of judgment: the extent to which one feels *worthy* of respect from others, and *competent* to face the challenges which lie ahead (Mruk, 1999). This theoretical perspective alerts us to a range of challenges to an individual's worth and competence which are likely to occur during this transition period. Central to the argument in this chapter is that, for some children and young people at least, transition can be legitimately considered 'a challenge of living' (Mruk, 1999).

Resilience has been chosen because it focuses on a range of factors (both within individuals and in their immediate environment) that influence whether these individuals cope with a period of adversity or threat—or fail to do so. As we explain later, for many children and young people transition does constitute such a period of potential threat. Resilience has been defined as a dynamic process encompassing positive adaptation within the context of significant adversity. As will be discussed later, research suggests that resilience during adverse situations is due to the internal attributes of the individual and protective factors in the family and the wider community (Luthar, 2006). In the resilience literature, self-esteem has been viewed as a personal characteristic of individuals who survive, or even thrive, in the face of adversity.

THE CONCEPT OF SELF-ESTEEM

At an everyday level, we have a clear enough idea of what we mean when we talk about self-esteem. However, when we come to define it, things are not so straightforward. Indeed, despite its prominent role in psychological theory, counseling, and teaching, there is little consensus in terms of definitions, models or measures (Tafarodi & Milne, 2002). Whereas writers in the area of self-concept tend to equate self-esteem with global self-concept (see, for example, Marsh & Craven, 2006), frequently writers will differentiate the terms (for example, Lawrence, 2006). The differences here are not insignificant, since in the former case self-esteem sits at the top of a hierarchy of self-perceptions, whereas with the latter it is self-concept which is the superordinate construct. The stance adopted in this chapter is informed by the literature on self-esteem rather than the work on self-concept, but even within this delineated field there is considerable variation in the way self-referent terms are conceptualized.

Indeed, the proliferation of self-related constructs and the associated lack of clarity are problems that have been commented on by various writers (see, amongst others, Blascovich & Tomaka, 1991; Emler, 2001; Lawrence, 2006; Tafarodi & Milne, 2002). A notable attempt to provide some clarity in this area can be found in the writing of Christopher Mruk (1999), who employed techniques from phenomenological psychology to address the problem. He points to some of the difficulties in arriving at a fundamental structure of self-esteem, including the fact that the topic is studied from both sociological and psychological perspectives, includes a wide variety of acceptable research methods, and involves some special measurement difficulties related to validity.

His analysis demonstrates that the main definitions of self-esteem have traditionally fallen into two categories: those which focus primarily on self-worth, and those which are based upon an individual's judgment of competence. For example, Mruk points out that although the writing of Coopersmith (1967) does make reference to competence, the main emphasis of his work has been on self-worth, as exemplified in his famous definition of self-esteem as being "a personal judgment of worthiness that is expressed in the attitudes [a person] holds towards himself" (1967, pp. 4–5). Certainly, the work of Rogers (1961) is clearly focused on the worth dimension. On the other hand, the seminal work of James (1890/1983) and the psychodynamic writing of White (1963) more clearly reflect a concern with competence.

As a result of his analysis, Mruk has developed a two-dimensional model of self-esteem, and has demonstrated that this is capable of incorporating the findings of the main work published in the field. This model reflects the belief that how people feel about themselves is dependent not only on whether they see themselves as worthwhile people who are accepted by others and lead a good life, but, importantly, also involves judgments about competence in a set of domains considered important to them[1]. Mruk therefore conceptualizes self-esteem as the integrated sum of self-worth and self-competence. In practice this means that for individuals to have high self-esteem they must feel confident both about their sense of self-worth ('I am a good person, entitled to care and respect from others') and their sense of self-competence ('I am able to meet the challenges I face in life'). According to this model, if individuals have a deficiency in one or other dimension, they may behave in ways which suggest high self-esteem, but such characteristics may in fact reflect what is called *pseudo* or *defensive* self-esteem.

According to Mruk's model, self-esteem conditions fall into one of four categories, each subdivided into clinical and non-clinical conditions. Two of these categories are consistent with what is generally known as high and low self-esteem. According to Mruk, individuals who are low both in self-competence and self-worth have classic low self-esteem; they are likely to behave in ways that are familiar to many teachers. They tend to be negativistic in outlook; they are reluctant to contribute to school activities, have negative perceptions of their own abilities, and low expectations of favorable outcomes. In clinical conditions this may result in depression and worse. In contrast, those who have a positive sense of worth and competence are described as having high self-esteem. (In fact, Mruk distinguishes between the majority of individuals in this category, whom he describes as medium self-esteem, and a much smaller minority who enjoy particularly high perceptions in both categories who are described as having *authentic* high self-esteem.)

An interesting aspect of Mruk's work is his conceptualization of the two other categories of self-esteem, and this can be seen to relate to notions of resilience; more specifically it can be seen to relate to the experiences which lead to vulnerability, and the self-perceptions of the individuals concerned. Mruk refers to the idea of defensive self-esteem, that is, where individuals act as though they have high self-esteem when in fact they have a serious deficiency in some important respect. He further divides this category into defensive type 1 and type 2. According to Mruk, the former have a sense of worth but not of competence. In a classroom, such children may feel secure in terms of being accepted and receiving positive messages about themselves *as individuals*, but have learned that they are often not able to perform age-appropriate tasks effectively. A consequence of this is that when the demonstration of some kind of competence is called for, such individuals may feel threatened and employ various avoidance and/or denial strategies.

In contrast, individuals who would be categorized as defensive type 2 are faced with a different set of self-appraisals and tend to display different behavior characteristics. Here a person may have a positive sense of competence, based on experiences of success, but a low sense of worth, because of distressing or traumatic events or a history of negative messages about their worth. According to Mruk, their behavior patterns are likely to include a range of anti-social behaviors, and although it is beyond the immediate scope of this chapter, extreme forms of this type of defensive self-esteem behavior have been linked to a range of deviant behaviors. (See Mruk pp.169–171 for further discussion.) The difference between these self-esteem conditions is central to the discussion in this chapter.

Mruk's analysis is certainly the most comprehensive articulation of the two-dimensional model of self-esteem, but further theoretical support for this perspective can be found in the writing of the humanistic psychologist Nathaniel Branden (1994). Additionally, factor analytical studies (Tafarodi & Milne, 2002; Tafarodi & Swann, 1995) have provided empirical support for a two-dimensional structure for self-esteem. Rosenberg's Self-Esteem Scale, an instrument considered by many to be the 'gold standard' in self-esteem research (see Blascovich & Tomaka, 1991), had been considered unidimensional in nature, but factor analyses by Tafarodi and Milne (2002) identified two correlated factors, labeled self-competence and self-liking. Although the terminology is not identical to that of Mruk, the similarity in terms of the underlying principle is clear: on one hand, performance-based judgments which contribute to feelings of self-competence, on the other, more subjective feelings of acceptance—what we might call internalized positive regard from others.

This brief outline of a two-dimensional perspective is worthy of further discussion than is possible here, but evidence of the growing acceptance of the duality of self-esteem is reflected in the adoption by NASE, the National Association for Self-Esteem, of such a definition (see Reasoner, 2004).

SELF-ESTEEM AND TRANSITION

The critical reader might reasonably ask: why should self-esteem be such a concern over the period of transition? Why now, specifically? The significance rests upon the belief that transition constitutes a 'challenge of living' (Mruk, 1999); that is, a period where an individual's sense of worth and competence are particularly vulnerable. Essentially, challenges of living are situations where individuals experience a series of significant events, find themselves in different and unfamiliar situations, and have to cope with new and sometimes difficult experiences. Many of these experiences and interactions are heavily loaded in terms of personal and emotional messages. Such ideas are reflected also in the work of Epstein (1979), whose studies led him to propose three major experiences which can significantly affect an individual's self-esteem: exposure to a new environment, being required to make new responses, and the establishment or loss of significant relationships. Clearly all of these are central to the process of educational transition.

For example, firstly in the case of transition to primary school, exposure to the new environment brings with it different learning experiences. As mentioned earlier, these are often more formal in nature, certainly when contrasted with child-initiated and free-flow play-based experiences which are the norm in most preschool contexts. New learning experiences are likely to be teacher-directed and consist of a greater number of less-active, seat-based tasks. Second, the requirement to make new responses can be related to new expectations from adults, both in terms of behavior (for example, there are likely to be more constraints on movement and choice) and 'work' (for example, the notion of 'required' performance, and an 'acceptable standard' of product). Associated with this we can see the development of social comparison, and possibly the first glimpse of norm-referencing, associated with grouping arrangements. All of these carry messages about worth and competence. Third, the establishment or loss of new relationships is clearly part and parcel of the transition period. The favorable adult–child ratio which is typical of preschool contexts is not the norm in most reception classes. The patterns of attachment change as young children leave behind their nursery 'helpers,' learn to interact with different adults, and begin to internalize the new messages received. Given what is generally believed about the importance of attachment, this is clearly a significant issue.

At the risk of oversimplification, the argument is that an individual with a healthy self-esteem is likely to be able to weather the storms which accompany such a difficult period. Self-esteem effectively acts as a buffer to help individuals cope with setbacks—both in terms of perceived self-worth and beliefs about their ability to meet life's new challenges (Mruk, 1999). Expectancies are important here, with several studies indicating that those with low self-esteem respond more negatively to experiences of failure, while those with higher self-esteem are more likely to persist in the face of difficulties (see Tafarodi & Vu, 1997, for discussion). In this respect, one can see links with the literature on stress, where appraisals of confidence and efficacy relate to an individual's ability to cope with stressors (see for example, Lazarus, 1999; Rowley, Roesch, Jurica, & Vaughn, 2005). Essentially, someone with a low self-esteem believes he or she has less in the way of resources to cope with these threats and challenges, and is consequently more vulnerable (Baumeister, 1993). Whereas those with a healthy self-esteem may cope with the rigors of transition, and benefit in terms of academic and personal growth, those without may emerge from the process uncertain about their worth, less confident about their ability to cope with the challenges that lie ahead of them—and possibly with the seeds of disaffection already sown.

To more fully understand how children and young people may be challenged—and how educational institutions may be able to help—we consider a selection of experiences which are an integral part of the transition process, and examine how such events may impact upon a child's self-esteem.

CHALLENGES IN TERMS OF WORTH AND COMPETENCE

The factors involved in the development and maintenance of self-esteem are many and sometimes complex, but there are some fundamental processes which have particular importance. Looking first at a sense of self-worth: this is strongly influenced by the quality of our relationships with others and the judgments we make about how we are living up to the standards expected of us. Simply stated, if we feel we are doing the 'right thing' in terms of behavior, and are receiving affirming messages from family, friends, and significant others, then our sense of worth is likely to be secure.

During transition, we see many events which have the potential to influence an individual's self-worth—and indeed, an important feature is that they often occur concurrently. The reassurance of old relationships is often lost. New and possibly different messages are being received from others—peers, older children, and teachers—about one's apparent worth. It is not difficult to appreciate that for some children, the messages from a new peer group may be less than positive, and may do little to compensate for the loss of friends with whom one has been in close daily contact for a significant period of time. Similarly, the messages (and the behaviors) of older children may not suggest to the newcomers that they are valued members of this new community.

In short then, these new messages affect our feelings of acceptance, and serve as an indication of the extent to which others see us as being worthy of their time and attention (Mruk, 1999). Support for the influence of such interpersonal messages can be traced back as far as Cooley in 1902, and have since been emphasized by Rogers (1961), Coopersmith (1967), and

Rosenberg (1965). Following empirical studies of significant life experiences which impact upon self-perceptions, Epstein (1979) concluded that the establishment or loss of significant relationships was one of the major causes of significant changes in self-esteem.

Inevitably, children face changes in how the social world appears to them, as the environment they have known so far gives way to a new, sometimes harder and less forgiving world. Judgments about right and wrong can become blurred as children are under pressure to follow behavior norms in their new situation. Tensions between previous codes of behavior and new ones may create uncertainty about 'the right thing to do'—and these have an impact upon a sense of worth. Certainly, as children develop, their judgments of personal worth and issues of right and wrong become more internalized and less influenced by the views of others. Nevertheless, Tafarodi and Swann (2001) remind us that,

> . . . at no point in development do we become numb to the moral judgment of those who we take an interest in. As social animals we cannot refrain from peering into the looking glass that others hold up to us, as much as we may distrust the images we see there. (p. 656)

Of course, the majority of children experience negative messages at times, and have to grapple with competing notions of right and wrong on occasion; most cope with them and learn from them. It is, after all, part of the process of growing up. However, for some children, the weight of such messages impacts upon an already fragile sense of worth, giving cause for concern.

There are many challenges also to self-competence, that is, an individual's belief that he or she can cope with the challenges which lie ahead in this new environment. Central to this is the nature of the learning situation. Among the many discontinuities are the significant changes in the nature of teaching and learning experiences. For example, after transfer from primary to secondary school, children now find that lessons happen in several different physical locations, with different lesson structures and teaching styles, and often with differing expectations and levels of challenge. Although schools are introducing measures to ease the change—such as improved liaison procedures, developments in the transfer of assessment information, 'bridging projects' and even changes in secondary pedagogy—difficulties remain here. We highlight just one factor.

There is evidence that secondary schools often favor a 'fresh start' approach to learning when pupils arrive in year one. Several factors are implicated here but a fundamental issue concerns assessment. In the past, secondary schools have argued that the assessment information which is passed on from the primary school is not reliable (see, for example, SEED, 1999) and this belief has been used to justify a fresh start approach. Whatever the cause, such discontinuity has often been linked with a recognized dip, not just in attainment but also in affective factors such as motivation, in the first year of secondary school (Boyd, 2005).

The links with self-competence are clear. Less-able children, accustomed to work which has been matched to their ability, can be faced with tasks that highlight their lack of understanding or competence. The difference between their performance and that of their peers may become very evident, not just to them, but also to their new peer group. Marsh's empirical studies into the 'big-fish-little-pond' (BFLP) effect (e.g., Marsh & Hau, 2003; Marsh, Hau, & Craven, 2004) highlight the importance of social comparisons on children's self-judgments. Although work on the BFLP effect is of particular interest to the selective schooling debate, the processes described are likely to apply to many children moving to a different type of classroom experience. Furthermore, it must be borne in mind that these 'academic' comparisons are being made at a time when many other new challenges are being faced; competence is demonstrated not just within the classroom, but on the playing fields and in the playground too. It is not difficult to appreciate how some individuals might be overwhelmed by negative messages.

But there are dangers for other children too in a fresh start approach. Perhaps surprisingly, those who are faced with work which is too *easy* may suffer in terms of self-esteem. Able children, receiving praise for work which they know is not particularly demanding for them, are likely to question the true nature of their ability. Work in the area of non-contingent success (for example, Thompson & Hepburn, 2003) alerts us to the fact that when individuals receive praise that appears disproportionate to their efforts, the uncertainty created can have negative effects on self-concept.

It is important to remember that for many children experiencing primary–secondary transition, these challenging events are happening in parallel with another momentous change in their lives: the onset of puberty. It is generally accepted that for many youngsters, particularly girls, the physical, emotional, and social changes can have significant effects on self-esteem (e.g., Williams & Currie, 2000).

Finally here, a two-dimensional perspective on self-esteem alerts us to the fact that one may have a sense of worth, based on secure relationships and a belief in leading a good life, but at the same time, not feel particularly competent—or vice versa. It follows that an individual may be able to cope with challenges to one aspect of self-esteem but be susceptible to challenges or threats in the other area. Such children may appear as though their self-esteem is secure, when in fact they are experiencing *pseudo* or *defensive* self-esteem as described earlier in this chapter. However, of greatest concern are the individuals who suffer from low self-competence *and* low self-worth—those with *authentic* low self-esteem. For such individuals, the range of potential threats during transition is increased, and importantly, so too are the potential consequences. These individuals pose even more of a challenge to schools, both from the learning and teaching perspective, and also in relation to pastoral care.

Before moving on, it is important to acknowledge that our conceptual model of self-esteem is not grounded in work with preschool children and requires further exploration. Much of the evidence base for a two-dimensional model of self-esteem comes from university students (for example, Tafarodi & Milne, 2002; Tafarodi & Swann, 2001) and other groups of adolescents and adults, such as patients suffering from eating disorders (Sassaroli & Ruggiero, 2005; Surgenor, Maguire, Russell, & Touyz, 2006) and children in the final years of primary school (Miller & Lavin, 2007; Miller & Moran, 2007). Unlike work in the area of self-concept (e.g., Marsh & Ayotte, 2003; Skaalvik & Hagvet, 1990), a two-dimensional model of self-esteem has not been employed in developmental studies.

In fact, Mruk (1999) points out that there is little 'hard evidence' in relation to the exact nature of self-esteem before age 5, and refers to 'developmental precursors' of self-esteem. He claims that the worthiness element precedes the competence element largely due to the environmental messages that the young child receives which relate to what is good, desirable and worthy—and what is not. According to Mruk it is not until the period of middle childhood, as children progress through primary school, that they begin to differentiate beliefs about competence and feelings of worth. This is consistent with work of other writers in the area. For example, it is believed that from age 7 onwards children begin to differentiate their self-perceptions in different domains, such as overall school performance, peer relations, and physical appearance (DuBois, 2003), and that they can discriminate judgments in areas such as academic achievement, conduct, and peer relationships (Harter, 1990). It would be inappropriate for us to apply the two-dimensional model to children's perceptions at age 4 in the same way as we feel is legitimate at age 11 or 12. Nevertheless, we retain the view that overall self-esteem is of central importance to healthy development, here as later on in life. We invite the reader to decide which of the processes we describe in relation to primary–secondary and secondary–post secondary transition are relevant also to that earlier transition.

THE CONCEPT OF RESILIENCE

The term resilience was introduced in scientific literature during the second half of the 20th century and has been recognized as an important construct from a theoretical and applied perspective (Luthar, 2006). In defining resilience as "a phenomenon or process reflecting relatively positive adaptation despite experiences of adversity or trauma," Luthar (2003, p. 6) explains that two conditions are critical: *exposure to significant adversity or threat*, and *achievement of positive adaptation despite that adversity or threat*. In fact, resilience research first gained prominence in pioneering work with children of schizophrenic mothers where it was found that among these children who were at high risk for psychopathology, were a number of children who had shown surprisingly healthy adaptive patterns (e.g., Garmezy, 1974, and Rutter, 1979, cited in Luthar, 2006). Further research was conducted with other groups, for example children exposed to naturally occurring stressors such as deaths or injuries in the family (Murphy & Moriarty, 1976) and Werner and Smith's (1982) work with infants at risk on the Hawaiian island of Kauai. These studies led to the identification of factors that seemed to be common amongst children who were successfully dealing with adversity, such as social charisma, and affectionate and strong ties with family and the wider community. Among other prominent publications, one that was particularly significant was an analysis of conceptual issues by Rutter (1987). He suggested four main *protective processes* which mediate risk at key life turning points. These are: to lessen the impact of risk by altering the experience of risk (e.g., preparing the child for the death of a family member) or exposure to the risk (e.g., by close supervision); to decrease the number of risk factors in order to avoid an accumulation of unmanageable risks; to increase self-esteem and self-efficacy (e.g., through positive and secure relationships, successful completion of tasks), in order to create a positive chain reaction in the young person's life; and to provide access to opportunities such as part-time work and out of school activities, to increase confidence and develop necessary life skills.

Gilligan (2000) expanded on Rutter's protective processes by stating the importance of five key areas which have to be addressed in order to understand resilience in at-risk young people and children. They are: decreasing the number of problems in the child's life; thinking about his or her life course in terms of a 'developmental pathway' which can be altered at any point by small incidents or experiences, whether positive or negative; providing him or her with a secure base (e.g., secure attachments with parents and siblings, enabling examination, and exploration of the greater environment); developing self-esteem through positive experiences, relationships, and success (e.g., performing well in sports); and finally, developing self-efficacy, by ensuring that he or she is involved in planning and preparation for any changes (e.g., involving in planning for the move to secondary school whilst the child is in primary school). He emphasized the importance of positive school experiences as a protective factor.

Catterall (1998) studied risk and resilience in primary–secondary transitions and presented some models on the basis of empirical research. He emphasized the need to move away from 'at risk groups' and instead to look at *individuals* who might be at risk of dropping out from school due to lowering of academic achievement and commitment. He used the terms 'commitment resilience' and 'academic resilience' and suggested that if we look at individuals and their performances, then we can see workings of risk over time. Importantly, he argued that the individual can move in and out of risk situations, indicating the dynamic nature of resilience. The concept of resilience has also been applied to early childhood transitions (Griebel & Niesel, 2001).

To summarize, if we take an overview of the research in the area of resilience, there appears to be a change in perspective, in that it is increasingly seen as a process that is dynamic, "having the capacity to emerge in later life after earlier periods of coping problems" (Newman & Blackburn, 2002, p. 10). As discussed earlier, this positive adaptation is seen to be the result of *protective factors* that are present within the individual and/or his or her environment. It is believed that the occurrence of such protective factors can negate the impact of risk factors, leading to resilience in individuals to any significant change in their life. Educational transition is clearly one such change. Despite differing views on many aspects of resilience, there seems to be a consensus on these two important sets of factors: the internal protective factors (e.g., child's internal attributes, self-esteem) and external protective factors (e.g., supportive family or community).

On the basis of extensively explored theoretical factors, Newman and Blackburn (2002) have suggested that resilience factors and risk factors operate in three dimensions: the individual (internal factor), the family (external factor), and the external environment (external factor). The authors have suggested that similar factors in a child's life can lead to the child being at risk (parent–child hostility) or can work as a protective factor (good parent–child relationships). They have further suggested that some of these factors are partly biogenetic and their sensitivity to change or manipulation is limited. However, most are variables known to professionals and present a wide range of possibilities for positive change. It is believed that if a child has a series of adverse circumstances/risk factors, compensatory resilience factors are required to promote resilience. For example, in the context of transition, an unpredictable crisis such as bullying can put a child at risk of underachieving or emotional distress. However, a supportive and positive family environment can promote resilience against the risk factors.

RESILIENCE AND TRANSITION

At this point the reader might question whether educational transition can be seen as traumatic enough to justify employing ideas from resilience theory. But, as can be seen from the previous example, research has already been conducted to look at risk and resilience in the context of preschool–primary school (Griebel & Niesel, 2001) and primary–secondary transition (Catterall, 1998). Further, research suggests that there is a difference in the perception of an adult and child regarding stressful and traumatic events (e.g., in the context of transition, see Akos, 2004; Brown & Armstrong, 1982). Although adults identify major life events as stressful, children see daily 'hassles,' such as conflicts with peers or school transition, as major stressors (Newman & Blackburn, 2002). Essentially, it is the number and frequency of apparently minor 'hassles' that make them traumatic.

If we look at transition research there seem to be several such stressors for a child at this time. For example, the issue of discontinuity has been highlighted in the context of primary–secondary transition in UK government reports (e.g., Galton, Gray, Rudduck, Berry, & Demetriou, 2003; SEED, 1999). Similarly, different researchers have focused on promoting continuity from preschool to school in different countries, for example, Bennett and Kell (1989), Fabian and Dunlop (2002), Ghaye and Pascal (1989) in the UK; Fthenakis (1998) in Germany; Broström (2002) in Denmark; Margetts (2002) and Dockett and Perry (1999, 2001) in Australia; and Peters (2000, 2003) in New Zealand. In fact, from the perspective of the child, there are a number of discontinuities which he or she has to cope with simultaneously. For example, in many situations, especially in the UK, there is a change in physical location coupled with changes in the way in which the learning environment is organized (Graham & Hill, 2003).

Importantly, the dominant pedagogic style is subject to change. While accepting the fact that approaches to teaching and learning are evolving, for many pupils, transitions are still characterized by shifts in pedagogy. At the risk of oversimplification, we can view the overall trend across the sectors to involve a shift from child-centered, activity-based, or experiential learning toward more didactic approaches, informed by different educational philosophies (Midgley, Feldlaufer, & Eccles, 1989). The expectations of teachers may differ, as will the nature of some important relationships between teachers and students (Midgley et al., 1989; Tonkin & Watt, 2003). For some children who might be experiencing problems in the family, the stable relationships or attachments formed with the primary school teacher, for instance, can be vital—but due to the large number of pupils and teachers in secondary schools (Jindal-Snape & Foggie, 2008) or tertiary education, these secure attachments can be more difficult to form. For some students, one negative experience can lead to a downward spiral in their motivation to attend school or tertiary education and can also have an impact on their self-esteem. Several studies in the rest of Europe (Kvalsund, 2000; Lohaus, Elben, Ball, & Klein-Hessling, 2004; O'Brien, 2003; Zanobini & Usai, 2002), the US (Akos, 2004; Eccles & Midgley, 1989; Pellegrini & Long, 2002; Wigfield et al., 1991), Australia (Tonkin & Watt, 2003), and elsewhere have emphasized similar issues.

Another stressor during transition seems to be that peer relationships are often in a state of flux. Children who have been together for several years can become strangers. The nature of peer status changes too, as children go from being 'big fish in a small pool' to minnows in an uncharted ocean. As they adjust to the new environment, the new organizational arrangements, the new relationships and the new sets of rules (both explicit and hidden), there may be conflict between social and educational agendas. Some 20 years ago, Measor and Woods (1984) highlighted that at this time children can experience a sense of loss—loss of the familiar, in terms of places, people, and routines. Despite the passage of time, this still seems true today (Tonkin & Watt, 2003).

Lucey and Reay (2000) point out that although any sense of loss is difficult, it is an integral part of the process of change. An important idea here is what Hallinan and Hallinan (1992) call the 'transfer paradox.' This refers to the fact that the transition process represents both a step up and a step down in terms of socially reflected maturity. Lucey and Reay (2000) argue that educational transition presents children with a dilemma central to the experience of growing up: that in order to gain a level of autonomy appropriate to their level of need, they must be able and willing to give up some protection. So, although anxiety and a certain amount of emotional impact are inevitable consequences of transition, they are central to the development of appropriate coping strategies. However, as educators we must ask, what happens if a child does not have the internal attributes or a supportive environment to help develop these coping strategies?

Newman and Blackburn (2002) encapsulate important issues here:

> Transitional periods in the lives of children and young people are times of threat but also of opportunity for change. If children possess adequate coping skills, are in environments that protect against excessive demands, but also have opportunities to learn and adapt through being exposed to reasonable levels of risk, then a successful transition is likely. If neither coping skills, nor an environment that is likely to promote them, are present then periods of transition may become points in the child or adolescent life span where serious developmental damage may occur. (p. 17)

Taking into account all of these factors, it is hardly surprising that for many children and young people this is a period of considerable uncertainty and potential stress. It is also important to remember that these changes occur at a time of great physical and emotional change: the onset of puberty in the case of primary–secondary, and from being a young person to an adult in the case of secondary to post-school. It is almost self-evident that all the changes referred to previously can have a significant effect on self-perceptions—specifically on an individual's sense of worth and competence—leading to stress and in some cases, trauma (Rudolph, Lambert, Clark, & Kurlakowsky, 2001).

In terms of previous resilience and transition research, the importance of the internal protective factors (for example, self-esteem) and external protective factors (such as positive relationships at home and school) to help reduce multiple 'risks' or 'stressors' at the time of transition, is obvious. Therefore, care needs to be taken to structure a supportive environment for children during transition, and we address this in the final section of this chapter. However, of equal importance is the need to understand what might be happening to the child's self-perceptions at this time.

SOME IMPLICATIONS FOR PROFESSIONALS
AND POLICY MAKERS

While not wishing to appear overcritical of current practice, we believe there is scope for educational institutions and parents to do more to prepare children and young people for transition. Central to this will be a clear focus on social and personal factors, as well as educational attainment and organizational processes.

An obvious place to start concerns the information being passed from one organization to another, for example, primary to secondary school: there is a need to look critically at this process. Information passed on at transfer should include more than details of academic attainment. Information needs to be provided about personal and social factors, in order to alert secondary schools to individuals who may, for a variety of reasons, be more vulnerable when they move on.

Of course, this means that nurseries and schools themselves need to be more aware of children and young people who may be at risk, either because of a lack of external support mechanisms on which they can call, or because of their internal characteristics (for example, in terms of self-esteem). Although we have been highlighting the importance of self-esteem at this time, identifying children at risk in this respect may be problematic; a recent study has suggested that teachers are not good at recognizing children who are low in self-esteem (Miller & Moran, 2005). It may be that teachers need a more sophisticated understanding of self-esteem, and focusing specifically on the primary–secondary transition Miller and Moran point to two areas here.

The first is recognition of the two-dimensional nature of self-esteem. This is particularly helpful because, as we have illustrated, it alerts us to the differing types of threat to self-esteem, and some possible sources of such threats. The second area where teachers need to develop a better knowledge of their students is in relation to the contingencies of their self-esteem. A contingency is defined as a "domain or category of outcomes on which a person has staked his or her self-esteem" (Crocker & Wolfe, 2001, p. 594). An important idea here is that individuals differ in terms of these contingencies, and the more strongly a person's self-esteem is contingent upon a particular outcome, the stronger the affective or emotional response to it. Clearly the more teachers learn about these, the better informed they are about children's views of themselves—and the better able to convey meaningful information to the colleagues in the receiving organization.

In terms of older children and young people, Miller and Daniel (2007) maintain that one of the important insights provided by the two-dimensional model relates to the phenomenon of defensive self-esteem, as outlined earlier in this chapter. The authors explain the need for teachers to recognize the symptoms of two different defensive self-esteem conditions.

This is important because each condition indicates distinctive types of negative self-evaluations, calling for different types of support.

Accordingly, Miller and Daniel discuss a range of teaching and learning approaches which can be employed to help build self-esteem. The key idea is that some of these strategies are known to impact on self-worth, and others to influence a sense of self-competence. Empirical support for their analysis can be found in Miller and Moran (2007), where the authors describe a controlled study which demonstrated differential effects for two different types of self-esteem enhancement strategies. Interestingly, although Miller and Daniel discuss strategies which specifically target each dimension, they also suggest that there are some classroom strategies which may impact upon both dimensions of self-esteem, notably peer tutoring (Topping, Campbell, Douglas, & Smith, 2003). One point that must be emphasized here is the need to be selective in the messages given to children/young people, basing strategies on a clear understanding of the needs of the individuals concerned, rather than simplistic notions of increasing a 'feel-good factor' (see also Miller & Moran, 2006, for discussion here).

Still focusing on curricular experiences, children's resilience can also be developed through involvement in simulated role plays, or creative drama. In this way, children and young people are provided with secure exposure to transition related issues and given opportunities to tackle them. Jindal-Snape and Foggie (2006) suggest that the child can be given opportunities to experience and engage with risk through creative drama in a supportive and safe environment. Gilligan (2000) also focused on school and spare time activities as important contexts for increasing resilience, one example being during a period of transition and change. Positive school experiences are not only valuable academically, but also socially and developmentally.

Both resilience and self-esteem theories would point to the importance of secure attachments in schools—with both adults and peers. It may be worth reviewing the pastoral care arrangements in schools, taking into account the perspectives outlined here. Secondary schools and tertiary education may wish to consider whether there are implications for their systems of guidance, counseling and pastoral support (through personal tutors at the university for instance). Similarly, attachments with peers might be examined. For example, there could be a system of providing non-stigmatizing secure attachments in nursery, schools, and tertiary education, especially for children and young people who come from unstable families. One method, employed in some schools, is via buddy systems, but as we indicate previously, there may also be social and personal gains from peer-tutoring arrangements.

The preceding discussion is necessarily limited in terms of the strategies identified. It is also limited in that it focuses specifically on the role of nurseries, schools, colleges, universities, and professionals in enhancing self-esteem and encouraging resilience. However, several of the issues already discussed are of interest and relevance to families too. Moreover, given that the family is one of the most important support networks of a child or young person, it almost goes without saying that professionals need to work with families to support the child or young person in understanding what transition involves. In so doing, all parties can enhance the social and emotional wellbeing of the children and young people.

IMPLICATIONS FOR FURTHER RESEARCH

As we have already noted, there is as yet little evidence of a two-dimensional model of self-esteem being employed in developmental studies. There is much to be learned about how self-esteem develops and is nurtured within nursery and early years contexts. There is a need also to investigate ways in which teachers can identify and support children at risk. This involves questions related to the predictive validity of the data collected, and practical issues related to the collection and sharing of information and the monitoring of subsequent provision.

A separate but related issue concerns a lack of clarity in some aspects of resilience theory—what Robinson (2000) has called 'conceptual blurriness.' Indeed, the ongoing quest for greater clarity has been noted by several prominent writers. In a critical analysis of resilience, Luthar, Cicchetti, and Becker (2000) comment on a lack of consensus about definitions and measurement of key constructs. One of the issues identified is that protective or vulnerability factors have been described—and operationalized—in varied and inconsistent ways.

As we have already pointed out, self-esteem has been identified both as a protective factor and an outcome of resilience. Consequently, individuals with high self-esteem are reported to be more resilient when faced with challenges—but equally, children and young people who survive such challenges are likely to emerge with higher self-esteem. Some readers may feel a sense of unease about what appears to be a circular issue of causality here. At one level, this reflects the dynamic nature of self-esteem; few writers in the area of self-perceptions would dissent from the view that an individual's self-esteem both influences—and is influenced by—interaction with others in social contexts. In fact, this is mirrored in changing perspectives on resilience, as where Margalit (2004) contrasts older conceptions of resilience as a trait with more recent views where it is seen as a dynamic process of adaptation. Nevertheless, at another level, it seems to us that there is a need for further investigation here also. Luthar et al. (2000) highlighted the need to further differentiate beneficial processes in different conditions of individual and context. We would agree, and there will be value in examining more critically the processes involved in stabilizing or enhancing self-esteem under different sets of personal and contextual conditions.

CONCLUSION

Clearly educational transition is a complex issue. It involves ideological issues as well as administrative processes and questions of attainment. We have focused primarily on the role played by the formal educational system, but an important message is that nurseries, schools, colleges, and universities should not neglect the beneficial impact on children and young people of informal support from families, peers, and the community. It is important to recognize and take advantage of the natural protective influences which stem from these three ecosystems—even if they can be the source of risk factors as well as protective factors (see Newman & Blackburn, 2002).

In essence, our argument has been that we need to be more aware of the social and personal messages which are conveyed in a range of experiences—experiences which occur with some rapidity in a concentrated period of time. It may be this very concentration that becomes overwhelming for vulnerable children and young people. Several of the issues discussed in this chapter may apply to all, but they undoubtedly have particular importance for those who find the process of transition daunting, or even traumatic. The literature on resilience points to a variety of protective factors which are important in helping children and young people to cope with transition. The internal attributes of the child or young person, a cohesive and supportive family, and an external support network in the form of nursery, school, or university, peers, and community all have a part to play in successful transition. We have highlighted internal attributes, in particular beliefs about worth and competence, as being of central importance.

In their overview of recent changes to middle schools in the US, Midgley and Edelin (1998) have pointed out that there can be dangers if educational institutions focus only on interpersonal relationships when trying to improve experiences for pupils after transition. In essence, this work suggests that self-esteem enhancement is an important concern during the transition process, but not sufficient in itself to ensure successful adaptation. Other factors are important also, not least improvements in attainment which can be brought about by more effective learning and teaching experiences. Our own position is completely consistent with this, and the perspective developed in this chapter requires that we attend both to the affective (e.g., feelings of worth) and the cognitive (e.g., judgments of competence which come from success in achieving goals).

As a final point, we would wish to emphasize that our aim is not the avoidance of risk for children. Discussing resilience factors, Rutter (1987, p. 318) points out, "Protection . . . resides, not in the evasion of risk, but in successful engagement with it . . . [it] stems from the adaptive changes that follow successful coping."

Successful coping is intimately related to self-esteem enhancement: the gain in feelings of competence which follow from meeting new challenges. Avoidance is not the issue; what is important, both educationally and ethically, is that we can help *manage* risk for those who might otherwise feel overwhelmed during transition—overwhelmed by exposure to a new environment, by being required to make new responses, and by establishing or losing significant relationships—in short, by this challenge of living. Knowledge of the issues highlighted in this chapter should enable us to do that more effectively.

Note: This chapter is based on a previous publication with kind permission from Springer Science and Business Media. Jindal-Snape, D., & Miller, D. J. (2008). A challenge of living? Understanding the psycho-social processes of the child during primary–secondary transition through resilience and self-esteem theories. Educational Psychology Review, 20, 217–236.

NOTES

1. The similarity with Bandura's concept of self-efficacy is immediately apparent. Although it is Bandura's view that self-efficacy is independent of self-esteem (Bandura, 1990), a two-dimensional model of self-esteem involves the belief that coping with the challenges one faces in life (or failing to do so) carries with it subjective feelings about the self. Tafarodi and Swann (2001) point out that experiences of success and failure do not simply influence a sense of agency at the cognitive level; they are experienced as a positive or negative *value*: "general self-efficacy, defined as global expectancy, and self-competence [. . .] are but two consequences of the same cumulative process. Namely, self-competence is the valuative imprint of general self-efficacy on identity" (p. 655).

REFERENCES

Adeyemo, D. A. (2007). Moderating influence of emotional intelligence on the link between academic self-efficacy and achievement of university students. *Psychology and Developing Society, 19(2),* 199–213.
Akos, P. (2004). Advice and student agency in the transition to middle school. *Research in Middle Level Education, 27,* 1–11.
Bandura, A. (1990). Conclusion: Reflections on nonability determinants of competence. In R. J. Sternberg & J. Kolligian Jr. (Eds.), *Competence considered* (pp. 315–362). New Haven, CT: Yale University Press.
Baumeister, R. F. (1993). *Self-esteem: The puzzle of low self-regard.* New York: Plenum Press.
Bennett, N., & Kell, J. (1989). *A good start? Four-year olds in infant schools.* Oxford: Blackwell.
Blascovich, J., & Tomaka, J. (1991). Measures of self-esteem. In J. P. Robinson, P. R. Shaver, & L. S. Wrightsman (Eds.), *Measures of personality and social psychological attitudes* (pp. 115–123). San Diego, CA: Academic Press.
Boyd, B. (2005). *Primary/secondary transition: An introduction to the issues.* Paisley: Hodder.

Branden, N. (1994). *The six pillars of self-esteem.* New York: Bantam Books.

Broström, S. (2002). Communication and continuity in the transition from kindergarten to school. In H. Fabian & A. W. A. Dunlop (Eds.), *Transitions in the early years: Debating continuity and progression for children in early education* (pp. 52–63). London: RoutledgeFalmer.

Brown, J., & Armstrong, R. (1982). The structure of pupils' worries during transition from junior to secondary school. *British Educational Research Journal, 8,* 123–131.

Catterall, J. (1998). Risk and resilience in student transitions to high school. *American Journal of Education, 106*(2), 302–333.

Coopersmith, S. (1967). *The antecedents of self-esteem.* San Francisco: Freeman.

Crocker, J., & Wolfe, C. T. (2001). Contingencies of self-worth. *Psychological Review, 108,* 593–623.

Dockett, S., & Perry, B. (1999). Starting school: What matters for children, parents and educators? *Australian Early Childhood Association Research in Practice, 6*(3), 1–16.

Dockett, S., & Perry, B. (2001). Starting school: Effective transitions. *Early Childhood Research and Practice, 3*(2). Retrieved September 16, 2008, from http://ecrp.uiuc.edu/v3n2/dockett.html.

DuBois, D. (2003). Self-esteem, early childhood. In T. P. Gullotta & M. Bloom (Eds.), *Encyclopedia of primary health prevention and health promotion* (pp. 937–945). New York: Plenum.

Eccles, J. S., & Midgley, C. (1989). Stage-environment fit: Developmentally appropriate classrooms for young adolescents. In C. Ames & R. Ames (Eds.), *Research on motivation in education: Goals and cognitions,* Vol. 3 (pp. 139–186). New York: Academic Press.

Emler, N. (2001). *Self-esteem: The costs and causes of low self-worth.* York: Joseph Rowntree Foundation and YPS.

Epstein, S. (1979). The ecological study of emotions in humans. In P. Pliner, K. R. Blankstein, & I. M. Spigel (Eds.), *Advances in the study of communication and affect, Vol. 5: Perception of emotions in self and others* (pp. 47–83). New York: Plenum.

Fabian, H. (2002). *Children starting school.* London: David Fulton Publishers.

Fabian, H., & Dunlop, A. W. A. (Eds.) (2002). *Transitions in the early years. Debating continuity and progression for children in early education.* London: RoutledgeFalmer.

Fabian, H., & Dunlop, A. W. A. (2006). *Outcomes of good practice in transition processes for children entering primary school.* Paper commissioned for the EFA Global Monitoring Report 2007, Strong foundations: early childhood care and education. Retrieved September 16, 2008, from http://unesdoc.unesco.org/images/0014/001474/147463e.pdf.

Fortune-Wood, J. (2002). Transitions without school. In H. Fabian & A. W. A. Dunlop, (Eds.), *Transitions in the early years. Debating continuity and progression for children in early education* (pp. 135–145). London: RoutledgeFalmer.

Fthenakis, W. E. (1998). Family transitions and quality in early childhood education. *European Early Childhood Education Research Journal, 6*(1), 5–17.

Galton, M., Gray, J., Rudduck, J., Berry, M., & Demetriou, H. (2003). *Progress in the middle years of schooling (7–14): Continuities and discontinuities in learning.* London: The Stationery Office for the DfES.

Galton, M., & Morrison, I. (2000). Concluding comments: Transfer and transition: The next steps. *International Journal of Educational Research, 33,* 443–449.

Ghaye, A., & Pascal, C. (1989). Four-year-old children in reception classrooms: Participant perceptions and practice. *Educational Studies, 14*(2), 187–208.

Gilligan, R. (2000). Adversity, resilience and young people: The protective value of positive school and spare time experiences. *Children and Society, 14*, 37–47.

Graham, C., & Hill, M. (2003). *Negotiating the transition to secondary school.* SCRE, Spotlight 89. Retrieved August 10, 2007, from www.scre.ac.uk/spotlight/spotlight89.html.

Griebel, W., & Niesel, R. (2001). *Transition to school child: What children tell us about school and what they teach us.* Paper presented at the 11th European Conference on Quality on Early Childhood Education. Alkmaar, The Netherlands, August 29–September 1, 2001.

Hallinan, P., & Hallinan, P. (1992). Seven into eight will go: Transition from primary to secondary school. *Australian Educational and Developmental Psychologist, 9*, 30–38.

Hargreaves, L., & Galton, M. (2002). *Transfer from the primary school: 20 years on.* London: Routledge.

Harter, S. (1990). Self and identity development. In S. Feldman & G. R. Elliott (Eds.), *At the threshold: The developing adolescent* (pp. 352–388). Cambridge, MA: Harvard University Press.

James, W. (1983). *The principles of psychology.* Cambridge, MA: Harvard University Press. (Original work published 1890)

Jindal-Snape, D., & Foggie, J. (2006). *Moving stories: A research study exploring children/young people, parents and practitioners' perceptions of primary-secondary transitions.* Report for Transitions Partnership Project, University of Dundee, Dundee.

Jindal-Snape, D., & Foggie, J. (2008). A holistic approach to primary–secondary transitions. *Improving Schools, 11*, 5–18.

Jindal-Snape, D., & Miller, D. J. (2008). A challenge of living? Understanding the psycho-social processes of the child during primary–secondary transition through resilience and self-esteem theories. *Educational Psychology Review, 20*, 217–236.

Kvalsund, R. (2000). The transition from primary to secondary level in smaller and larger rural schools in Norway: Comparing differences in context and social meaning. *International Journal of Educational Research, 33*, 401–423.

Lawrence, D. (2006). *Enhancing self-esteem in the classroom.* London: Paul Chapman Publishing.

Lazarus, R. S. (1999). *Stress and emotion.* London: Free Association Books.

Lohaus, A., Elben, C. E., Ball, J., & Klein-Hessling, J. (2004). School transition from elementary to secondary school: Changes in psychological adjustment. *Educational Psychology, 24*, 161–173.

Lucey, H., & Reay, R. (2000). Identities in transition: Anxiety and excitement in the move to secondary school. *Oxford Review of Education, 26*, 191–205.

Luthar, S. S. (Ed.) (2003). *Resilience and vulnerability. Adaptation in the context of childhood adversities.* Cambridge: Cambridge University Press.

Luthar, S. S. (2006). Resilience in development: A syhnthesis of research across five decades. In D. Cicchetti & D. J. Cohen (Eds.), *Developmental psychopathology: Risk, disorder, and adaptation* (pp. 739–795). New York: Wiley.

Luthar, S., Cicchetti, D., & Becker, B. (2000). The construct of resilience: A critical evaluation and guidelines for future work. *Child Development, 71*, 543–562.

Margalit, M. (2004). Second-generation research on resilience: Social-emotional aspects of children with learning disabilities. *Learning Disabilities Research & Practice, 19*(1) 45–48.

Margetts, K. (2002). Transition to school: Complexity and diversity. *European Early Childhood Education Research Journal, 10*(2), 103–114.

Marsh, H. W., & Ayotte, V. (2003). Do multiple dimensions of self concept become more differentiated with age? The differential distinctiveness hypothesis. *Journal of Educational Psychology, 95*, 687–706.

Marsh, H. W., & Craven, R. G. (2006). Reciprocal effects of self-concept and performance from a multidimensional perspective. *Perspectives on Psychological Science, 1*(2), 133–166.

Marsh, H. W., & Hau, K. T. (2003). Big fish little pond effect on academic self-concept: A crosscultural (26 country) test of the negative effects of academically selective schools. *American Psychologist, 58*, 364–376.

Marsh, H. W., Hau, K. T., & Craven, R. (2004). The big-fish-little-pond effect stands up to scrutiny. *American Psychologist, 59*, 269–271.

Measor, L., & Woods, P. (1984). *Changing schools: Pupil perspectives on transfer to a comprehensive.* Milton Keynes: Open University Press.

Midgley, C., & Edelin, K (1998). Middle school reform and early adolescent well-being: The good news and the bad. *Educational Psychologist, 33*, 195–206

Midgley, C., Feldlaufer, H., & Eccles, J. S. (1989). Student/teacher relations and attitudes toward mathematics before and after the transition to junior high school. *Child Development, 60*, 981–992.

Miller, D. J., & Daniel, B. (2007). Competent to cope, worthy of happiness? How the duality of self-esteem can inform a resilience-based classroom environment. *School Psychology International, 28*(5), 605–622.

Miller, D. J., & Lavin, F. M. (2007). "But now I feel I want to give it a try": Formative assessment, self-esteem and a sense of competence. *The Curriculum Journal, 18*(1), 3–23.

Miller, D. J., & Moran, T. R. (2005). One in three? Teachers' attempts to identify low self-esteem children. *Pastoral Care in Education, 23*, 25–30.

Miller, D. J., & Moran, T. R. (2006). Positive self-worth is not enough. Some implications of a two-dimensional model of self-esteem for primary teaching. *Improving Schools, 9*, 7–16.

Miller, D. J., & Moran, T. R. (2007). Theory and practice in self-esteem enhancement. Circle-time and efficacy-based approaches: a controlled evaluation. *Teachers and Teaching: Theory and Practice, 13*(6), 601–615.

Mruk, C. (1999). *Self-esteem: Research, theory and practice.* London: Free Association Books.

Murphy, L. B., & Moriarty, A. (1976). *Vulnerability, coping and growth: From infancy to adolescence.* New Haven, CT: Yale University Press.

Newman, T., & Blackburn, S. (2002). *Transitions in the lives of children and young people: Resilience factors.* Edinburgh: Scottish Executive Education Department.

O'Brien, M. (2003). Girls and transition to second-level schooling in Ireland: 'moving on' and 'moving out.' *Gender and Education, 15*, 249–267.

Pellegrini, A. D., & Long, J. D. (2002). A longitudinal study of bullying, dominance and victimization during the transition from primary school through secondary schools. *British Journal of Developmental Psychology, 20*, 259–280.

Peters, S. (2000). *Multiple perspectives in continuity in early learning and the transition to school.* Paper presented at 10th European Early Childhood Conference, University of London, August 29–September 1.

Peters, S. (2003). "I didn't expect that I would get tons of friends . . . more each day": Children's experiences of friendship during the transition to school. *Early Years, 23*, 1, 45–53.

Reasoner, R. (2004). *The true meaning of self-esteem.* National Association for Self-Esteem. Retrieved December 15, 2007, from http://www.self-esteem-nase.org/whatisselfesteem.html.

Robinson, J. L. (2000). Are there implications for prevention research from studies of resilience? *Child Development, 71*(3), 570–572.

Rogers, C. R. (1961). *On becoming a person.* Boston: Houghton Mifflin.

Rosenberg, M. (1965). *Society and the adolescent self-image.* Princeton, N.J.: Princeton University Press.

Rowley, A. A., Roesch, S. C., Jurica, B. J., & Vaughn, A. A. (2005). Developing and validating a stress appraisal measure for minority adolescents. *Journal of Adolescence, 28*(4), 547–557.

Rudolph, K. D., Lambert, S. F., Clark, A. G., & Kurlakowsky, K. D. (2001). Negotiating the transition to middle school: The role of self-regulatory processes. *Child Development, 72*, 929–946.

Rutter, M. (1987). Psychosocial resilience and protective mechanisms. *American Journal of Orthopsychiatry, 57*, 316–331.

Sassaroli, S., & Ruggiero, G. M. (2005). The role of stress in the association between low self-esteem, perfectionism, and worry, and eating disorders. *International Journal of Eating Disorders, 37*, 135–141.

SEED. (1999). *Review of assessment in preschool and 5–14.* Edinburgh: HMSO.

Skaalvik, E. M., & Hagvet, K. A. (1990). Academic achievement and self-concept: An analysis of causal predominance in a developmental perspective. *Journal of Personality and Social Psychology, 58*, 292–307.

Surgenor, L. J., Maguire, S., Russell, J., & Touyz, S. (2006). Self-liking and self-competence: Relationship to symptoms of anorexia nervosa. *European Eating Disorders Review, 15*(2) 139–145.

Tafarodi, R. W., & Milne, A. B. (2002). Decomposing global self-esteem. *Journal of Personality, 70*, 443–483.

Tafarodi, R. W., & Swann, W. B. Jr. (1995). Self-liking and self-competence as dimensions of global self-esteem: Initial validation of a measure. *Journal of Personality Assessment, 65*, 322–342.

Tafarodi, R. W., & Swann, W. B. Jr. (2001). Two-dimensional self-esteem: theory and measurement. *Personality and Individual Differences, 31*, 653–673.

Tafarodi, R. W., & Vu, C. (1997). Two-dimensional self-esteem and reactions to success and failure. *Personality and Social Psychology Bulletin, 23*, 626–635.

Thompson, T., & Hepburn, J. (2003). Causal uncertainty, claimed and behavioral self-handicapping. *British Journal of Educational Psychology, 73*, 247–266.

Tonkin, S. E., & Watt, H. M. G. (2003). Self-concept over the transition from primary to secondary school: A case study on a program for girls. *Issues in Educational Research, 13*(2), 27–54.

Topping, K. J., Campbell, J., Douglas, W., & Smith, A. (2003). Cross-age peer tutoring in mathematics with seven- and eleven-year-olds: Influence on mathematical vocabulary, strategic dialogue and self-concept. *Educational Research, 45*(3), 287–308.

White, R. (1963). Ego and reality in psychoanalytic theory: A proposal regarding independent ego energies. *Psychological Issues, 3*, 125–150.

Wigfield, A., Eccles, J. S., Mac Iver, D. J., Reuman, D. A., & Midgley, C. (1991). Transitions during early adolescence: Changes in children's domain-specific self-perceptions and general self-esteem across the transition to junior high school. *Developmental Psychology, 27*, 552–565.

Williams, J. M., & Currie, C. E. (2000). Self-esteem and physical development in early adolescence: Pubertal timing and body image. *Journal of Early Adolescence, 20*, 129–149.

Werner, E. E., & Smith, R. (1982). *Vulnerable but invincible: A study of resilient children.* New York: McGraw-Hill.

Yeboah, D. (2002). Enhancing transition from early childhood phase to primary education: Evidence from the research literature. *Early Years, 22*(1), 51–68.

Zanobini, M., & Usai, M. C. (2002). Domain-specific self-concept and achievement motivation in the transition from primary to low middle school. *Educational Psychology, 22*, 203–217.

3 Educational Transition and Emotional Intelligence

David A. Adeyemo

INTRODUCTION

As people make the transition from childhood to adolescence and from adolescence to adulthood, similarly they make transitions from one level of education to another (i.e., nursery, kindergarten, primary or elementary school, junior or middle school, senior secondary or high school, college or university). These are educational ladders individuals have to scale in the course of their educational career. Most people, if not everybody, at one time or the other have experienced a situation synonymous to transition. For example, when people change location or are transferred in their place of work, they experience transition. Anyone that has had this experience will know and understand well how difficult transition can be. Moving from known and relative comforts of one's home and environment to an unfamiliar terrain can, at least for a short while, create psychological disequilibrium.

Educational transition is a process of change that children, adolescents, and adults experience from one level of education to another. As defined by Wesley (2001), transition implies change from one style, from one state, or from one place to another. It involves changes in relationships, teaching style, environment, space, time, context for learning, and learning itself, all of which combine together at the time of transition to make intense and accelerated demands on the lives of students (Fabian & Dunlop, 2005). When students make transitions, they experience the so-called top-dog phenomenon. This phenomenon as conceptualized by Fabian and Dunlop (2005) has to do with: (i) circumstance of moving from top position in elementary school to lowest position in high school and from being high school seniors to fresh undergraduate in the university; (ii) these positions are characterized by being oldest, biggest, and most powerful versus youngest, smallest, and least powerful.

The examination of existing perspectives on transition will further heighten our understanding of transition. As conceived by Bronfenbrenner (1979) transition is an interlocking set of systems of home, nursery, and school through which children travel in their early years of education. This perspective, as beautiful as it is, fails to take into account the transition from high school to university. Other theoreticians have viewed transition as a 'rite of passage' (Van Gennep, 1960), as border-crossing (Campbell, 2000), and as rites of institution (Webb, Schirato, & Danaher, 2002). Yet another perspective situated transition within the context of life course theory which places children and families within the context of social structure, culture, and population which affect them over time and place (Elder, 2001).

Transition is a mixed-blessing in the sense that it brings along with it a great level of excitement, a sense of worth and pride, and accomplishment for children and their parents. For example, when children move to primary schools, there may be concern about missing friends, parents, siblings, preschool teachers, and the home environment. The 'honeymoon' which initially characterized transition from home to school later gives way to thinking about the uncertainties in the new environment. Although many students make these transitions with little or no difficulty, it is clear that most parents experience varying degrees of problems with transition. Some students also experience academic, social, and emotional challenges as they navigate transitions. The failure to cope effectively with such challenges can produce in the students life-shaping consequences (Center for Mental Health in Schools at UCLA, 2008). For students to negotiate transitions successfully, they need to be equipped with psychological skills or resources that will help them to adjust effectively to people, situations, and events. This is because they need such skills to relate with peers, teachers or lecturers, and other personnel in the school system, and also to understand themselves and use such understanding to relate with others.

It is in view of the above that an emotional intelligence intervention was developed and implemented for first year university students in a Nigerian university. The program could also be implemented for pupils and students at other levels of education. The rest of this chapter focuses on fresh university students with a view that the information provided therein and the intervention proposed are equally useful to pupils/students at the other levels of education.

Entering the university creates a lot of excitement for freshmen and women. This is particularly so when the competitive nature of admission into the university is considered. The joy and the bravado associated with gaining admission into tertiary institution are not limited to the students alone as their parents and relatives are part of the celebration.

As fresh students enter the university environment, however, they might find that there is a huge gap between their initial expectation and the situation on the ground. The discrepancy between the conceptualization of what the university might be and what it actually is becomes quite obvious (Breder, 1997). Adjustment, therefore, becomes a vital recourse. Adjustment to university life is a transitional experience with varying consequential effects for the people involved.

As a person is leaving home to attend university, s/he is faced with the challenges of coping with environmental demands, decrease in parental supervision, very different daily experiences, different academic structure, and the need to adjust to new social relationships. The transition to university, which necessitates the need for the student to repackage his/her personality so as to meet the emerging demands and realities, can indeed impact significantly on his/her physical and mental health (Tao, Dong, Pratt, Hunsberger, & Pancer, 2000). This fact is recognized by the universities all over the world as it is evidenced in the various orientation programs put in place for the fresh students so that they can navigate successfully their transition from high school to the university.

The transition into the university is further heightened by the fact that the adolescents are at the same time making a transition into adulthood. This developmental transition is further accentuated by the additional stressors of university life. These stressors range from environmental adjustment to psychological and psychosocial adaptation. Corroborating the preceding view, Gall, Evans, and Bellerose (2000) identified novel living arrangement, establishing social network, and meeting the expectation of academic demands as examples of a few of the challenges to which students must adapt.

Having reviewed a plethora of studies on the subject, Schwitzer, Griffin, Ancis, and Thomas (1999) summarized that fresh university students face four demands as they navigate the transition from high school and home environment to college life: (i) academic adjustment to college level educational requirements; (ii) institutional adjustment or commitment to college pursuit, academic goals, and eventual career direction; (iii) personal emotional adjustment or the need to independently manage one's own emotional and physical well-being; and (iv) social adjustment to roommate, peer, faculty, and other interpersonal relationships. In a study conducted by Lisa, Lisa, and Rosina (2004), academic issues, student stress, social integration issues, homesickness, and alcohol use are parts of the transitional challenges encountered by first year university students.

The view that fresh university students encounter overwhelming odds is an established fact. Various strategies for dealing with the problems have been suggested. Schwitzer et al. (1999), for instance, advocated a three-pronged approach to helping students in transition namely: prevention, developmental intervention, and consultation. In the college/university setting preventive intervention strategies are usually used when there is possible or probable susceptibility to a particular problem in order to forestall or prevent the onset of adjustment difficulties (Drum & Lawler, 1988). Based on the preceding premise, the present study was designed to facilitate adjustment of fresh university students using emotional intelligence intervention.

Emotional intelligence as conceptualized by Salovey and Mayer (1990) is the set of abilities that underlie competency in dealing with and acting upon emotion-relevant information. It encompasses the ability to perceive, appraise, and express emotion accurately and adaptively; the ability to understand emotion and emotional knowledge; the ability to use feeling to facilitate cognitive activities and adaptive action; and the ability to regulate emotion in oneself and others. This postulation has been empirically validated in several studies (e.g., Adeyemo, 2005, 2007). In these studies, it was established that emotional intelligence is crucially important in school adjustment and academic success. Research evidence has demonstrated that emotional intelligence skills are critical factors in student achievement, retention, and personal well-being (Goleman, 1995; Jaeger & Eagan, 2007; Low & Nelson, 2004; Nelson & Low, 2003; Nelson & Nelson, 2003; Vela, 2003). Among university students, emotional intelligence has been found to impact positively on quality of social interaction, adjustment, and academic success (e.g., Boyle, 2003; Elkins & Low, 2004; Potter, 2005).

Emotional intelligence competencies can contribute to students' social adaptation and academic adjustment in a number of ways. In the first instance, school/university work and cultivation of intellectual competencies demand the ability to use and regulate emotion to facilitate thinking, enhance concentration, control impulsive behavior, perform effectively under stress, and nurture intrinsic motivation (Adeyemo, 2008; Baumeister, Heatherton, & Tice, 1994). Two, adjustment requires establishing meaningful relationship with people such as teachers and peers, and in this case emotional intelligence skills are important. Considering the many benefits of emotional intelligence, it is expected that an intervention program based on the construct would benefit university freshmen in terms of equipping them with the skills that would enable them to cope with the demands of higher education.

Another variable of interest in the study is academic (self-efficacy). Academic self-efficacy was used as a moderating variable in the study. As has been argued consistently and strongly by Bandura (1984, 1986, 1991), the confidence one brings to a specific task mediates the effect of other variables on performance and is a potent predictor of behavior related to that task. Based on this premise, it is expected that students transiting from high school to university would be influenced by their beliefs in their capability to execute relevant academic tasks in the university. It was anticipated that academic self-efficacy would mediate the effect of the intervention on the adjustment of university freshmen.

The aforementioned expectations are not borne out of the blue. For example Lent, Brown, and Larkin (1984) found that efficacy beliefs of students participating in a science and engineering career planning course were related to their grade in the subsequent year. Students with higher efficacy beliefs received higher grades and persisted longer in related majors. Other studies (Bonffard-Bonchard, 1989; Pajares, 1996; Schunk, 1991) have further affirmed the relevance of academic self-efficacy. Students with high sense of academic self-efficacy are characterized by the ability to: undertake more challenging tasks; put in greater effort; show increased persistence in the face of obstacles; demonstrate lower anxiety levels; display flexibility in the use of learning strategies; self-regulate better than other students; demonstrate accurate self-evaluation of their academic performance; display greater intrinsic interest in scholastic matters; and attain higher intellectual achievement. In this study, it is postulated that this construct will mediate the causal link between emotional intelligence intervention and adjustment of fresh university students.

Purpose of the Study

The objective of the study was to use an emotional intelligence intervention to facilitate adjustment of fresh university students. The study also examined the moderating effect of academic self-efficacy on the causal link between emotional intelligence intervention and adjustment of fresh university students.

Hypotheses

Based on the articulated objectives of the study, it was hypothesized that the experimental group will not be significantly different from the control group on the measure of adjustment.

METHODOLOGY

Design

The study used a pretest–posttest control group quasi-experimental design with 2 by 3 factorial matrix. The row consisted of emotional intelligence and control group. The row was crossed with academic self-efficacy varied at three levels (high, moderate, and low).

Participants

Participants were 200 fresh university students randomly drawn from two faculties in a Nigerian university. One hundred and ten participants were male and the remaining ninety female. Their age ranged from 16 to 28 years with a mean age of 18.4 years and standard deviation of 0.76.

Instrumentation

Adjustment to University

Adjustment was assessed with the 'Student Adaptation to College Questionnaire' (SACQ) developed by Baker and Siryk (1984). The instrument assessed four dimensions of college adjustment, namely: academic, personal, social–emotional, and goal commitment–institutional attachment. Academic adjustment subscale measures how well student manages the educational challenges in the university. Social adjustment assesses student's capacity to deal with interpersonal experiences at the university level. Personal–emotional adjustment is a measure of the extent to which a student experiences general psychological distresses or the somatic consequences of distress. The goal commitment institutional adjustment, which is the fourth subscale, measures the degree of institutional affiliation the student feels toward the university. The scale has a total of 67 items with response format arranged on a 9-point Likert scale. The composite score constitute overall adjustment score and the higher the score, the higher the perceived adjustment. The authors had used two independent samples to establish the psychometric properties of the scale. For the two independent samples, Cronbach alphas values of 0.91 and 0.92 were reported (Baker & Siryk, 1984). The subscales have Cronbach alpha values ranging from 0.79 to 0.92. Indication of the criterion validity of the scale was provided by the predicted significant correlation with attrition, use of psychological services, Grade Point Average (GPA), and participation in social activities.

Academic Self-efficacy

For the purpose of measuring academic self-efficacy, the college academic self-efficacy scale (CASES) developed by Owen and Froman (1988) was utilized. It is a 33-item, 5-point Likert type scale which assesses the amount of confidence a student has in relation to taking notes, answering questions, writing, attending class on regular basis, using computer, participating in extra-curricular activities, and so on.

The students responded to the items by circling letters a, b, c, d, e which ranged from high confidence to low confidence. Each letter corresponds to a value ranging from 5 which is equal to a lot of confidence and 1 which implies no confidence at all. To establish the psychometric property of the instrument, it was first administered to 93 undergraduate educational psychology students and later to another group of 88 educational psychology students twice over an 8-week interval. Alpha internal consistency estimates for the two occasions were 0.90 and 0.92. The 8-week stability estimate was 0.85.

Two different criteria, which are in compliance with self-efficacy theory, are frequency of performing each task and enjoyment of each task. In two separate studies the students were asked on 5-point self-ratings for frequency and enjoyment for each of 33 items on CASES (Owen & Froman, 1988). These studies were arranged as incremental validity research. To predict mean item of frequency, GPA was entered into regression equation first and thereafter the CASES score. The analyses of each of the samples described earlier gave very similar results. Academic self-efficacy demonstrated an incremental validity over and above that explained by GPA. To further ascertain the concurrent validity of the scale, the two samples were combined and the scores regressed hierarchically against GPA and CASES. This resulted in the increase in r value of CASES from 0.62 to 0.81.

Emotional Intelligence

This was assessed with the emotional intelligence questionnaire developed by Schutte et al. (1998). The instrument has a total of 33 items with a 5-point response format. It has a Cronbach's alpha of 0.87. Also, a 2-week test–retest showed that the scale has a reliability coefficient of 0.70. Evidence was also provided by the author for the predictive and discriminant validity of the scale. The scale was used as a monitoring device to gauge the progress of the participants in the course of the training program.

Procedure

The training program was conducted in the first semester of the session among fresh undergraduate students in a Nigerian university. The study was done in four phases: pre-sessional activities, pretest, treatment, and post-test. Pre-sessional activities included the recruitment and random assignment of participants to experimental and control group. At the pre-test stage, college adjustment questionnaire, college academic self-efficacy, and emotional intelligence questionnaire were administered to the participants. The post-test was administered following the conclusion of the training program. Participants in the experimental group were exposed to 5 weeks of treatment consisting of two sessions per week. Each session lasted for one hour as a regular lecture. Though the control group was not treated, they were given lecture on study skills technique after the post-test. The College Adjustment Questionnaire (CAQ) was administered to the experimental and control groups as criterion measure.

Emotional Intelligence Training Program

The approach employed in this study is fashioned after the emotional intelligence psychotherapy group developed by Pennington (2001). The goal of the model is to educate and train participants in being emotionally intelligent so that they can enhance their learning potential in school/university, their interpersonal relationship, and the way they cope with emotional discomforts such as adjustment challenges. In this approach, emphasis is also placed on equipping participants with skills with which they can understand themselves, those around them and their circumstances better. The goal of the therapy include: (a) provision of accurate information about the adaptive functions of emotion; (b) assisting group participants in identification of feelings and their appropriate expression particularly the negative or toxic feelings; (c) educating about emotions and their respective meanings; and (d) identifying helpful and adaptive mood or emotional regulation strategies in managing unpleasant feelings and enhanced pleasant feelings. The training program lasted for 10 sessions of 1 hour each.

Session 1: The therapist gave orientation to the participants as to the nature of the program. Specifically, the goal of the session, main concept, and intervention strategies were discussed. Following introduction to the group, the therapist briefed the participants about the time, duration, group structure, group process, goals, and rules and regulations governing participation. Participants were asked to respond to the arrangement. This was followed by self-introduction. Participants were asked what motivated their participation in the program and what they hoped to gain. To elicit participation of all the members, participants were given time to ask questions from the respondents. This was followed by summarization of the issues discussed during the session.

Session 2: The major activities here were the identification of emotion in one's physical state, feeling and thought, and ability to identify emotion in other people. They were asked to identify stressful events as they experienced them in their new environment and their ways of coping with them. They were asked to identify positive and negative emotional states. Participants were further asked to demonstrate the thought they were having and what was it like. They were also asked to demonstrate the physical signs resulting from their emotional experience. Participants were also exposed to problem-solving skills.

Session 3: The focus was on the perception, appraisal and expression of emotion. Participants were asked to describe their feelings following the occurrence of a particular event. The exercise was scripted. Three basic steps were involved namely: (a) description of the situation in factual term; (b) communication of feeling with a single statement; and (c) specification of wants or needs.

Session 4: The session was dedicated to emotional facilitation. The capability of emotion to prioritize thinking by directing attention to important information was demonstrated. The use of emotion to complement judgment and memory concerning feelings was practicalised. Participants were asked to narrate stories and compose songs depicting various emotional states for the next meeting.

Session 5: The session commenced with a review of previous activities and assignments. Psycho-educational activities and materials showing how emotional mood-swinging affects individual's life were presented and provided. Such emotional mood-swinging provides individuals with the opportunity to explore several points of view and alternatives. These points of view could range from optimism to realism and to pessimism. Participants learned how certain emotional states, for instance happiness or joy could be used to inductive creative problem solving. The therapist demonstrated how negative emotions which they may perceive as stressful could help in deductive reasoning skills. A group assignment involving brainstorming which allowed for generation of ideas and feelings for creative problem solving was given.

Session 6: The session involved checking the assignment and a review of past activities. The focus of the session was on how to label emotion and the recognition of the relations among the words and emotion. Therapeutic activities during the session emphasized the understanding of the meanings emotions convey with particular reference, for instance, happiness which is a positive emotion may convey a sense of accomplishment while sadness could be indicative of a sense of loss. Participants were asked to mention other emotional states and their possible interpretation. The participants were told the importance of understanding emotion. For instance, understanding our emotions will enable us to regulate them and be more skilful in managing our lives and relate effectively and productively with people, situations, and events.

Session 7: Activities during the session centered on understanding emotions. Participants' scores on an emotional intelligence questionnaire were presented and discussed. Didactic information was presented on the complex nature of feeling and examples presented. Participants were also asked to give examples.

Session 8: Therapeutic activities during the session involved management of emotion. To assist participants to understand the impact of cultural and familial factors on emotional management, participants were asked to write about how emotions were managed in their homes. The therapist asked questions and gave minimal prompts to facilitate the exercise.

Session 9: This session was spent on discussion of strategies for handling strong emotions which are perceived as stressful. These techniques are presented using didactic approach.

i. Develop emotional self-awareness. This could be achieved by identifying and classifying your emotional strength and skills and the aspect that requires improvement. Being conscious of one's emotional state can provide an avenue for self-monitoring and emotional management.

ii. It should be borne in mind that feeling is symptomatic of important experiences. When strong emotional state occurs, it may signal that something important is occurring. For example, transition stress may trigger withdrawal cognition. Though the occurrence of such a feeling may be transient, it certainly conveys a message. Such feelings could be managed by using 'thought stopping.' For instance, if you have the feeling of leaving the university, you can act promptly by telling yourself that you will not leave the university no matter how difficult. You can also develop empathic assertion to deal with such feelings.

iii. Label your emotion. For emotions to be properly regulated or managed, they would need to be identified and labeled appropriately. Whether you experience positive or negative emotions, make self-statement to that effect. If you are happy, just say so and if you are sad, or anxious, tell yourself in a statement what you are feeling. Identifying and labeling emotion appropriately has therapeutic effect.

iv. Emotion should be expressed in a healthy manner. This can be achieved by setting appropriate and achievable goals, using problem-solving skills generating several alternatives, exploring options, and embarking on behavioral course of action.

Session 10: This session was dedicated to the review of the entire program. Participants were asked evaluative questions concerning what they had gained from the program. They were also allowed to ask questions about the entire program. Thereafter, the college adjustment scale was administered to the participants as post-tests. The therapist having completed the post-test administration thanked the participants for their perseverance, cooperation and support throughout the duration of the program. This was followed by exchange of addresses and phone numbers.

Data Analysis

Analysis of covariance is the major statistical tool employed in this study.

RESULTS

As indicated in Table 3.1, the analysis of covariance of the participants' post-test scores on adjustment using their pretest as covariates indicates that there was significant main effect of treatment ($F(1,199) = 1258.3$, $p< 0.05$).

Consequent upon this result the null hypothesis which states that there would be no significant difference in the adjustment score of experimental and control group was rejected. There was also a two-way interaction of treatment with the academic self-efficacy of the participants ($F(2,199) = 12.75$; $p < 0.05$). What the result is suggesting is that emotional intelligence program was effective in enhancing the adjustment of fresh university students and that the causal link between the treatment and criterion measure was mediated by academic self-efficacy.

The Multiple Classification Analysis (MCA) as can be seen in Table 3.2 shows the adjustment score of the two groups. The experimental group has the highest adjusted post-test mean score ($x = 297.67$) while the control group recorded adjusted posttest mean score of ($x = 8.85$). These values were obtained by summing the grand means ($x = 153.26$) with respective adjusted deviation.

The MCA as shown in Table 3.2 also indicates that the multiple R^2 is 0.956 while the multiple R is 0.978. Thus the treatment program accounted

Table 3.1 Analysis of Covariance (ANCOVA) on Adjustment Between Treated Participants and Control Group With Pretest as Covariate

Source of variation	Sum of squares	Df	Mean Square	F	Sig. of F
Covariates	996144.316	1	996144.316	974.516	.000
PRETEST	996144.316	1	996144.316	974.516	.000
Main Effects	3858692.408	3	1286230.803	1258.304	.000
Treatment	3825440.237	1	3825440.237	3742.381	.000
Academic Self-efficacy	33252.171	2	166626.085	16.265	.000
2-Way Interactions	26068.273	2	13034.136	12.751	.000
Treatment Academic Self-efficacy	26068.273	2	13034.136	12.751	.000
Explained	4880904.997	6	813484.166	795.822	.000
Residual	197283.483	193	1022.194		
Total	5078188.480	199	25518.535		

Table 3.2 Multiple Classification Analysis of Posttest Score of Participants According to Treatment and Academic Self-efficacy on Adjustment Scores

Grand Mean = 153.26

Variable + Category TRTGRP	N	Unadjusted		Adjusted or Independents + Covariates	
		Dev'n	Eta	Dev's	Beta
1. Experimental	100	152.26		144.41	
2. Control	100	-152.26		-144.41	
			.96		.91
ACADEMIC SELF-EFFICACY					
1. Low	70	25.60		17.61	
2. Moderate	70	-13.06		-6.68	
3. High	60	-14.63		-12.74	
			.12		.08
Multiple R Squared					.956
Multiple R					.978

for 95.6% of the variance of the criterion measure (adjustment) while the remaining 4.4% are due to other unexpected sampling error.

DISCUSSION

The findings of the present study have once again established the effectiveness of emotional intelligence intervention in enhancing college adjustment of university freshmen. These findings are in tandem with previous research works (Potter, 2005; Vela, 2003). The probable explanation for this result could be due to the acquisition of emotional intelligence skills which are the combination of intrapersonal and interpersonal factors which would help individuals cope not only with their own emotions but also other's. Such skills include: (a) the ability to recognize, understand, and express emotions and feelings; (b) the ability to understand how others feel and relate to them; (c) the ability to manage and control emotions; (d) the ability to manage change, adapt, and solve problems of a personal and interpersonal nature; and (e) the ability to generate positive affect and be self-motivated (Bar-On, 2006). People who are adept in these skills would be able to interact meaningfully and productively with people, situations, and events. Suffice to say that emotionally intelligent individuals have the capacity to cope with intrapersonal and interpersonal challenges, and thus are able to adjust to environmental demands and people as it has happened in the case of the participants in the present study.

Another important finding worthy of note in the present study is the moderating influence of academic self-efficacy on the causal link between the intervention and the criterion variable (adjustment). Academic self-efficacy has been reported to be a potent factor in academic success and adjustment (Chemers, Hu, & Garcia, 2001; Hirose, Wada, & Watanabe, 1999). The finding is also an empirical validation of Bandura's (1997) postulation that strong self-efficacy beliefs enhance human accomplishment and personal well-being. According to him, people with a strong sense of personal competence in a domain, approach difficulty in that domain as challenges to be mastered rather than as danger to be avoided, have greater intrinsic interest in activities, and set challenging goals and maintain a strong commitment to them. Further explanation for the finding can also hinge on the fact that students with a high sense of efficacy are characterized by the ability to undertake more challenging tasks, demonstrate low anxiety levels, self-regulate better, and demonstrate accurate self-evaluation of their general performance.

CONCLUSION AND RECOMMENDATIONS

The efficacy of emotional intelligence as a veritable tool for enhancing the adjustment of university freshmen has been demonstrated in the present study.

The existing practices for fostering adjustment of students in transition lack the depth and theoretical grounding of emotional intelligence intervention. Educational institutions would therefore need to integrate emotional intelligence training program into the orientation program for fresh students. For effective accomplishment of the goals and expectations of education, there is a need for the intentional integration and fostering of emotional intelligence competencies in teacher education program and school curriculum.

As academic self-efficacy has been identified as a core issue in student adjustment, an intervention program aiming to boost student efficacy should be delivered simultaneously with emotional intelligence intervention for greater impact. There are some resources for developing self-efficacy that could be beneficial to students in transition; vicarious experience from the sophomores who have been able to successfully overcome college adjustment concerns can have a soothing effect on the transition experience of freshmen. College/university counselors can help freshmen to relay and relive their experience of success as a way of counterbalancing adjustment difficulties.

REFERENCES

Adeyemo, D. A. (2005). The buffering effect of emotional intelligence on the adjustment of secondary school students in transition. *Electronic Journal of Research in Educational Psychology, 3*(2), 79–90.
Adeyemo, D. A. (2007). Moderating influence of emotional intelligence on the link between academic self-efficacy and achievement of university students. *Psychology and Developing Society, 19*(2), 199–213.
Adeyemo, D. A. (2008). Measured influence of emotional intelligence and some demographic characteristics on academic self-efficacy of distance learners. *Perspectives in Education, 24*(2), 105–112.
Baker, R., & Siryk, B. (1984). Measuring adjustment to college. *Journal of Counselling Psychology, 31*, 179–189.
Bandura, A. (1984). Recycling misperception of perceived self-efficacy. *Cognitive Therapy and Research, 8*, 231–255.
Bandura, A. (1986). *Social foundation of thought and action: A social cognitive theory.* Englewood Cliffs, NJ: Prentice Hall.
Bandura, A. (1991). Social cognitive theory of self-regulation. *Organizational Behavior and Human Decision Process, 50*, 248–287.
Bandura, A. (1997). *Self-efficacy: The exercise of control.* New York: Freeman.
Bar-On, R. (2006). The Bar-On model of emotional–social intelligence (ESI). *Psychothema, 18*, Supl. 13–25.
Baumeister, R. F., Heatherton, T. F., & Tice, D. M. (1994). *Losing control: How and why people fail at self-regulation.* San Diego, CA: Academic Press.
Bonffard-Bonchard, T. (1989). Influence of self-efficacy on performance in cognitive task. *Journal of Social Psychology, 130*, 353–363.
Boyle, J. R. (2003). *An analysis of emotional intelligence skills development training program and student achievement and retention.* Unpublished raw data, Texas A & M University—Kingsville.
Breder, S. (1997). *Addressing the issue of social and academic integration for first year students.* Retrieved June 12, 2008, from http://ultibase.rmt.edu.au/article.dec(.9)beder.htm.

Bronfenbrenner, U. (1979). *The ecology of human development. Experiment by nature and design.* Cambridge, MA: Harvard University Press.

Campbell, C. S. (2000). Work family border theory: A new theory of work family balance. *Human Relations, 53*(6), 747–770.

Center for Mental Health in Schools at UCLA. (2008). *Transitions: Turning risks into opportunities for student support.* Los Angeles, CA: Author. Retrieved April 5, 2009, from http://smhp.psych.ucla.edu/pdfdocs/transitions/transitions.pdf.

Chemers, H. M., Hu, L., & Garcia, B. F. (2001). Academic self-efficacy and first year college students' performance and adjustment. *Journal of Educational Psychology, 93,* 55–64.

Drum, D. L., & Lawler, A. C. (1988*). Developmental intervention: Theories, principles and practice.* Columbus, OH: Merill Publishing.

Elder, G. H. (2001). Families, social change and individual lives. *Marriage and Family Review,* 177–192.

Elkins, M., & Low, G. (2004). *Emotional intelligence and communication competence: Research pertaining to their impact upon the first year experience.* Unpublished raw data, Texas A & M University—Kingsville.

Fabian, H., & Dunlop, A. (2005). The importance of play in the transition to school. In J. R. Moyles (Ed.), *The excellence of play, 2nd edition* (pp. 228–241). Berkshire: Open University.

Gall, T., Evans, L., & Bellerose, S. (2000). Transition to first year university: Patterns of change in adjustment across life domains and homes. *Journal of Social and Clinical Psychology, 19,* 544–567.

Goleman, D. (1995). *Emotional intelligence: Why it can matter more than IQ for character, health and lifelong achievement.* New York: Bantam Press.

Hirose, E. I., Wada, S., & Watanabe, H. (1999). Effects of self-efficacy on adjustment to college. *Japanese Psychological Research, 41*(3), 163–172.

Jaeger, A. J., & Eagan K. (2007). Developing emotional intelligence as a means to enhance academic performance. *NASPA Journal, 44*(4), 512–537.

Lent, R. W., Brown, S. D., & Larkin, K. S. (1984). Relation of self-efficacy expectation to academic achievement and persistence. *Journal of Counselling Psychology, 31,* 356–362.

Lisa, C., Lisa, C., & Rosina, P. (2004). *The first year experience: Transition.* Retrieved May 22, 2008, from *Chat charleton.Ca/taeix/chapte2.html*

Low, G. R., & Nelson, D. B. (2004). Emotional intelligence: The role of transformative learning in academic excellence. *Texas Study Magazine for Secondary Education* (Spring 2004). Retrieved April 5, 2009, from http://www.tamuk.edu/edu/kwei000/Research/Articles/Article_files/EI_TransformativeLearning.pdf.

Nelson, D., & Low, G. (2003). *Emotional intelligence: Achieving academic and career excellence.* Upper Saddle River, NJ: Prentice Hall.

Nelson, D., & Nelson, K. (2003). *Emotional intelligence skills: Significant factors in freshmen achievement and retention.* (ERIC Document Reproduction Service No. CG032375)

Owen, S. V., & Froman, R. D. (1988). *Development of a college academic self—efficacy scale.* Paper presented at the annual meeting of the National Council on Measurement in Education, New Orleans, LA.

Pajares, F. (1996). Self-efficacy beliefs in academic setting. *Review of Educational Research, 66,* 543–578.

Pennington, R. S. (2001). A time-limited psychotherapy group model for developing emotional intelligence: The EIPG model for counseling. Retrieved May 28, 2008, from http://www.eq.org.

Potter, G. (2005). *The impact of emotional intelligence intervention program on freshmen at a South Texas Higher Education Institutions.* Unpublished doctoral dissertation, Texas A & M University—Kingsville.

Salovey, P., & Mayer, D. (1990). Emotional intelligence. *Imagination, Cognition and Personality, 9*, 185–211.

Schunk, D. H. (1991). Self-efficacy and academic motivation. *Educational Psychologist, 26*, 207–231.

Schutte, N. S., Marlouff, J. M., Hall, L. E., Haggerty, D. D., Cooper, J. T., Golden, C. J., et al. (1998). Development and validation of measure of emotional intelligence. *Personality and Individual Differences, 25*, 167–177.

Schwitzer, A. M., Griffin, C. T., Ancis, J. R., & Thomas, C. R. (1999). Social adjustment experiences of African American college students. *Journal of Counselling and Development, 77*, 189–197.

Tao, S., Dong, Q., Pratt, M. W., Hunsberger, P. S., & Pancer, S. M. (2000). Social support, relationship to coping and adjustment during the transition to university in the people's Republic of China. *Journal of Adolescent Research, 15*, 123–144.

Van Gennep, A. (1960). *Rites of passage* (M. B Vizedom & G. L Caffee, Trans.) London: Routledge and Kegan Paul.

Vela, R. (2003). *The role of emotional intelligence in the academic achievement of first year college students.* Unpublished doctoral dissertation, Texas A & M University—Kingsville.

Webb, J., Schirato, T., & Danaher, G. (2002). *Understanding Bourdieu.* London: Sage Publications.

Wesley, P. (2001). *Smooth moves to kindergarten.* Chapel Hill: Chapel Hill Training Outreach Project Incorporated.

Part II

Transition from Early Years Setting to Primary School

4 Small Steps

Perspectives on Understanding and Supporting Children Starting School in Scotland

Elizabeth Hannah, Heather Gorton, and Divya Jindal-Snape

EARLY YEARS EDUCATION IN SCOTLAND

In Scotland, children in the age range birth to 5 years experience a range of informal and formal learning opportunities in the home and other settings. These settings typically include parent and toddler groups, playgroups, nurseries (schools and classes), and family centers (Scottish Office, 1999). The importance of early years provision has been recognized by the present Scottish Government (Scottish Government, 2008a; Scottish Government, 2008b; Scottish Government 2008c; Scottish Government, 2008d) and, previously, by the Scottish Executive (Scottish Executive, 2002).

The Standards in Scotland's Schools etc. Act 2000 places a legislative duty on local authorities to provide free part-time preschool education for all eligible children. In 2002, the Scottish Executive issued guidance on Section 34 of the Act and introduced free part-time early years education for 3- and 4-year-old children (Scottish Executive, 2002; Scottish Government, 2008a) with 3-year-old children entitled to start preschool the term following their 3rd birthday. In 2008, the Scottish Government reaffirmed its commitment to improving the lives of young children by increasing access to free preschool education for this preschool group (Scottish Government, 2008b). A recent survey, conducted between April 2006 and March 2007, of a sample of Scottish children born between June 2002 and March 2003 found that 94% of the children had preschool placements. Of these, 85% were in local authority and 15% in private or voluntary provision (Scottish Government, 2008a). Local education authorities receive funding from the government to deliver this education either through their own provision or by working in partnership with voluntary and private organizations. As of August 2007, every 3- and 4-year-old child was entitled to 475 hours of preschool education per year, which could be supplemented by additional hours, paid for by parents/carers, to accommodate parents' work and other family commitments. The Scottish Government is committed to a further increase to 570 hours per annum as of August 2010 (Scottish Government, 2008c).

The compulsory age of starting school in European countries ranges from 4 to 7 years, although children may start school before then (Eurydice at NFER, 2007). Relative to other European countries, the UK has a low statutory age of entry to school, with Northern Ireland having the lowest at 4 years. In Scotland, the Education Act 1872 made education compulsory from the age of five years (Anderson, 2003). Given that there is a single intake in August, the typical age range of those commencing primary school is 4.5 to 5.5 years (Hughes & Kleinberg, 2003).

The terms 'delayed' and 'retained' are applied to children who stay on in preschool when they could start school. Currently, children who are 5 by March 1st may start school in the preceding August, however parents of children with January and February birthdays have the right to request a delay in school entry and are entitled to a funded early years placement for an additional year (automatic deferral). In contrast, parents of children whose birthdays fall between mid-August and December 31st have the right to request delayed entry but have to provide supporting evidence for additional funding to the local council (discretionary deferral; Edinburgh City Council, 2007). Retention is a term applied to a minority of children who are 5 years of age by August; where there are concerns about their development; and a decision has been made to retain them in early years' provision.

The educational curriculum for 3- to 5-year-olds in Scotland is informed by national guidance, namely The Curriculum Framework for Children 3–5 (Scottish Office, 1999). This informs practitioners of the learning needs of young children and suggests ways of planning, implementing, and evaluating the curriculum to complement other learning opportunities. This guidance will in due course be succeeded by A Curriculum for Excellence, which provides a single curriculum covering the age range 3 to 18 years (Scottish Executive, 2004). A key component of this strategy is to improve continuity through the different phases of preschool and school education. In an international review of early years education, Stephen (2006) reports that children moving into primary school tend to experience curricular and pedagogical discontinuity. A Curriculum for Excellence recommends the adoption of active learning methods in the first year of primary school to address such concerns and facilitate the transition process.

SCHOOL READINESS

Four approaches to conceptualizing school readiness emerge from the literature, namely school readiness as a function of the child's maturation; proficiency with a set of skills; meanings and values assigned by an individual school community; and an interactionist approach which tries to integrate children's strengths, with the school's capacity to adapt educational experiences according to individuals' strengths and needs (Meisels, 1998). In this chapter we have focused on maturationist and interactionist approaches.

Scotland is in a unique position within the UK as children start school later than their English, Welsh, and Northern Irish counterparts and Scottish parents have more flexibility in deciding when their child will start school. Many parents choose to delay their child's school entry and educational psychologists are often involved in decisions about retaining children in a nursery setting.

A common argument for delaying children's school entry to ensure their readiness to start formal schooling is that of maturation (Marshall, 2003). Adults putting forward this argument are of the view that delaying a child's school entry or retaining them in an early years setting will maximize their later progress. Follow up of delayed entry children suggests that they make better educational progress initially although not always significantly (Katz, 2000; Malone, West, Flanagan, & Park, 2006; March, 2005; Stipek, 2002) whereas the retained group do not appear to make better progress (Guevermont, Roos, & Brownwell, 2001; Malone et al., 2006; National Center for Education Statistics (NCES), 2000; Stipek, 2002). Studies confirm that both delayed and retained children are at risk of leaving secondary education before their education is complete and may also be more at risk of emotional, social, and behavioral difficulties (Stipek, 2002; Wils, 2004).

Findings regarding whether younger children are more vulnerable to social, emotional, and behavioral difficulties are more mixed. Some studies find no effect whereas others find an impact (Ford & Gledhill, 2002; Stipek, 2002). Where an impact is found, caution is needed in interpreting this as often the finding is based on teacher/parental ratings rather than direct observations of a child's behavior. Some studies find that relatively younger children are more likely to be registered as having special education needs (Wilson, 2000), referred to Psychological Services (Menet, Eakin, Stuart, & Rafferty, 2000; Wilson, 2000) or diagnosed as having ADHD (Ford & Gledhill, 2002). These findings need to be interpreted with caution as when children's actual performance is looked at more closely there are often other contributory factors such as teacher bias and length of schooling. Parents and teachers seem to hold strong beliefs about the importance of age in determining school readiness (Graue & Di Perna, 2000; Marshall, 2003). A range of international studies (Bedard & Dhuey, 2006; Ford & Gledhill, 2002; NICHD, 2007; Sharp, 2002; Stipek, 2002; Tymms, Jones, Merrell, Henderson, & Cowie, 2005) show that relatively older children initially achieve better attainments in literacy and sometimes maths. This effect is evident whether children start school at age 4 or at age 7 suggesting that it may occur because of the way that school systems are organized. Therefore, it appears that there is no one optimal age for starting school but instead a variation in performance by age that may reduce by the end of primary school or possibly persist into higher education. Increasing or reducing the age that children start school is not likely to remove the effect; it would just shift it to a different group of children. This suggests that we should be more concerned about finding ways to reduce the relative age effect rather than hunting for an 'optimal school starting age.' Further, studies that look at a range of other factors such as socioeconomic and/or ethnic background of parents, length and quality of preschool education, and length of schooling find that these factors actually hold greater importance in determining the progress a child makes.

In conclusion, professionals are becoming increasingly aware of the limitations of both the maturationist argument and the benefits of delayed and retained entry. The interactionist approach appears to offer a more effective model for conceptualizing children's school readiness and planning for and supporting their entry into school. There is an argument that rather than focusing on school readiness, appropriate measures need to be established to ensure a successful school transition for every child.

EVIDENCE OF A RELATIONSHIP BETWEEN AN EFFECTIVE TRANSITION PROCESS AND A SUCCESSFUL START TO SCHOOL

There appear to be relatively few studies of preschool to primary transition which have investigated the relationship between an effective transition process and child outcomes. In the UK, Smith (2003) evaluated the impact of a 13-week intervention program, implemented during the two terms before the transition to school, aimed at promoting the children's social and emotional development so that they became more adaptive to the challenges of the new context. The range of positive outcomes identified in the intervention group included knowledge of playtime rituals, confidence in exploring the environment, and having a special friend. Limitations of the study include the small sample size and the lack of an established evidence base for the intervention program.

Taking an international perspective, an Australian study by Margetts (2002) measured the success of transition programs in terms of children's social adjustment to school. The findings support the hypothesis that children in schools with a high number of transition activities adjust better initially than children in schools with a limited number of transition activities. Further evidence for the relationship between the frequency of transition activities and children's adjustment was found in a US study by LoCasale-Crouch, Mashburn, Downer, and Pianta (2008). They confirmed the effect on social adjustment and, in addition, found an impact on the children's academic competencies using kindergarten teacher completed rating scales. Perceived limitations of these studies are their reliance on teachers' ratings (LoCasale-Crouch et al., 2008) and on teachers' and parents' ratings (Margetts, 2002). Furthermore, they do not provide a longitudinal perspective as to whether these gains are sustained. Clarke (2007) measured the longer-term impact of a transition intervention using quantitative and qualitative measures. This study, conducted in Singapore, investigated ways of empowering parents to become more involved in their children's learning during the final semester in preschool and during the transition to school. One of its aims was to increase the children's cognitive and language skills. In terms of measured child outcomes, the children in the two parent intervention groups (parent and child interactive learning sessions; parent-only evening workshops) evidenced an increase in skills compared to the contrast group (no additional parent sessions). However, the differences found at the end of the preschool year had reduced by the end of the first year in primary school.

THEORETICAL MODELS USED BY RESEARCHERS AND POLICY MAKERS TO CONCEPTUALIZE THE TRANSITION FROM PRESCHOOL TO SCHOOL

A number of theoretical models have been utilized by researchers and policy makers to conceptualize the transition from preschool to school. These have included medical, maturationist, interactionist, social constructivist, environmental, social, sociocultural, and ecosystemic perspectives (Deckert-Peaceman, 2006; Dockett & Perry, 2002; Einarsdóttir, 2007; Stephen & Cope, 2003).

Bronfenbrenner's (1979) ecological systems model or its derivatives appear to have had a major influence on research, policy, and practice since it was published 30 years ago. Taking an international perspective, it has been used by an array of researchers to conceptualize the transition process from preschool to school and to inform their research activities (for example, Broström, 2000; Dockett & Perry, 2001; Ledger, Smith, & Rich, 2000; Margetts, 2007; Pianta, Cox, Taylor, & Early, 1999). Bronfenbrenner (1992), in a personal critique of his original ecological paradigm, reaffirms the basic theorems and proposes some changes to some of the corollaries based on scientific evidence and argument. He refers to the following definition as the 'cornerstone' of his theory:

> The ecology of human development is the scientific study of the progressive, mutual accommodation, throughout the life course, between an active, growing human being, and the changing properties of the immediate settings in which the developing person lives, as this process is affected by the relations between the settings, and by the larger contexts in which the settings are embedded. (Bronfenbrenner, 1992, p. 188)

Bronfenbrenner (1979) conceptualized his ecological systems paradigm in terms of hierarchical systems ranging from those proximal to the individual to those most remote or distal. These were termed the microsystem, mesosystem, exosystem, and macrosystem. In his 1992 reformulation of the microsystem, Bronfenbrenner emphasizes the importance of the unique and distinctive characteristics of individuals in the person's immediate environment (e.g., parents of a child) within a bidirectional influential relationship. The mesosystem remains unchanged and refers to interactions between two or more settings within which an individual could be situated (e.g., child's home and school). Similarly, the retained definition of the exosystem refers to two or more settings one of which is in the individual's immediate environment and one of which is remote to, but has an influence on, that setting (e.g., relationship between child's home and parent's employment). Finally, Bronfenbrenner (1992) reformulates his definition of the macrosystem drawing on two 'context-oriented' views of development, namely sociohistorical and belief systems. Although the new definition retains reference to cultural and subcultural characteristics, it highlights the importance of elements considered to have a direct causal relationship on development such as belief systems and lifestyles. Finally, Bronfenbrenner (1992) draws attention to a key omission from his original thesis, namely temporal elements which later investigators employed in their research and which Bronfenbrenner refers to as 'chronosystem models.' He notes that these temporal aspects may refer to changes in the individual (e.g., chronic illness) or in the environment (e.g., starting school) either of which create a dynamic change in the relationship between the individual and the environment.

It is argued that the utility of Bronfenbrenner's ecological systems theory as applied to the child's transition to school lies in its ability to capture the multiplicity of interrelated factors which may influence a child's development; the bidirectional nature of the interactions between the child and his/her environment; and dynamic features of the process, including temporal aspects, which reflect changes in the individual and/or the setting. We have utilized this model to frame the following case study.

CASE STUDY OF PARENTS' VIEWS ABOUT THE TRANSITION OF THEIR CHILDREN FROM PRESCHOOL TO A SCOTTISH PRIMARY SCHOOL

The third author collected data from some parents after nearly 4 months of their children moving to the first year of primary school in a city in Scotland. The sampling frame was 50, out of which 20 parents responded to a questionnaire, a response rate of 40%. The questionnaire involved a number of closed questions, primarily requiring their agreement to statements, some factual and some that were related to their experience. It also had eight open questions seeking detailed responses about their experiences. Overall, out of the 20 parents, 5 reported that their children had faced difficulties during transition. Of the 20 parents, 18 thought that the preparation from primary school staff was helpful for their child and interestingly 16 thought that it was helpful for them. On further investigation, it was found that one parent felt that the preparation was good for the child but not for them and one parent had ticked both agree and disagree regarding the preparation for them as a parent and so had been considered under the category 'Don't Know.' It was interesting to note that the 2 parents above also reported that their child did not experience any problems. Looking at further data from these 2 parents as to what the school could have done to make the move better for them, it is clear that more information, and additional opportunities to visit the school and talk with the teachers would have helped them. Although 17 parents reported that they were happy that the primary school staff did all they could to make the move smooth, 3 reported that they were not.

Further data has been presented in accordance with Bronfenbrenner's ecological systems theory with more emphasis on parents' voices rather than quantitative data. Direct quotes from the parents' responses are in italics.

Microsystem

Child–home

Having a child starting school is a significant event in a family. Taking a sociocultural perspective, there are associated family rituals during the child's preparation for school (Deckert-Peaceman, 2006). Niesel and Griebel (2001) describe transition to school as a common experience for the whole family involving a co-construction by the child, parents, and others. The child and parent develop new identities as a school child and the parent of a school child (Niesel & Griebel, 2001). It has been suggested that strong emotional arousals are associated with this change process and that the influential nature of the parent–child interaction should be acknowledged and addressed through transition practices (Griebel & Niesel, 2000).

In the current study, parents highlighted their need for support to help prepare their child for the transition to primary school. Good communication with teachers was a key component, including feedback regarding how their child was settling in, and more and timely information about the school systems, routines, and procedures. The following parental quote illustrates these sentiments and suggests that parents want to play an important part in the transition process.

> *I would have liked to be more familiar with what my child is being taught, homework, school diaries etc. Didn't know if clear folders had to be returned every day or just once a week on Thursday. Felt a bit useless.*

Recognition of the importance of the first day of school for parents and the value of having people with whom they can engage is reflected in the following parental quote.

> *More communication on the first day so I could put my child at ease if I knew what was happening. For instance on arriving in the classroom although the teacher spoke to our child she ignored us. She didn't introduce herself or explain what to do with coats or bags. We also were not told where to pick our children up when we came back. As parents we were left hanging around like spare parts and ruined the experience of our child's first day at school.*

These findings highlight the perceived importance of the parental role during the child's transition to school. This resonates with research studies which have demonstrated the effectiveness of parent empowerment programs (Clarke, 2007) and those which have highlighted the emotional support provided to children by home artifacts (Fabian, 2000). Furthermore, there is a need to recognize the transition which parents undergo from being the parent of a preschool child to being the parent of a school child, and to provide support during this process of change in personal identity (Niesel & Griebel, 2001).

Child–school

A key component of a transition program is helping a child adjust to a new learning environment that includes both physical/organizational elements and relationships (adults and peers). This importance of the former was emphasized by one parent in this study.

> *You go from a nursery setting where you know the staff to having to line up with a class of strangers and the parents having to stand back—a huge change! . . .*

It has been suggested that teachers can help children adjust to this new environment by explicitly teaching expected behavior and using other children as role models (Fabian, 2000). One parent in the present study highlighted the importance of letting children practice something before it is implemented.

> *The school lunches, and in particular the way in which orders are taken, could have been explained to us, so we could make sure our child understood it. At first, he was very puzzled and got the wrong meal a few times. Maybe children could practice this in the week before they go full time.*

Eight parents suggested that the school visit could be made longer and extended over a period of time. The following quote is illustrative.

> *Rather than one 4 hour morning where the children visit the school— would be better if it was maybe 1 hour a week for 4 weeks prior to them starting school. . . . gives the children a familiarity with going to school and lets them meet their classmates on a regular basis.*

In terms of teacher–child relationships, this study found that the parents thought it was very important not only for a child to be familiar with the teacher but also to start forming a relationship before s/he started school. Sixteen parents reported that the school visits had been very useful. Seven parents further commented on the usefulness of booklets provided about the school, especially the ones that had photos of teachers. They reported that this helped familiarize the child with the teacher prior to starting school. The following quotation illustrates such views.

> *My child visiting to familiarise themselves with the surroundings [was beneficial]. Also the booklet about the school with photos so yet again you can discuss what they will be doing and who the people are.*

This finding concurs with other research which has demonstrated that parents not only value the child–teacher relationship (Fabian, 2000) but emphasize the two-way nature of the relationship in contrast with early childhood educators (Dockett & Perry, 2001). This has important implications for transition activities suggesting that there should be a greater emphasis on teacher–child contact.

Child–peer group

Children value peer relationships during their first year of school (Margetts, 2006). Child participants report the importance of developing pro-social peer relationships (including friends) and of dealing with anti-social peer relationships (such as bullying). In terms of outcomes, Margetts (2002), in a large scale Australian study of factors which impact on children's adjustment during the first year of school, reports a positive relationship between the presence of a familiar playmate in the same class and teacher and parent ratings of behavior at home and in school. In a UK study which involved interviewing 50 children, their parents and teachers, Fabian (2000) notes that children who start school with a friend are happier; those who start school with a new class rather than an established class find it easier to adjust; circle time and registration helps children to get to know each other; and children learn by asking friends and watching other children. In contrast, in an ethnographic, participant observation study in New Zealand, Ledger et al. (2000) report that adjustment to school does not appear to be related to having friends or familiar peers on school entry. However, the authors acknowledge that the system of school entry in New Zealand means that children usually start school alone. They note that "only two instances of continuing friendships were observed in this study, so it was hard to make a clear connection between ease of transition and stable friendships" (p. 67).

In the current study, quantitative data analysis did not show any significant relationship between moving with peers from an early years setting to primary school, however comments from parents highlighted its importance.

> *. . . on the first day the teacher understood that sitting next to your best friend was important.*

The negative impact on the child of not moving with friends was emphasized by the 2 parents who reported that their children faced difficulties during transition.

> *Such a completely alien environment for both me and my child—child knew no other children in P1 and I knew no other parents . . .*

> *My son only knew one child in his class (who attended the same private nursery) and was extremely clingy for the first two weeks or so, not wanting to line up and having to be prised off me a few times— mainly a little separation anxiety but also not knowing anyone.*

Mesosystem

Home–school

The nature and function of the relationship between parents and school staff over the transition period has been the subject of previous research (Dunlop et al., 2008; Fabian, 2000; Griebel & Niesel, 2000; Pianta et al., 1999; Russell, 2005). In the present study, several parents commented on the importance of a good relationship between parents and school professionals.

> *'Head Teacher' was fantastic—from completing the placing request to showing us round the school . . . gave us so much confidence in the management of the school.*

The importance of good communication between school staff and parents has been highlighted in a number of studies. This communication can be achieved in a variety of ways, including visits, meetings in school, information giving and information sharing (Dunlop et al., 2008; Fabian,

2000). Although in the current study, parents were positive about the visits, meetings, and information they had received from school staff, similar to Dunlop et al. (2008), they expressed the need for further communication.

> *Opportunities to talk to the teacher in the early days would have been appreciated. I was very conscious of delaying the teacher as she brought the line in, therefore we avoided opportunities such as this to talk through minor concerns. Informal visits to the classrooms in the early days would have been helpful, though I appreciate that this is difficult to manage.*

This resonates with the findings from a small-scale longitudinal study of parents' expectations as their disabled child started school (Russell, 2005). In that study, the largest proportion of unrealized expectations was linked to parents' relationships with the school and, in particular, the need for ongoing accurate information, greater knowledge of schools, and opportunities to discuss expectations.

Preschool–school

Exploration of communication and other forms of liaison between staff in early years establishments and primary schools, as one component of the transition process, has been the focus of a number of studies (Broström, 2000; LoCasale-Crouch et al., 2008). In the present study, children had moved from a variety of early years settings into the school. Out of 20 children, 8 were from the nursery attached to the school (feeder nursery), 2 from another local authority nursery, 7 from private nurseries in the same city, 2 from nurseries outside the city (school has a big international population), and 1 child went part-time to a private and part-time to the feeder nursery. Of the 20 parents, 12 felt the communication was good, 3 said it was not good, and 5 said that they did not know. Of the 12 who thought communication was good, 6 children went to feeder nurseries, 3 to private, and 3 to other early years settings. Of the 3 who disagreed, their children were in feeder, private and other settings. Of the ones who said they did not know, 1 child was at a feeder nursery, 3 at private nurseries, and 1 at another nursery.

This is an interesting finding as there is a common assumption that there is better communication between feeder nurseries and the receiving primary school; however this did not seem to be the case here. Importantly, it highlights that this is an area where the early years establishments and schools need to put in more effort, especially as several parents commented that the reciprocal visits and exchange of information between nursery and school was one of the most beneficial aspects of the work done to prepare the child for transition. In research exploring teachers' views of communication practices (hypothetical and actual) between early years staff and school staff, it appears that there is greater emphasis on the sharing of written records and discussions about specific children than on visits (LoCasale-Crouch et al., 2008) and the coordination of the two curricula and coordinated teaching (Broström, 2000).

Exosystem

Parent–Parent relationship

An interesting finding from the current study concerned the ways in which parents can support each other during transitions. Parents were very positive about the role that other parents had played as reflected in the following quotes.

> . . . this [parents and Parent Council] is a positive aspect of school community.

> . . . all the information I get was from the parent chats in the playground.

Two parents reported that they had found the communication with other parents to be helpful.

> *The majority of parents have been very friendly and happy to share information.*

The value placed on support from other parents in relation to the transition to school has been reported in other studies. Niesel and Griebel (2001) report that for parents of first-born children the main source of school information was other parents with older children. This reflected the importance of the family's social network rather than formal institutions.

The Scottish Schools (Parental Involvement) Act 2006 (Scottish Government, 2006) changed arrangements for parental representation. All parents/carers are members of the Parent Forum and can set up a Parent Council (from August 2007) to represent and act on their behalf. Given this recent development, the third author wanted to explore the potential role of Parent Councils in facilitating transition.

Seven parents made suggestions as to how other parents and the Parent Council could support a child making the transition and his/her parents. The following quotes are typical.

> *It would be good if in the first few weeks of school, members of the Parent Council (or other parents) were available to and advertised at drop-off times to answer practical questions from new parents.*

Facilitate parents and children getting to know each other—when the letters are sent out to parents telling them what class their children will be in, why not also offer a service whereby parents can add their e-mail address to a distribution list—play dates at parks etc can then be scheduled through the summer and parents and children turn up if they want to/when they can. I'm sure this is something that the Parent's Council could manage. Would really strengthen the feeling of the school community and children would recognise and know each other when school starts. Same could apply for October holidays. I find it extremely difficult to get to know other parents and arranging play dates is just something I'm not yet confident enough to do. I am very aware that other parents collect every day and have got to know each other—is a very rare option for me.

These quotations exemplify the perceived importance of parents in the wider school community. They suggest that other parents can impact indirectly on the success or otherwise of an individual child's transition to school.

CONCLUDING COMMENTS

In this chapter, the authors discuss school readiness and transition issues within the Scottish context. Different ways of conceptualizing school readiness are considered and they conclude that an interactionist approach appears to offer a more effective model than a maturationist approach. Questions are raised about the benefits of delayed and retained school entry. The authors propose a focus on measures which will ensure a successful school transition. There appears to be some evidence from research conducted in the UK and further afield of a relationship between an effective transition process and positive child outcomes.

Theoretically, the authors argue that Bronfenbrenner's ecological systems model provides a useful conceptual framework to consider school transition as it reinforces the complex, multi-faceted, and dynamic nature of the process. A case study of parents' views of their children's transition to a Scottish primary school provides a focus for exploring the utility of this framework. At the microsystem, the importance of a range of individuals (parents, teachers, and peers) in the child's immediate environment was highlighted. The mesosystem was exemplified by consideration of home–school and preschool–school interactions. In relation to the former, parents commented on the importance of good communication with school staff. In relation to the latter, although parents appeared to value reciprocal visits and the exchange of information between nursery and school staff, there was evidence of a need to further develop these transition activities. Finally, the exosystem was reflected in parent–parent relationships. Parents were very positive about the supportive role played by other parents, not just those with children making the transition but also those with older children, with specific reference to the value of information sharing. This is an interesting finding given the emphasis in a recent Scottish Government publication, The Early Years Framework, on the key role of parents and the wider community in achieving positive outcomes for children and on the importance of building family and community capacity (Scottish Government, 2008c).

At a local policy and practice level, the findings from the case study have informed specific recommendations to the school's senior management team and Parent Council members. For example, in response to the case study findings, a web forum has been set up to increase communication between the parents of children about to make the transition and other parents, as well as between parents and teachers. Further research within the Scottish context is suggested. Areas of interest to the authors include further exploration of the role of parents and the wider community in supporting a child's transition to school. Furthermore, it is acknowledged that one of the limitations of this case study was the sole focus on the parents' voices and that it is important to take cognizance of children's views. Hence, it is planned to undertake research that will encapsulate the child's unique perspective of transition.

Note: The authors would like to thank the research participants and the Parent Council members for their input in the Scottish case study.

REFERENCES

Anderson, R. (2003). The history of Scottish education, pre-1980. In T. G. K. Bryce & W. M. Humes (Eds.), *Scottish education: Post devolution, 2nd Edition* (pp. 219–228). Edinburgh: Edinburgh University Press.
Bedard, K., & Dhuey, E. (2006). The persistence of early childhood maturity: International evidence of long-run age effects. *Quarterly Journal of Economics, 121,* 1437–1472.
Bronfenbrenner, U. (1979). *The ecology of human development. Experiments by nature and design.* Cambridge, MA: Harvard University Press.
Bronfenbrenner, U. (1992). Ecological systems theory. In R. Vasta (Ed.), *Six theories of child development* (pp. 187–249). London and Philadelphia: Jessica Kingsley Publishers.
Broström, S. (2000). *Transition to school.* Paper related to poster symposium on "transition" at EECERA 10th European Conference on Quality in Early Childhood Education, University of London.
Clarke, C. (2007). Parent involvement in the transition to school. In A.-W. Dunlop & H. Fabian (Eds.), *Informing transitions in the early years: Research, policy and practice* (pp. 120–136). Maidenhead: Open University Press.
Deckert-Peaceman, H. (2006). *"Big kids go to big school." Changing transitions from early childhood to school. Some methodological considerations towards an international comparison.* AARE Conference 2006, University of South Australia.

Dockett, S., & Perry, B. (2001). Starting school: Effective transitions. *Early Childhood Research and Practice, 3*(2). Retrieved October 16 2008 from http://ecrp. uiuc.edu/v3n2/dockett.html.

Dockett, S., & Perry, B. (2002). Who's ready for what? Young children starting school. *Contemporary Issues in Early Childhood, 3*(1), 67–89.

Dunlop, A.-W., Lee, P., Fee, J., Hughes, A., Grieve, A., & Marwick, H. (2008). *Positive behavior in the early years: Perceptions of staff, service providers and parents in managing and promoting positive behavior in early years and early primary settings.* Retrieved January 8, 2009, from http://www.scotland.gov.uk/ Publications/2008/09/12112952/0.

Edinburgh City Council. (2007). *Is your child ready for primary school?* Edinburgh City Council: Children and Families Department.

Einarsdóttir, J. (2007). Children's voices on the transition from preschool to primary school. In A.-W. Dunlop & H. Fabian (Eds.), *Informing transitions in the early years: Research, policy and practice* (pp. 74–91). Maidenhead: Open University Press.

Eurydice at NFER. (2007). *Compulsory age of starting school in European countries 2007.* Retrieved December 6, 2008, from http://www.nfer.ac.uk/ eurydice.

Fabian, H. (2000). Small steps to starting school. *International Journal of Early Years Education, 8*(2), 141–153.

Ford, J., & Gledhill, T. (2002). Does season of birth matter? The relationship between age within the school year (season of birth) and educational difficulties among a representative general population of children and adolescents (aged 5–15) in Great Britain. *Research in Education, 68,* 41–47.

Graue, M., & Di Perna, J. (2000). Redshirting and early retention: Who gets the 'gift of time' and what are the outcomes? *American Educational Research Journal, 37*(2), 509–634.

Griebel, W., & Niesel, R. (2000). *The children's voice in the complex transition into kindergarten and school.* Paper presented at 10th European Conference on Quality in Early Childhood Education, London, United Kingdom.

Guevermont, A., Roos, N., & Brownwell, M. (2001). Predictors and consequences of grade retention-examining data from Manitoba Canada. *Canadian Journal of School Psychology, 22*(1), 50–67.

Hughes, A., & Kleinberg, S. (2003). Early education and schooling. In T. G. K. Bryce & W. M. Humes (Eds.), *Scottish education: Post devolution, 2nd Edition* (pp. 342–351). Edinburgh: Edinburgh University Press.

Katz, L. (2000). Academic redshirting and young children. Retrieved November 24, 2008, from http://ceep.crc.uiuc.edu/eecearchive/digests/2000/katzred00.pdf.

Ledger, E., Smith, A. B., & Rich, P. (2000). Friendship over the transition from early childhood centre to school. *International Journal of Early Years Education, 8*(1), 57–69.

LoCasale-Crouch, J., Mashburn, A. J., Downer, J. T., & Pianta, R. C. (2008). Pre-kindergarten teachers' use of transition practices and children's adjustment to kindergarten. *Early Childhood Research Quarterly, 23,* 124–139.

Malone, L., West, J., Flanagan K., & Park, J. (2006). The early and mathematics achievement of children who repeated kindergarten or who began school a year late. Retrieved November 24, 2008, from http://nces.ed.gov/pubs2006/2006064. pdf.

March, C. (2005). Academic redshirting: Does withholding a child from school entrance for one year increase academic success? [Electronic version]. *Issues in Educational Research, 15*(1), 69–85.

Margetts, K. (2002). Transition to school: Complexity and diversity. *European Early Childhood Education Research Journal, 10*(2), 103–114.

Margetts, K. (2006). *Teachers should explain what they mean: What new children need to know about starting school.* Paper presented at the EECERA 16ᵗʰ Annual Conference, Reykjavik, Iceland, 2006.

Margetts, K. (2007). Understanding and supporting children: Shaping transition practices. In A.-W. Dunlop & H. Fabian (Eds.), *Informing transitions in the early years: Research, policy and practice* (pp. 107–119). Maidenhead: Open University Press.

Marshall, H. (2003). Opportunity deferred or opportunity taken? An up-dated look at delaying kindergarten entry [Electronic version]. *Young Children, 58*(5), 84–93.

Meisels, S. J. (1998). *Assessing readiness.* Retrieved March 30, 2009, from http://eric.ed.gov:80/ERIC/data/ericdocs2sqp/content_stirage_01/0000019b/80/17/84/26.pdf.

Menet, F., Eakin, J., Stuart, M., & Rafferty, H. (2000). Month of birth and effect on literacy, behaviour and referral to psychological service. *Educational Psychology in Practice, 16*(2), 225–233.

National Center for Education Statistics (NCES). (2000). Children who enter kindergarten late or repeat kindergarten: Their characteristics and later school performance. Retrieved November 24, 2008, from http://nces.ed.gov/pubs2000/2000039.pdf.

National Institute of Child Health and Human Development (NICHD). (2007). Age of entry to kindergarten and children's academic achievement and socioemotional development [Electronic version]. *Early Education and Development, 18*(2), 337–368.

Niesel, R., & Griebel, W. (2001). *Transition to schoolchild: What children tell about school and what they teach us.* Paper presented at 11ᵗʰ European Conference on Quality in Early Childhood Education, Alkmaar, Netherlands, 2000.

Pianta, R. C., Cox, M. J., Taylor, L., & Early, D. (1999). Kindergarten teachers' practices related to the transition to school: results of a national survey. *The Elementary School Journal, 100*(1), 71–85.

Russell, F. (2005). Starting school: The importance of parents' expectations. *Journal of Research in Special Educational Needs, 5*(3), 118–126.

Scottish Executive. (2002). *Standards in Scotland's schools etc Act 2000, Section 34: Guidance on preschool education.* Retrieved December 6, 2008, from http://www.scotland.gov.uk/Publications/2006/08/gpse/1.

Scottish Executive. (2004). *A curriculum for excellence.* Edinburgh: Scottish Executive. Retrieved December 6, 2008, from http://www.scotland.gov.uk/Resource/Doc/26800/0023690.pdf.

Scottish Government. (2006). *Scottish schools (Parental Involvement) Act 2006 asp8.* Retrieved March 13, 2009, from http://www.opsi.gov.uk/legislation/scotland/acts2006/pdf/asp_20060008_en.pdf.

Scottish Government. (2008a). *Growing up in Scotland: Year 2.* Retrieved December 6, 2008, from http://www.scotland.gov.uk/Resource/Doc/212225/0056476.pdf.

Scottish Government. (2008b). *Moving Scotland forward: The government's program for Scotland 2008–09.* Retrieved December 6, 2008, from http://www.scotland.gov.uk/Resource/Doc/236931/0065009.pdf.

Scottish Government. (2008c). *The early years framework.* Edinburgh: Scottish Government.

Scottish Government. (2008d). *The early years framework: Part II.* Edinburgh: Scottish Government.

Scottish Office. (1999). *A curriculum framework for children 3 to 5.* Dundee: Scottish Consultative Council on the Curriculum.

Sharp, C. (2002). School starting age: European policy and recent research. Retrieved November 24, 2008, from http://www.nfer.ac.uk/publications/

other-publications/conference-papers/school-starting-age-european-policy-and-recent-research.cfm.

Smith, N. (2003). *Transition from nursery to school playground: an intervention program to promote emotional and social development.* Paper presented at 13th European Early Childhood Education Research Association (EECERA) Conference, University of Strathclyde, Glasgow.

Stephen, C. (2006). *Insight 28. Early years education: Perspectives from a review of the international literature.* Retrieved March 15, 2009, from http://www.scotland.gov.uk/Publications/2006/01/26094635/1.

Stephen, C., & Cope, P. (2003). An inclusive perspective on transition to primary school. *European Educational Research Journal, 2*(1), 262–276.

Stipek, D. (2002). At what age should children enter kindergarten? A question for policy makers and parents [Electronic version]. *Society for Research in Child Development Social Policy Report, 16*(2), 3–17.

Tymms, P., Jones, P., Merrell, C., Henderson, B., & Cowie, M. (2005). Children starting school in Scotland. Retrieved June 1, 2008, from http://www.scotland.gov.uk/Publications/2005/02/20634/51601.

Wils, A. (2004). Late entrants leave school earlier: Evidence from Mozambique. *International Review of Education, 50*(1), 17–37.

Wilson, G. (2000). The effects of season of birth, sex and cognitive abilities on the assessment of special educational needs. *Educational Psychology, 20*(2), 153–166.

5 Shifting the Lens

Re-Framing the View of Learners and Learning During the Transition From Early Childhood Education to School in New Zealand

Sally Peters

Each year, around the world, children enter the school system for the first time. In New Zealand enrollment is continuous throughout the year and children usually start school on or just after their 5th birthday. A high proportion of these children will have attended one or more early childhood services (Ministry of Education, 2008). Curriculum documents are one of the many interwoven aspects of the sociocultural milieu as children make the transition from early childhood education to school. The impact of curriculum will be discussed in this chapter, drawing on findings from a number of research projects that the author has been involved in. These projects include a 3-year Teaching and Learning Research Initiative exploring learning dispositions and key competencies in early childhood and school settings (Carr et al., 2008) and a 3-year Centre of Innovation project looking at transitions and 'border crossing' (Hartley, Rogers, Smith, Peters, & Carr, forthcoming). Findings from these recent studies will be compared with earlier data from the author's Ph.D., an interpretive study of the children making transition to school (Peters, 2004). The chapter highlights the potential of the 2007 New Zealand school curriculum (Ministry of Education, 2007), with its focus on key competencies, for re-framing views of learners, supporting children's transitions, and opening dialogue between teachers in the 'borderland' between sectors. Although the research is based in New Zealand, the theoretical ideas have relevance in other contexts.

CROSSING THE BORDER—LEARNERS' STORIES

The following descriptions draw together case study data from a variety of sources (interviews with the children, their parents, and teachers, and observations at kindergarten and school) to provide possible 'first person' vignette accounts of the backgrounds and first few days at school of 4 of the 23 children in a New Zealand study of children starting school (see Peters, 2004, for details). All the children described had attended kindergartens prior to school entry. Kindergartens are sessional early childhood services where all the teachers are qualified and registered. The children's kindergartens all ran three afternoon sessions for younger children (usually 3-year-olds), with the children moving to five morning sessions around age 4. The children moved to school when they turned 5, meaning that the kindergarten groups constantly changed with children moving to the morning session as places became available, and new enrolments taking their places in the afternoon sessions.

Child 1

I'm one of six children. My mum has had a hard life. She's now separated from Dad and we're struggling to make ends meet. Mum wants us girls to experience a much better life than she has had, and sees education as our ticket to success. She puts a lot of thought and effort into enhancing our chances. Mum recently moved my two middle sisters to a new school for a fresh start. At their old school they got a lot of hassle and put downs because we don't have a lot of flash things. I'm going to the new school with them. Mum's going to be a lot more careful about how we are seen here, and what people get to know about us.

I was bored at home, not very interested in kindergarten, and keen to 'have a turn at school'. I had my school bag ready for weeks. Mum made sure I have all the right gear for school so that I'll fit in with the richer kids. She enrolled me but won't come in and meet my teacher because she doesn't want the teacher to look down on her, in case that affects my chances. When I first got to school it wasn't what I expected. My sisters couldn't stay with me. They weren't even supposed to play with me at lunchtime—even though my big sister had my lunch in her bag. I was supposed to make my own friends but I didn't know anyone here. It's hard to focus; I just seem to be crying all the time.

Child 2

I've got one older brother. We came to New Zealand because Dad got offered an important new job here. I don't speak any English although I've been in New Zealand for a few months now and I have heard it being spoken. I'm starting to understand some of what I hear. I went to kindergarten for 6 hours a day in Japan and I loved it. New Zealand kindergarten was a bit more challenging for me because I couldn't talk to anyone and I felt very shy.

I visited school with my kindy [kindergarten] teacher, and then again with Mum. Mum translated a lot of the instructions, like where the toilets were and where to eat lunch. When I started school I found that the work was quite easy. If I don't understand the instructions I can usually tell what to do by watching others. Sometimes I make up extra activities to make things a bit harder and to fill in time until the others have finished. There are so many interesting ways I can do this, so I'm never bored. I still feel a bit shy though, especially when people tease me. I don't know the English words to ask them to stop.

Child 3

I'm the middle child of three (although I think Mum's pregnant again). Dad has a good job but he works long hours and Mum's very wrapped up with my baby sister and doesn't have a lot of time for school things. I spent most of my time at kindergarten playing outside on the trolleys and the climbing equipment. I'm usually in perpetual motion. Mum would have liked me to paint pictures and things when I was at kindergarten but I was so busy I usually forgot. My parents were really worried about how I'll get on at school. My older sister was quiet and bidable, interested in books and puzzles. Her teachers all think she's wonderful. I've been described as more 'search and destroy'. I'm very determined. Adults seem to find that a bit of a challenge but it can be a good thing. I finished the fun run even though I had blisters on my feet. For the last few months of kindy all my friends kept going to school. Each time I managed to make new friends but I was quite glad when it was time for me to start school too.

Mum and I used to collect my sister from school, and sometimes I'd be invited to join in with the activities, so I already knew my teacher and the classroom. So far school seems ok, and it means I can start after-school gym class with my sister—at last!

Child 4

I'm the oldest of two. My parents are quite well off and because Dad works shifts he's often around during the day. I do lots of practical things with my Dad and my granddad. I know how to change the oil in a car, I have my own vegetable patch and I have been helping to renovate a caravan. Mum and Dad take me and my sister on lots of trips to science museums or the beach. My parents are amazed at all the things I know how to do, and the information I can remember. When I went to kindergarten I liked the teachers but I didn't always get on very well with the other children. I found the things they liked to do quite boring. Now I am at school there seems to be a lot of sitting around. I like solving problems and thinking about things. The work isn't too hard but holding a pencil makes my fingers ache, so I don't finish my writing. It's very noisy with lots of kids talking. I don't say much. I hope my little sister won't mess with my garden while I am here.

Just four stories remind us of the diversity a teacher is faced with. Intuitively, even from these brief details, the reader might start to develop opinions about how successful these different learners will be at school. However, what happens next is difficult to predict. The nature of their individual journeys will depend on a complex interplay of many different factors.

COMPLEX JOURNEYS

Starting school is a "dynamic, multifaceted, interactive process between all participants involved" (Ghaye & Pascal, 1988, p. 206). Case studies of children in my Ph.D. research illustrated how the complex interweaving of characteristics of individual children, and their immediate and more remote environments, led to different patterns of experiences (Peters, 2004). Bronfenbrenner and Morris's (1997) ecological model was useful in considering how the dispositions, resources, and demand characteristics of the child interacted with features of the environment that appeared to inhibit, permit, or invite engagement. External factors, from the levels Bronfenbrenner (1979, 1986) referred to as the exosystem and macrosystem, also contributed to each individual's cycle of experience. For example, the ways in which children were viewed (e.g., the nature of norms in a setting), the influence of capital (Bourdieu, 1993, 1997), access to scaffolding (Bruner, 1985), and the nature of that scaffolding (van der Veer & Valsiner, 1994), were just some of the influences on their experiences.

Within the overall journey, the first day at school was a point at which many changes occurred. At the time, the many differences between early childhood and school settings meant that the transition to school could be thought of as the border between different 'cultures,' each with its own habitus (acquired patterns of thought, behavior, and taste that becomes an integral part of a person; Bourdieu, 1997). In addition to learning curriculum content, there was an ongoing process of 'becoming a pupil' as the children adapted to the new culture of school.

BECOMING A PUPIL: LEARNING TO 'DO' SCHOOL

Children have to acquire a body of "school specific, social knowledge" (Fields, 1997, p. 7) and this involves internalizing the many rules that define the teacher's expectations and the children's role in the setting. "Children need to become aware of the expectations and demands of the school situation so that their own learning will become appropriate to the constraints of the situation in the classroom" (Jackson, 1987, p. 81). This can include very subtle behaviors, such as children learning to hold their bodies in certain ways that signal listening and attention (Hill, Comber, Louden, Rivalland, & Reid, 1998). It is interesting to speculate on the ease with which the children in the vignettes at the start of this chapter might pick up on these norms and adapt their behaviors accordingly.

Learning the culture of the school, and their role within it, that is, what it means to 'do school,' has been shown to be a necessary step before children could focus on the *content* of schooling (Hill et al., 1998). During the first year of school, children are therefore learning to become pupils *and* learning curriculum content. The two aspects are closely interrelated, and it follows that the children who already 'know' and can 'do' school, or who pick this up quickly are thus advantaged in the classroom right from the outset (Brooker, 2002; Kamler & Comber, 2005; Thomson & Hall, 2008).

For other children the new role may be so different that they must unlearn their first notions of participation, developed in home and early childhood settings, in order to adapt to the new requirements of school (Fernie, 1988). Brooker's (2002) study of Anglo and Bangladeshi children starting school in England illustrated this. She observed that sometimes the children with the largest adjustment to make seemed to have given up trying to understand what was expected of them.

Teachers in Brooker's (2002) study had very little understanding of the children's home background when this was different to their own. The children who were able to access the highest level of teacher support were those who appeared to need it least, while those children, who, in the teachers' eyes were seen as lacking the attributes for learning, received very little support from teachers and other adults. Similarly, Stephen and Cope (2003) found that teachers located problems, when they occurred, in the children not the school, and did not talk about adapting their practices in response to difficulties that children experienced. It is therefore not surprising to find that in some cases the gap between the advantaged and the disadvantaged has been shown to grow on entry to school (Thomson & Hall, 2008).

VIEWS ABOUT LEARNERS AND LEARNING

The demands of the change in role on entry to school may help to explain why there are sometimes wide discrepancies between school teachers' views of the capabilities of children, and their early childhood teachers' assessment of the same children (see, for example, Dunlop, 2002; Norris, 1999; Peters, 2004; Robinson, Timperley, & Bullard, 2000). Sadly it is not unknown for a child to go from being what Norris (1999) described as the "Star of Crèche" to "a new entrant with problem behavior" (p. 188).

Another reason why children might go from being viewed as competent and accomplished in early childhood settings to incompetent novices at school is simply because teachers in the two settings have different ideas about children as learners (Dunlop, 2002). Stephen and Cope's (2003) study of 27 children entering Scottish schools is likely to resonate with other contexts. Four of the children were described by their teachers as ideal pupils or very near to ideal and 12 were considered to have 'adjusted well to school' and to have met teacher expectations. Interestingly the teachers' descriptions of these children seemed to fit closely with their ability to 'do' school and grasp the structural requirements of the classroom. This appeared to be more about conformity and 'fitting in' behaviors rather than approaches to learning.

In my 2004 study, although (when interviewed) the teachers said that they valued the children's approaches to learning, these were not highlighted in planning, assessment or reporting. Instead the teacher-created new-entrant assessments were of the type that Carr (2001, p. 3) described as a "folk model" of assessment, where children's achievements are checked against a list of skills. When deficits were revealed, such as the inability to name more than a few letters of the alphabet, this became a major focus for intervention that overshadowed much of the child's experience. Elsewhere I have written about how quickly a child could be positioned as having problems, and how well-meaning attempts to drill the missing skills could lead to a dislike of school (Peters, 2004, 2005). These assessments overlooked the many strengths and interests of the children involved that could have provided a basis for learning at school.

Phillips, McNaughton, and MacDonald (2002, p. 48) have also described pressure "to achieve and to bridge gaps that exist on entry to school" as a feature of teaching to the clearly defined tasks to be learned in the primary school curriculum. Although the school curriculum documents did not prescribe what children of a certain age should know, assessment against particular achievement objectives contributed to the view of individual children. The following section outlines some of the documents that help to shape practice in New Zealand.

POLICY CONTEXT IN NEW ZEALAND

New Zealand's first early childhood curriculum *Te Whāriki* (Ministry of Education, 1996) was developed in the early 1990s. The draft version of the early childhood curriculum (Ministry of Education, 1993a) and the *New Zealand Curriculum Framework* (NZCF) for schools (Ministry of Education, 1993b) were developed in the same time frame and context, but took very different approaches to learning.

Pressure to align *Te Whāriki* with the school curriculum was resisted (Carr & May, 1993) and much of the motivation for developing an early childhood curriculum reflected resistance to the downward influence of the school curriculum (May, 2001). In the final document, links between each strand and learning in school were described, but the overall aspirations for children in *Te Whāriki* were broader than just preparation for what was seen, at the time, as a very narrow view of learning at school. The early childhood curriculum aspirations were for children to:

> *... grow up as competent and confident learners and communicators, healthy in mind, body and spirit, secure in their sense of belonging and in the knowledge that they make a valued contribution to society.* (Ministry of Education, 1996, p. 9)

Learning outcomes emphasized children's development of working theories and learning dispositions.

Te Whāriki (Ministry of Education, 1996) is still the curriculum for early childhood but there have been significant changes to the school curriculum in recent years, beginning with a major stocktake of the New Zealand school curriculum in 2000 (Ministry of Education, 2002). Extensive consultation as part of the *New Zealand Curriculum/Te Marautanga o Aotearoa Project* followed the Stocktake (see Cubitt, 2006, for details). The result was a much shorter core school curriculum, with a lot more freedom for schools to design and implement their own curriculum "so that teaching and learning is meaningful and beneficial to their particular communities of students" (Ministry of Education, 2007, p. 37).

With regard to starting school, one of the important changes to the school curriculum included the introduction of 'key competencies,' which align with the strands of the early childhood curriculum, *Te Whāriki*. The theoretical base for the key competencies drew from OECD, which, as Rychen and Salganik (2003) explained, focused on "competencies that contribute to a successful life and a well-functioning society." Key competencies were deemed to be "relevant across different spheres of life and important for all individuals" (p. 54).

The New Zealand Curriculum (Ministry of Education, 2007) identifies five key competencies:

- Thinking
- Using language, symbols and texts
- Managing self
- Relating to others
- Participating and contributing

The competencies are dispositional in nature and draw on "knowledge, attitudes and values in ways that lead to action" (Ministry of Education,

2007, p. 12). The curriculum acknowledges that the development of key competencies occurs over time, "shaped by interactions with people, places, ideas, and things" (p. 12). The key competencies therefore not only align with the strands of *Te Whāriki,* there are also many synergies with the dispositional focus in early childhood and commonalities in the way learning is framed and discussed in the two curriculum documents (see Carr et al., 2008, for details).

The school curriculum also includes explicit recommendations for teachers to connect with and build on early childhood learning experiences. In addition it acknowledges that fostering a child's relationships with teachers and other children, consideration of the child's whole experience of school and being welcoming of families, helps to support the children's transition to school (Ministry of Education, 2007).

However, the move from policy or curriculum level change to practice is not seamless. For example, in England, Wood (2004) noted that practitioners have shown resistance, adaptation, and mediation as they work toward finding a 'best fit' between their personal theories, beliefs, and pedagogical knowledge, and policy frameworks. In Scotland, Stephen and Cope (2003) noted that practice around equity and inclusion fell short of the commitment articulated in policy, and in Australia, Britt and Sumsion (2003) were interested in the tensions and experiences of those who are negotiating their way through the "mysterious gap between hope and happening" (Kenway & Willis 1997, cited in Britt & Sumsion, 2003, p. 116). Nevertheless, the current New Zealand context includes a commitment to supporting children's learning through the transition to school and potentially reframes the view of learners and learning.

RE-FRAMING VIEWS OF LEARNERS AND LEARNING

Identifying and building on prior learning, and fostering the development of key competencies, precludes deficit models and the location of problems within individual children. Whilst previous practices may have focused on children learning to 'do' school, and problematized children and families whose approaches and practices differ from those of their teachers, increasingly what is valued in schools has been the focus of critique.

Similar to Bourdieu's (1997) notion of habitus, Thomson (2002) proposed children come to school with virtual school bags filled with knowledge, experiences, and dispositions. Although in some contexts school only draws on the contents of selected bags, "those whose resources match those required in the game of education" (Thomson & Hall, 2008, p. 89), ideally schools will recognize and celebrate the learning and experiences that all children bring to school (Thomson, 2002). Putting this into practice, teachers in Kamler and Comber's (2005) Australian study began to think about what might be hidden away in children's virtual school bags and became ethnographers of communities to learn about cultural resources. This helped teachers reassess their students' potential and design pedagogies to connect them to the literacy curriculum.

OPENING THE BACKPACKS: CENTRE OF INNOVATION RESEARCH

Teachers at Mangere Bridge Kindergarten in New Zealand have recently completed a 3-year research study, funded by the Ministry of Education, which explored the transition to school. One aspect of this study examined the use of children's early childhood portfolios as a tool for 'opening their virtual backpacks' in the school setting. This is explained in detail in the report from the project (Hartley et al., forthcoming).

In brief, the teachers came to think of the children's portfolios as a suitcase (Broström, 2005) or a virtual school bag (Thomson, 2002), full of cultural and linguistic resources gained at home and in early childhood education. Children were encouraged to take their kindergarten portfolios to school, where they were shared with the teacher and other children in the class. For the new entrant teacher this helped to meet the curriculum requirement to build "on the learning experiences that children bring with them" (Ministry of Education, 2007, p. 41). As one teacher noted:

> *what the kindy books [kindergarten portfolios] do is tell me so much more . . . it gives me an insight into where the child is socially—who their friends are, what their interests are—which for me as a new entrant teacher is far more valuable because I can find out myself easily enough if they can write their name or know their colors . . . but in fact their interests and personality takes a lot longer to get to know. (Teacher 1, First video interview, cited in Hartley et al., forthcoming)*

> *. . . this little boy brought his portfolio in and he was a very quiet boy, ESOL (English as a second or other language), didn't speak a word for probably a week or so and then he brought his kindy book [kindergarten portfolio] in and it was like a new child emerged and it was like 'this is me and this is who I am and even though I don't necessarily have the language to tell you I can show you with pictures . . . ' and I would turn around at all times of the day and hear little murmurings and laughing and there would be pockets of children sitting around this little boy with his kindy book. (Teacher 1, First video interview, cited in Hartley et al., forthcoming)*

The power of portfolios as a tool for fostering belonging and empowerment was also evident:

I guess it's like us starting a new job and moving to a new country, everything is new but if they come with this little treasure, that's something that's theirs, something they can talk about, something they share and particularly for children who are really shy or having English as a second language, they don't even need to talk, they can just sit and show and share and often you see that happening and you realize they are really valuable and really powerful. (Teacher D, Final Interview, p. 10, cited in Hartley et al., forthcoming)

I've noticed that even the most shy of children when they've got their portfolio with them they just seem to have this sense of confidence, it's that ownership over something and the fact that the other children in the class are acknowledging their prior learning and lots of rich experiences for the kids in that the children here remember friends from the kindergarten, they remember the teachers. (Teacher C, Final Interview, p. 12, cited in Hartley et al., forthcoming)

In valuing each child's prior learning the Mangere Bridge research found the use of the portfolios at school contributed to the child's sense of self as a strong, capable, interesting and competent learner. This was in contrast to the children in my Ph.D. research, whose identity and reputations as learners at school was initially very much dependent on their performance on the narrow range of tests carried out by their teachers (Peters, 2004).

KEY COMPETENCIES—BROADENING THE VIEW OF LEARNING

A recent 3-year Teaching and Learning Research Initiative [TLRI] project explored the key competencies in the New Zealand school curriculum and what they might mean in practice (Carr et al., 2008). The sociocultural basis of the key competencies places both teacher and learner at the heart of the learning process. This contrasts sharply with the view noted earlier of problems being located within a child. Further, it became clear during the project that it was not possible to interpret or trace learning dispositions or key competences without reference to the teachers' and the learners' intentions and interests. This relates to Rogoff's (2003) descriptions of intersubjectivity, and 'bridging and structuring' understanding and meaning.

Teachers in one school became interested in documenting the co-constructed nature of children's learning. Narratives were used to capture the learning in context and collected in individual portfolios documenting children's learning journeys, and also shared on classroom display walls, which tracked and connected learning within the group over time.

"Virtual school bags" of knowledge from home were again opened and shared, with both children and their families documenting activities from home in their school portfolios. For example, one child, Kaleb, had been pursuing an interest in Maui, a central figure in many Māori stories. This interest was expressed in reading, writing, and dance. Later his mother contributed an entry to his portfolio describing how, while at the beach, Kaleb found a piece of driftwood that he said looked like the north island. He decided to make a shell and wood sculpture representing Maui in the story where he fished up the north island of New Zealand. The completed sculpture was shared at school and was the inspiration for Kaleb to organize and lead a shell sculpture workshop for all the children in his class.

In the report (Carr et al., 2008), we concluded that Kaleb's exploration of the Maui stories was an example of his engagement in meaningful relations with: other people, his own prior experiences, a range of ways of representing and communicating his ideas, a number of creative ways of thinking, and communities beyond the school. His work over several months illustrated all five of the key competencies in action.

Overall the research highlighted that learning dispositions and key competencies are 'fuzzy,' and not easy to define. It was important for teachers and learners to co-construct meanings and make these available and transparent in documentation. The documentation also indicated the integration of learning areas and key competencies. Feedback to children and their families demonstrated that approaches to learning as well as knowledge and skills were valuable. The lens had shifted from content only, to highlight this interaction.

KEY COMPETENCIES AND THE CONTRIBUTION OF ASSESSMENT TO 'LIFE JACKETS'

The key competencies required a new way of thinking about learning, and the ways in which learning might progress. Case studies were used to illustrate this in practice. Documentation over time significantly re-framed the focus on learning from a compliance or skills-based focus to the key competencies in action. One example was of a child's 'Participating and contributing' key competency, which initially focused on trying new things. The following are excerpts from some of the entries in this child's portfolio and on the classroom wall:

Diana has really taken to the idea of participation, particularly the idea of making the most of new opportunities. In this instance she is engaging in a new activity she has really enjoyed. The lazy river [at the local swimming pools] is now a place where Diana can add to her 'repertoire of places'. (Learning Story, 9 March, 2007, cited in Carr et al., 2008, p. 62)

Today Diana told me [teacher] she had been thinking about the word participation and decided to try karate for her 'making things, doing things' workshop. She said she was the only girl from her Homebase to attend this workshop but thought it was okay because she was trying something new.

She said, "I was a little scared of the kids from other Homebases but then I wasn't. I kept on doing it and it didn't make me feel nervous anymore. There is one girl in the karate workshop and her name is Katherine. I remember her from camp. She got her face painted when I was with my mum. That was when we painted my mum."

Teacher Analysis: Diana is developing a strong understanding of the word participation. She is doing this by actively exploring what it means to participate. Diana's risk taking and her sense of belonging is helping her to trust herself and others, even when she feels scared or nervous. (Learning Story, 15 March, 2007, cited in Carr et al., 2008, p. 63)

Later the teachers commented that Diana was seeking more opportunities to participate, and beginning to create opportunities for other children's learning and participation. For example, at a dance workshop in May, Diana suggested that the whole group work to become a waka [Māori canoe]. Together they determined how this should be shaped, how to paddle and how to get into place.

Analysis of Diana's learning over several months illustrated how the key competencies can become part of a learner's identity, and how these can be strengthened. Teachers described the ways in which weaving an accumulation of identity stories appeared to provide a 'life jacket' (that tells something of the child's life).

The strengthening of key competencies was demonstrated in increasing *mindfulness* or *agency* as Diana looked for new opportunities to participate and *breadth* was reflected in the key competencies, especially participating and contributing, being connected to a widening number of places (classroom, swimming pool, school-wide karate workshop). Teachers noticed the increased *frequency* of Diana's willingness to try things she had not done before. *Complexity* increased (e.g., from floating in the 'lazy river' at the local pools to working in a team to develop a dance routine), with later activities showing greater integration of key competencies, and an increasing number of people and ways of thinking involved (Carr et al., 2008).

However, the teachers concluded that while the 'life jacket' is reflected in ways of participating, and provides the continuity from place to place, it is not permanent. It can wash away unless reified. Another way of thinking about this is that dispositions or key competencies are not acquired;

instead, a person becomes "more or less disposed" to respond in a particular way (Claxton & Carr, 2004, p. 88).

TEACHERS 'BORDER CROSSING' AND
IN THE 'BORDER LANDS'

Curriculum documents alone will not change practice in schools, but these
New Zealand projects have illustrated the ways in which a change to the
school curriculum could legitimize and foster a reframing of the ways in
which learning, and therefore learners are viewed in the primary school
classroom. In the first project (Peters, 2004) the early childhood and school
sectors were different 'cultures' and children were required to navigate a
change in role in order to 'do' school and adopt learning practices that were
more akin to 'fitting in' than active learning.

Although starting school will still require some adaptations, recent
New Zealand research, such as Hartley et al. (forthcoming) and Carr et
al. (2008), has shown the potential for greater connections between early
childhood and school, and the opportunity provided by the inclusion of
key competencies in the school curriculum to reframe the view of learners and learning. This shifting lens on learning also re-frames views of
teaching. Elsewhere I have written about the exciting opportunities for
teachers to make connections between the strands of *Te Whāriki* and the
key competencies in ways that respect the existing 'cultures' of both early
childhood education settings and school, whilst offering a powerful framework for crossing the border between the two, so that children's learning
is enhanced (Peters, 2005). This notion of border crossing underpinned my
thesis (Peters, 2004) and the Hartley et al. (forthcoming) study. However, it
is important to remember that the cultural border between early childhood
education and school is socially constructed. As Clandinin and Connelly
(1995) noted, "borders are abstractions. They exist as clear demarcations
of territory but do not show up in real world" (cited in Clandinin & Rosiek,
2007, p. 57).

One of the teachers in Britt and Sumsion's (2003) research offered
an interesting alternative to border crossing with a metaphor of early
childhood and primary sectors being two houses, with a shared basement. On the surface it appears that they are totally separate and a long
way apart. However, in the dark, messy, basement, which people do not
usually share with visitors, there is some common ground. This teacher
spoke about bumping into each other occasionally in the basement. Writing about narrative therapy Clandinin and Rosiek (2007) also describe
"bumping places," conceptual spaces where particular ideas intersect
with other ways of thinking, and traversing borderlands, as opposed to
crossing borders. Borderlands are "those spaces that exist around borders
where one lives with the possibility of multiple plotlines" and which do

"not have a sharp divide line where one leaves one way of making sense for another" (p. 59).

The notion of a borderland seems to offer great potential for the transition to school. Britt and Sumsion (2003) explored the possibility of a shared 'space between' early childhood and school, a border land.

> *We can now look for and work toward connections and intersections between two different places—points of negotiation, of cohabitation, meshing, transforming, combining. Whereas before, the focus was on the gap between early childhood education and primary education as a void, as state of non existence (because within that model you are either one/or the other, never both or between the two), now it is a valid site of connection, intersection and overlap. The borderland is a space not only of existence, but of coexistence.* (Britt & Sumsion, 2003, p. 133)

While historically and physically schools and early childhood centers do have clear divisions, the notion of borderlands offers a new way of conceptualizing and discussing learning during the transition between the two.

CONCLUSION

The alignment between the early childhood and school curriculum, through the links between learning dispositions and key competencies, has opened a new space for teachers to reframe thinking about learners and learning. Instead of the move to school representing a whole new culture, with children having to learn to 'do school' and fit within a narrow construction of being a pupil, teachers have been exploring interesting ways of acknowledging, celebrating, and building on the diverse strengths and interests that children bring with them. The work is not without its challenges and there is more to be done to fully explore the potential offered by the current school curriculum. However, in both Carr et al. (2008) and Hartley et al. (forthcoming) early childhood and school teachers were engaged in joint research, finding points of contact and shared understanding in the borderlands and 'bumping spaces' that offer new ways to think about the transition to school.

Note: I acknowledge with thanks the funding from the Ministry of Education for the Teaching and Learning Research Initiative (Carr et al., 2008) and Centre of Innovation (Hartley et al., forthcoming) projects discussed in this chapter. It is important to note that the views expressed in relation to these projects are those of the author and not the New Zealand government. I am also very grateful to the colleagues, teachers, children and families involved in these projects and my Ph.D. study, who have allowed their work and experiences to be shared.

REFERENCES

Bourdieu, P. (1993). *Sociology in question*. London: Sage.

Bourdieu, P. (1997). The forms of capital. In A. H. Halsey, H. Lauder, P. Brown, & A. S. Wells (Eds.), *Education, culture, economy and society* (pp. 45–58). Oxford: Oxford University Press.

Britt, C., & Sumsion, J. (2003). Within the borderlands: Beginning early childhood teachers in primary schools. *Contemporary Issues in Early Childhood*, 4(2), 115–136.

Bronfenbrenner, U. (1979). *The ecology of human development*. Cambridge, MA: Harvard University Press.

Bronfenbrenner, U. (1986). Ecology of the family as a context for human development: Research perspectives. *Developmental Psychology*, 22, 723–742.

Bronfenbrenner, U., & Morris, P. A. (1997). The ecology of developmental processes. In W. Damon & R. M. Lerner (Eds.), *Handbook of child psychology: Vol. 1. Theoretical models of human development, 5th edition* (pp. 993–1029). New York: John Wiley.

Brooker, L. (2002). *Starting school—Young children's learning cultures*. Buckingham: Open University Press.

Broström, S. (2005). Transition problems and play as transitory activity. *Australian Journal of Early Childhood*, 30(3), 17–25.

Bruner, J. (1985). Vygotsky: A historical and conceptual perspective. In J. V. Wertsch (Ed.), *Culture, communication and cognition: Vygotskian perspectives* (pp. 21–34). Cambridge: Cambridge University Press.

Carr, M. (2001). *Assessment in early childhood settings: Learning stories*. London: Paul Chapman.

Carr, M., & May, H. (1993). Choosing a model: Reflecting on the development process of *Te Whāriki*: National early childhood curriculum guidelines in New Zealand. *Journal of Early Years Education*, 1(3), 7–21.

Carr, M., Peters, S., Davis, K., Bartlett, C., Bashford, N., Berry, P., et al. (2008). *Key learning competencies across place and time. Kimihia te ara tōtika, hei oranga mō to aō*. Wellington: Teaching and Learning Research Initiative. Retrieved April 20, 2009, from http://www.tlri.org.nz/ece-sector/

Clandinin, J., & Rosiek, J. (2007). Mapping a landscape of narrative inquiry Borderland spaces and tensions. In J. Clandinin (Ed.), *Handbook of narrative inquiry* (pp. 35–75). London: Sage.

Claxton, G., & Carr, M. (2004). A framework for teaching learning: The dynamics of disposition. *Early Years*, 24(1), 87–97.

Cubitt, S. (2006). The draft New Zealand curriculum. *Curriculum Matters*, 2, 195–212.

Dunlop, A.-W. (2002). Perspectives on children as learners in the transition to school. In H. Fabian & A.-W. Dunlop (Eds.), *Transitions in the early years* (pp. 98–110). London: RoutledgeFalmer.

Fernie, D. E. (1988). Becoming a student: Messages from first settings. *Theory Into Practice*, XXVII(1), 3–10.

Fields, B. A. (1997). The nature and function of rules. *Australian Journal of Early Childhood*, 22(3), 7–12.

Ghaye, A., & Pascal, C. (1988). Four-year-old children in reception classrooms: Participant perceptions and practice. *Educational Studies*, 14(2), 187–208.

Hartley, C., Rogers, P., Smith, J., Peters, S., & Carr, M. (forthcoming). *Across the border: A community negotiates the transition from early childhood to primary school*. Centre of Innovation Final Report to the Ministry of Education.

Hill, S., Comber, B., Louden, W., Rivalland, J., & Reid, J. (1998). *100 children go to school: Connections and disconnections in literacy development in the year prior to school and the first year of school.* Canberra: Department of Employment, Education, Training and Youth Affairs.

Jackson, M. (1987). Making sense of school. In A. Pollard (Ed.), *Children and their primary schools: A new perspective* (pp. 74–87). New York: The Falmer Press.

Kamler, B., & Comber, B. (2005). Designing turn-around pedagogies and contesting deficit assumptions. In B. Comber & B. Kamler (Eds.), *Turn-around pedagogies: Literacy interventions for at risk students* (pp. 1–13). Newtown, Australia: Primary English Association.

May, H. (2001). *Politics in the playground.* Wellington: Bridget Williams with NZCER.

Ministry of Education. (1993a). *Te Whāriki: Draft guidelines for developmentally appropriate programs in early childhood services.* Wellington, New Zealand: Learning Media.

Ministry of Education. (1993b). *The New Zealand curriculum framework.* Wellington, New Zealand: Learning Media.

Ministry of Education. (1996). *Te Whāriki. He Whāriki Mātauranga mö ngā Mokopuna o Aotearoa: Early Childhood Curriculum.* Wellington, New Zealand: Learning Media.

Ministry of Education. (2002). *Curriculum stocktake report.* Wellington, New Zealand: Ministry of Education.

Ministry of Education. (2007). *The New Zealand Curriculum: The English-medium teaching and learning in years 1–13.* Wellington, New Zealand: Learning Media.

Ministry of Education. (2008). *Licensed services and licence-exempt groups 2008.* Retrieved April 20, 2009, from http://www.educationcounts. govt.nz/statistics/ece/ece_staff_return/licensed_services_and_licence-exempt_groups/34821.

Norris, J. A. (1999). *Transforming masculinities: Boys making the transition from early childhood education to school.* Unpublished MA thesis. Wellington, New Zealand: Victoria University of Wellington.

Peters, S. (2004). *"Crossing the border": An interpretive study of children making the transition to school.* Unpublished Ph.D. thesis. Hamilton, New Zealand: University of Waikato.

Peters, S. (2005). Making links between learning in early childhood education and school using the 'key competences' framework. *Teachers and Curriculum, 8,* 9–15.

Phillips, G., McNaughton, S., & MacDonald, S. (2002). *Picking up the pace: Effective literacy interventions for accelerated progress over the transition into decile 1 schools.* Auckland: The Child Literacy Foundation and Woolf Fisher Research Centre.

Robinson, V., Timperley, H., & Bullard, T. (2000). *Strengthening education in Mangere and Otara evaluation: Second evaluation report.* Auckland: The University of Auckland.

Rogoff, B. (2003). *The cultural nature of human development.* Oxford and New York: Oxford University Press.

Rychen, D. S., & Salganik, L. H. (Eds.). (2003). *Key competencies for a successful life and a well-functioning society.* Göttingen: Hogrefe & Huber.

Stephen, C., & Cope, P. (2003). An inclusive perspective on transition to primary school. *European Educational Research Journal, 2*(2), 262–276.

Thomson, P. (2002). *Schooling the rustbelt kids: Making the difference in changing times.* Sydney: Allen & Unwin.

Thomson, P., & Hall, C. (2008). Opportunities missed and/or thwarted? 'Funds of knowledge' meet the English national curriculum. *The Curriculum Journal, 19*(2), 87–103.

van der Veer, R., & Valsiner, J. (Eds.). (1994). *The Vygotsky reader*. Oxford: Blackwell.

Wood, E. (2004). *The impact of national curriculum policies on early childhood teachers' thinking and classroom practice*. Unpublished Ph.D. thesis. Exeter, UK: University of Exeter.

6 The Transition to Formal Schooling and Children's Early Literacy Development in the Context of the USA

Kelley L. Mayer, Steven J. Amendum, and Lynne Vernon-Feagans

The transition to kindergarten (*first year of formal schooling in this context*) in the United States occurs around the age of 5, and is generally thought of as a child's entry into formal schooling. It is an important time in the life of the child, his or her family, and the school. Often the concept of transition is closely related to the concept of "readiness," particularly in the professional literature (e.g., Meisels, 1999). Ensuring that children begin kindergarten ready to learn requires that families, school professionals, and researchers alike pay close attention to a complex and significant change for young students (Bohan-Baker & Little, 2004). In fact, in the past, researchers seldom acknowledged the transition to kindergarten as a complex process involving children, families, schools, and communities, and instead focused on individual characteristics of the child as important in the transition to school. A transition to school framework which integrates contextual factors over time is viewed as a more accurate portrayal of children's experiences than a framework centered on child factors alone and this framework has been embraced by recent reviews of the literature, special journal issues, and national consensus reports (Bohan-Baker & Little, 2004; Lewitt & Baker, 1995; National Association of State Boards of Education, 1991; Pianta, Cox, & Snow, 2007; Vernon-Feagans & Blair, 2006; Vernon-Feagans, Odom, Panscofar, & Kainz, 2008). Such a framework recognizes the importance of families, schools, and communities to the transition process in addition to child factors.

There are many understandings as to what defines *transition*. For some, transition is a single event experienced by programs, families, and children at the end of one time period (e.g., a visit by parents and children to the kindergarten setting prior to beginning), while for others transition reflects an ongoing effort to link children's families with programs (Kagan & Neuman, 1998). Finally, Kagan and Neuman (1998) state that for some, transition is "the manifestation of the developmental principles of continuity, that is, creating pedagogical, curricular, and/or disciplinary approaches that transcend, and continue between, programs" (p. 366).

The first major transition for most children in the United States is the transition to school. This transition has major implications for children's entire school trajectory since a number of studies have shown that children's performance in kindergarten and first grade significantly predict their later performance in school (Alexander & Entwisle, 1988). Thus, there has been a focus on getting children ready for this transition to school. Though the term, "school readiness" has been around for over 50 years, the issue began receiving increased national attention with the formation of the National Education Goals Panel (NEGP) in 1989. The NEGP (1993) proposed that by the year 2000, all children will start kindergarten ready to learn. The panel focused on defining "ready children" as those who are healthy and have appropriate motor skills, demonstrate social–emotional maturity, positive approaches to learning, ability to communicate effectively, and those who demonstrate basic knowledge. While the NEGP argued children should be ready to learn, Pianta and Cox (1999) argued schools should be ready for children. Vernon-Feagans (1996, in press) similarly had stressed this call and emphasized that schools should be ready for *all* children.

Piotrowski, Botsko, and Matthews (2000) define readiness at levels beyond the child, including the community, school, and family. Ready communities provide affordable, high-quality child care, access to libraries, and safe playgrounds and streets. Ready schools provide strong leadership, transition programming, parent-involvement activities, professional development for teachers, and individual instruction for children. Ready families provide rich literacy experiences in the home, nurturing parenting practices, financial resources, and social support for child rearing.

In addition, readiness may be locally determined (Graue, 1992). Children in low-income neighborhoods may need to have different skills upon kindergarten entry given the lack of support services and resources in the schools and communities they have access to. These may include access to health care, high-quality preschool programs, and educational materials in the home, to name a few. On the other hand, particular skills and characteristics of children may be less important in high-income communities where schools and communities generally have more than enough resources to support individual differences in children upon kindergarten entry.

Although school readiness and the transition to school began receiving increased national attention in the past 20 years, results from a large research study of over 20,000 children entering kindergarten in 1999 funded by the Institute of Educational Statistics, a bureau of the U.S. Department of Education (2000), demonstrated that many children were not ready for kindergarten. In fact, over a third of the children participating in the study were not able to recognize letters and did not demonstrate positive approaches to learning.

A successful transition to kindergarten is particularly important for children's early literacy development. The academic demands of the kindergarten literacy curriculum can be challenging, especially for children with few literacy experiences prior to entering school. Children who receive support from parents, teachers, and school systems during the transition to kindergarten perform better on standardized literacy measures (Ramey & Ramey, 1999). On the other hand, children who experience ineffective transitions to kindergarten are at a greater risk for difficulty in school, especially in literacy (Coyner, Reynolds, & Ou, 2003; Juel, 1988). Effective transition practices are particularly important for children and families in poverty. Children from low-income families, on average, have difficulty in the transition to school. More often they exhibit early and persistent academic failure, behavior problems, and lower parental involvement in school (Gutman, Sameroff, & Cole, 2003; Rimm-Kaufman, Pianta, & Cox, 2000; Vernon-Feagans, 1996). However, effective transition practices were found to moderate the effect of poverty on individual child outcomes including academic achievement (Schulting, Malone, & Dodge 2005). Schulting and colleagues (2005) examined whether transition practices had an increased effect on child outcomes during kindergarten and whether this effect varied across socioeconomic groups. Results indicated school-level transition practices were a significant predictor of academic achievement at the end of children's kindergarten year. Child socioeconomic status was a significant moderator of this association, indicating school transition practices made a greater difference for children from low-income backgrounds. The transition practice having the strongest impact on children's academic achievement was the opportunity for parents and children to visit the kindergarten classroom prior to kindergarten entry. Also, school transition practices had a positive effect on parent involvement in schools. Involvement partially mediated the effect of transition practices on academic achievement. Apparently, as parents felt greater awareness and knowledge of what to expect in kindergarten classrooms, they were more likely to become involved in their child's school, which in turn was related to better academic progress for children. That transition practices are especially important for children and families in poverty highlights the necessity to offer more transition practices in schools serving low-income families, especially since these are often the schools which offer the fewest transition practices.

As previously mentioned, the transition to school has received increasing attention from researchers in the past 20 years. However, the topic is approached from a variety of perspectives. It is clear there are multiple influences on the success of children's transition to school in the United States. While research has tended to focus on the effects of transitions on child outcomes, less attention has been paid to the specific impact the transition to kindergarten makes for students struggling with literacy acquisition. The purposes of this review are to: (a) review research on the transition to school, with particular attention to children's literacy outcomes; (b) identify gaps in the research; and (c) recommend future practices for schools and communities that might better address the particular needs of children who struggle with literacy development.

RESEARCH REVIEW

This review is organized to first present research on child characteristics and skills identified as important in the transition to school. Next, research on the role of the family in the transition to school is addressed. Then we follow with a review of the research on the teacher's role. Finally, research on school and community contexts and practices that support successful transitions to school is presented. The research reviewed was conducted from a variety of perspectives, as all are generally considered key informants in better understanding the transition to school.

Theoretical Frame

Much of the early research on children's transition to school focused on characteristics of the child that were deemed important in preparing the child to be "ready for school." Teachers often list a variety of characteristics and skills as important for children's success in kindergarten, including knowledge of the alphabet, ability to identify shapes and colors, and counting from 1 to 10. However, many agree social and emotional skills are even more important than academic skills (Heaviside & Farris, 1993).

Later research began looking beyond the characteristics of the child and emphasized the importance of contextual influences on the transition. These contextual influences may include parent–child relationships, opportunities for learning available in the home, and quality of care prior to school entry, along with many others. Kraft-Sayre and Pianta's (2000) ecological model of transition, based on Bronfenbrenner's (1979) ecological model of development, emphasizes that the transition to kindergarten involves multiple people in the child's life, including the child's teachers, peers, family, and community members. In this model, transition is viewed as a process rather than an event. The child's teachers, family, community members, and peers each influence the transition as they interact with one another and with the child. Emphasis is put on how these interactions change over time to further support children's individual needs as the transition from preschool to kindergarten takes place and continues into the child's kindergarten year.

Vernon-Feagans et al. (2008) extended this thinking to include the influence of the family's work and neighborhood settings on children's transition to school. Important aspects of the work setting were a family's work schedules and support for child rearing. For instance, Han (2005) found that mothers' work schedules were associated with infant cognitive and language development. Infants at 24 and 36 months with mothers who reported working irregular hours performed less well on cognitive and language measures (Han, 2005). In addition, early papers from the Family Life Project (Burchinal, Vernon-Feagans, & Cox, 2008; Vernon-Feagans, Garrett-Peters, Willoughby, & Mills-Koonce, under review) suggest that especially low-income mothers' irregular and non-standard work hours may impact their children by creating the context of unpredictability that may prevent mothers from being involved in their children's schooling. Important aspects of the neighborhood setting were neighborhood violence and access to print resources through libraries and other sources. Neuman and Celano (2001) found children in low-income neighborhoods had less access to print in the environment, including less access to book stores and libraries. Additional neighborhood factors which influence children's development include the presence of environmental toxins. Low-income neighborhoods, on average, contain higher levels of lead in the environment, which has been associated with cognitive delays (Evans, 2004). In addition, children and families living in poverty have less access to healthy foods (Evans, 2004). Community violence, a common problem in low-income neighborhoods, is associated with child health problems (Jones, Foster, Forehand, & O'Connell, 2005). Violence is also negatively associated with preschoolers' cognitive development, and the association is mediated by children's ability to cope with distress (Farver, Natera, & Frosch, 1999).

Vernon-Feagans and colleagues (2008) also emphasized the influence of oppression and discrimination in the lives of poor and minority children and families in the United States where there has been hundreds of years of discrimination that created inequality in schools and jobs for minority families. However, few studies have addressed the influence of oppression and discrimination on parenting. Hughes and Chen (1997) argue that children are socialized by their parents about African American culture. Parents attempt to prepare children for experiences with prejudice and promote out-group mistrust (Hughes & Chen, 1997). Murry, Brown, Brody, Cutrona, and Simons (2001) found mothers who experienced more racial discrimination tended to have higher rates of depression and lower quality relationships with their children. Such factors may be important to consider in studying children's later experiences during the transition to school.

Relationships Between Child Characteristics and the Transition to School

Researchers have examined relationships among various child characteristics and skills and the transition to school. Findings from such studies highlight the importance of child behavioral characteristics, age at kindergarten entry, factors related to unsuccessful transitions, and parent and teacher beliefs about important factors for the transition to school. Teachers indicate a variety of skills as important in the transition to school. These may include paying attention to the teacher, following directions, listening during group exercises, following classroom routines, communicating needs, playing well with others, being emotionally mature, being physically healthy and demonstrating appropriate self-care and self-regulation (Graue, 1992). Schoen and Nagle (1994) found kindergarten teachers value persistence, low activity, and low distractibility as most related to success in kindergarten. Additional child characteristics found to be important include the ability to express emotions appropriately and being sensitive to others (Lin, Lawrence, & Gorrell, 2003).

Child age at kindergarten entry is associated with children's learning and development in the transition to school. Early research suggested younger children were at risk of poorer academic performance (Brenitz & Teltsch, 1989; Davis, Trimble, & Vincent, 1980). However, later research by Morrison and colleagues has shown that any advantages afforded to older children are lost by the later grades (McClelland, Morrison, & Holmes, 2000; Morrison, Griffith, & Alberts, 1997). It is likely that younger children gain just as much from formal kindergarten programs as do their older classmates (Morrison, Bachman, & Connor, 2005).

Rimm-Kaufman et al. (2000) surveyed teachers to assess their perceptions of why children struggle in the transition to kindergarten. Furthermore, they were interested in discussing how these reported struggles were related to particular school characteristics, such as school poverty level and student minority composition. Teachers reported approximately 50% of students experienced a successful transition to kindergarten. However, approximately 30% of students experienced moderately successful entry into kindergarten, and 15% had difficulty at kindergarten entry. Teachers indicated lack of academic skills and difficulty following directions as the most common problems affecting children's transition (Rimm-Kaufman et al., 2000).

Parents and teachers differ in their beliefs of what is important in the transition to kindergarten. Preschool and kindergarten teachers and parents in a low-income, urban community were surveyed about their beliefs about what is important in the transition to kindergarten (Piotrowski et al., 2000). The survey measured their beliefs on the importance of both children's general readiness resources (e.g., self-regulation, social interaction with peers, interest, and engagement), and their classroom readiness resources (e.g., ability to follow the teacher's directions and adjust to classroom routines). The sample included primarily Hispanic and Black parents whose children received subsidized lunch. Parents and teachers rated most of the general readiness skills similarly in terms of their importance with the exception of the significance of motor skills. They agreed playing well with other children, communicating needs and feelings in their home language, and emotional maturity were absolutely necessary for a successful transition to kindergarten. Kindergarten teachers tended to rate motor skills as less important than preschool teachers and parents (Piotrowski et al., 2000). While the teacher/parent groups generally agreed on the importance of general readiness skills, they differed in their beliefs on the importance of classroom readiness skills. All agreed that compliance with teacher authority was absolutely necessary, but parents tended to rate this as more important than teachers (Piotrowski et al., 2000). Parents also thought compliance to school rules was more important than both preschool and kindergarten teachers. For basic knowledge, parents thought it was absolutely necessary; preschool teachers thought it was important but not absolutely necessary; and kindergarten teachers did not see it as important. Parents also placed greater emphasis on basic knowledge than interest and engagement while teachers thought the opposite. There were also differences with respect to race. Hispanic parents put more emphasis on their children's ability to communicate needs and feelings in their home language, emotional maturity, and interest and engagement than did Black parents (Piotrowski et al., 2000).

Children's reading growth during the transition to kindergarten is associated with key child characteristics. Kainz and Vernon-Feagans (2007) found child's age, race, and gender to be associated with higher reading scores at kindergarten entry. Children who were older at kindergarten entry began school with higher reading skills, as did children who were White. Girls were found to make higher gains in reading at the beginning of the year. However, these gains decreased over the school year (Kainz & Vernon-Feagans, 2007). The one variable that was most associated with reading growth over the first three years of school was minority segregation, suggesting the importance of understanding subtle aspects of racism as they impact early school transitions.

Relationships Between Family Characteristics and the Transition to School

Researchers have investigated how family characteristics are related to the transition to school. Findings from such studies illustrate the influence of Head Start (preschool) experience, family oral language use and vocabulary development, parent support and beliefs, and parent characteristics. Ramey, Gaines, Phillips, and Ramey (1998) studied how children in Head Start classrooms fared during the transition to kindergarten, taking into account the perspectives of the child and family in measuring the child's success in the transition to school. Head Start is an intervention program designed to meet the needs of children and families living in poverty. Head Start provides early childhood education services to children up to age 5, as well as adult and parenting education services to the families of children attending the program. Ramey and colleagues (1998) interviewed family members and children to gauge their perspective on the transition to school. Teachers rated children's academic competence and children completed the Peabody Picture Vocabulary Test (PPVT; Dunn & Dunn, 1997) to measure vocabulary knowledge. The researchers found that most children rated school and teachers positively, with girls rating their experiences slightly higher than boys. Children who reported negative school experiences were more likely to report not being good at school and reported difficulty interacting positively with peers. This same group who reported negative experiences, on average, had lower scores on the PPVT and had younger mothers. Significantly more parents of these children predicted their child would have difficulty in the transition to school than did parents of children with more positive views of school (Ramey et al., 1998).

Children's experiences in families are particularly salient in predicting later success in school, especially when investigating children's language development. A revolutionary study by Hart and Risley (1995) recorded language used in the homes of 42 families from low-, middle-, and high-income families. One of the most striking results was that quantity of language heard by children was more influential than quality. The quality of verbal interactions across socioeconomic levels was similar; the amount was most influential with *parents* in the low-income group talking only as much as *children* in high-income families. Children in high-income families spent an average of 55 minutes per hour interacting with their parents or siblings compared to children of low-income families who spent as little as 7 minutes per hour interacting with others, and these differences were found to be stable over time. Therefore, it is likely that children in middle- and high-income families hear more oral language and therefore may likely acquire larger vocabularies. On the other hand, children in some low-income families may hear very complex oral language. In a study of rural low-income children in North Carolina, Vernon-Feagans (1996) and Feagans and Haskins (1986) found that low-income kindergarten children had more complex language and storytelling than their middle class counterparts in conversations in their neighborhoods. Their findings along with others (Heath, 1983) suggest that there may be other more complex issues beyond language that are related to children's school language and later adjustment in school.

Parents influence children's experiences during the transition to school and have the opportunity to provide support to children during the transition. In one study of children and families in Head Start programs, 20% of parents reported supporting children by providing learning opportunities in the home. Over 10% of parents also reported talking about and playing school as ways to support their child's transition to kindergarten. More than 10% indicated that their decision to send their child to Head Start resulted from a desire to help the child prepare for kindergarten (Ramey et al., 1998).

When making decisions about their own child's entry into kindergarten, parents often express different concerns than when asked about their general beliefs surrounding kindergarten readiness. In a nationally representative survey study of over 2,500 families, parents indicated both academic and social–emotional skills were important for children's success in kindergarten (Diamond, Reagan, & Bandyk, 2000). However, when asked what would be important in making the decision to delay their own child's kindergarten entry, a majority of parents placed greater weight on their child's academic ability over their social–emotional skills.

Kainz and Vernon-Feagans (2007), in an analysis of children in poverty in the Early Childhood Longitudinal Study–Kindergarten (ECLS–K) sample, found that parent education, income, and parent reported preschool literacy experiences were associated with higher emergent literacy at kindergarten entry but the influence of the home decreased over time as teacher instructional practices were more important in predicting literacy growth over the early elementary school years. It seems the influence of family factors on children's literacy development, while important at kindergarten entry, does decrease over time. Perhaps, classroom and school level variables become greater influences than do family variables once children enter kindergarten (Kainz & Vernon-Feagans, 2007).

Relationships Between Teacher Characteristics and the Transition to School

Researchers have examined relationships among various teacher characteristics and the transition to school. Findings from such studies demonstrate the influence of teacher/student relationship quality, teacher support, communication with families, and the amount and type of transition activities provided by teachers for the transition to school. A positive relationship with one's kindergarten teacher is important for a child's successful transition to kindergarten. Baker (2006) was interested in the effect of teacher–child relationship quality on children's school adjustment. Baker found closeness to be moderately positively associated with children's reading grades and work habits. However, conflict in the relationship was even more robustly negatively related to children's reading grades. The association between teacher–child relationship quality and children's reading grades was moderated by child behavior. Children who exhibited externalizing behavior problems (such as, hyperactivity or aggression) and had close relationships with teachers outperformed children with externalizing behavior problems in conflictual teacher–child relationships. In addition, the importance of teacher–child relationship quality tends to be consistent over the child's transition to kindergarten. Children in conflictual teacher–child relationships in preschool also experienced conflict in their relationship with kindergarten teachers (Birch & Ladd, 1997; Howes, Phillipsen, & Peisner-Feinberg, 2000). Children in conflictual relationships reported liking school less and were reported to be less cooperative and less self-directed in the classroom (Birch & Ladd, 1997).

Close teacher–child relationships may serve as a protective factor for students who exhibit high amounts of externalizing problem behaviors in the transition to kindergarten. Silver, Measelle, Armstrong, and Essex (2005) found children with a conflictual teacher–child relationship in preschool exhibited more externalizing behaviors in kindergarten. However, when able to establish a close teacher–child relationship once the child reached kindergarten, the growth trajectory of these behaviors decreased over time (Silver et al., 2005).

A lack of support during the process of transition to kindergarten may be particularly salient for children with special needs. A qualitative researcher (Jewett, 1998) collected and analyzed preschool teachers' journals regarding their experiences of supporting children with special needs and their families during the transition to kindergarten. From analysis of these journals, the researcher concluded that teachers found the transition stressful and often discussed barriers to successful transitions. Teachers felt overwhelmed by the variety of needs children presented and were worried about the lack of training and preparation they received in responding to those needs in a timely manner. They were also discouraged by the way children were treated, with the focus too often placed on children's weaknesses as opposed to their strengths. Teachers emphasized the importance of building relationships with families and relied on family members to share how the child's needs could best be met. The preschool teachers also described their roles as advocates for children in communicating children's needs to the kindergarten teacher (Jewett, 1998).

Teachers report communication with parents as an important transition practice to help children and families feel comfortable in the transition to school. A sample of over 4,000 teachers was surveyed to measure the prevalence of transition practices in schools. Survey results indicated communicating with families about the transition was the most common activity used by the surveyed teachers (Pianta, Cox, Taylor, & Early, 1999). However, a majority indicated this communication occurred after the school year had started. Only 17% of kindergarten teachers mentioned visiting preschool classrooms and only 20% indicated that specific efforts were made to coordinate the preschool and kindergarten curricula in their schools. In addition, schools classified as more urban, with more children of low-income and minority backgrounds, reported offering fewer transition activities. Results from a similar survey study indicated the most common transition practice used by teachers was kindergarten orientation (Love, Logue, Trudeau, & Thayer, 1992), where children and families had the opportunity to visit kindergarten classrooms and meet the teachers.

The amount and type of transition activities may vary depending on teachers' experience. Overall, preschool teachers tended to provide more transition activities than kindergarten teachers (La Paro, Kraft-Sayre, & Pianta, 2003). Kindergarten teachers who had previous experience of working in preschools reported contacting parents more often (La Paro et al., 2003). It may be that preschool experience raises teachers' awareness of the need for such communication. Preschool teachers with more experience in general reported contacting parents more often than their less experienced colleagues (La Paro et al., 2003). This increased contact may come with greater confidence in interacting with parents as teachers accumulate experience in the field.

Relationships Between Peer Characteristics and the Transition to School

The theoretical model from which we have framed this review includes peers as an important influence during the transition to school, yet the influence of peers on the transition to school in the United States has not been deeply researched. Researchers have suggested children who do not make effective transitions to kindergarten often struggle in building friendships with their classmates (Ramey & Ramey, 1994). On the other hand, children who made successful transitions to kindergarten made friends easily and demonstrated appropriate social skills when interacting with peers and adults (Ramey & Ramey, 1994). Children who entered school with friends also tended to make better gains in their academic performance (Ladd, 1990). At the same time, peer rejection was associated with a negative attitude toward school and poor school adjustment.

Some have argued the mere presence of familiar peers is not as important as the quality of friendships children have during the transition to school. Ladd and Kochendorfer (1996) were interested in better understanding the influence of friends versus acquaintances on children's adjustment to and attitude toward school. They found no association between the number of acquaintances the child reported and attitude toward school. However, children's positive attitude toward school was significantly associated with friendship (Ladd & Kochendorfer, 1996).

There are several studies conducted abroad that may also inform peers' influence on the transition to school. For example, research done in Australian schools found a positive association between children who reported the presence of a friend in class and measures of positive adjustment in school (Margetts, 2000). However, additional research conducted in New Zealand early childhood classrooms found adjustment to school was not associated with having friends or familiar peers upon school entry (Ledger, Smith, & Rich, 1998). Similarly, as mentioned in Chapter 4 of this book, quantitative data did not show a relationship between successful transition and moving to school with friends from the same preschool setting, despite parents' perception that it would make a difference.

Relationships Between School/Community Characteristics and the Transition to School

Researchers have investigated how school/community characteristics are related to the transition to school. Findings from such studies support the influence of school demographics, school grade span, quality of pre-kindergarten care, classroom demographics, and characteristics of "ready" schools on the transition to school.

Teachers' reports of problems during the transition to school vary depending on school metropolitan status, district poverty level, and school minority composition. Specific problems reported included difficulty following directions, lack of academic skills, disorganized home environments, difficulty working independently, lack of preschool experience, difficulty working as part of a group, problems with social skills, immaturity, and difficulty communicating. Higher rates of school poverty level and minority composition predicted higher-levels of teacher reported difficulty in school (Rimm-Kaufman et al., 2000). Both were significantly related to a majority of the problems described. Whereas, rural school status, when compared to urban and suburban school contexts, only predicted higher rates of disorganized home environments.

Research on school grade span has begun to inform research on the transition to kindergarten. A study conducted with a large longitudinal sample from the ECLS–K dataset found grade span to be an important predictor of children's success in school (Burkam, Michaels, & Lee, 2007). When children went to the same school for preschool and kindergarten, they experienced greater success in the acquisition of literacy skills. When compared with students who attend preschool and kindergarten in the same setting, children who attend preschool and kindergarten in different settings, on average, learn less in literacy and math as measured by standardized achievement tests (Burkam et al., 2007). This is likely a result of greater communication between preschool and kindergarten teachers given the convenience of working in the same building.

Quality of care (either in a formal preschool classroom or another day-care setting) prior to kindergarten entry is an important factor in measuring children's success in the kindergarten year. Children who receive higher quality care generally fare better in the transition to school than children who do not receive high quality care. Pigott and Israel (2005) were interested in whether children in Head Start classrooms performed better than children without Head Start experience. When compared with children who experience similar economic circumstances, Head Start children outperformed other children who did not attend Head Start on measures of print familiarity, letter recognition, vocabulary knowledge, and comprehension. However, when compared with children coming from higher socioeconomic homes, the Head Start children were still disadvantaged on the same measures. In addition, Head Start children appeared to function adequately in kindergarten classrooms due to the similarity between Head Start and kindergarten classrooms in the way they are structured and managed (Skinner, Bryant, Coffman, & Campbell, 1998). However, one difficulty lies in the differences between Head Start classrooms and public school kindergarten classrooms. Typically, both are operated under different agencies, and communication and collaboration across settings between teachers and staff becomes difficult.

With respect to classroom demographics, researchers have found that children in classrooms with higher percentages of children reading below grade level tended to have lower reading scores. In addition, minority segregation was significantly negatively related to children's reading scores, and this association became stronger over time (Kainz & Vernon-Feagans, 2007).

Research on "ready schools" helps administrators and teachers better understand policies and practices that are important for children's successful experiences in the transition to school. Pianta and colleagues (1999) define ready schools as those that "reach" in different directions to support children and families. Ready schools "reach out" to establish effective links with families and local preschools through communication and collaboration between teachers and across school settings. Ready schools "reach" back in time to establish connections before the first day of school so children and families know what to expect beforehand and feel welcome in the new environment. Finally, ready schools "reach" with intensity to establish close, personal connections with families through home visits.

IMPLICATIONS FOR PRACTICE

Based on the research review in the previous section, we now turn to implications for practice. We present four main implications for practice: an expanding conceptualization of readiness, increased communication between preschool and kindergarten teachers, earlier communication between kindergarten teachers and new families, and parallel professional development in literacy for preschool and kindergarten teachers. In the following paragraphs we provide a brief discussion of each implication in turn.

We begin with an implication of the theory and research presented in the previous sections which requires an expanding understanding for teachers, parents, and preschool and elementary school administrators of school readiness, a concept intertwined with the transition to school in the United States. Vernon-Feagans and colleagues (2008) provide a way to conceptualize readiness which puts the definition of readiness, not within the child, but at the "interaction and fit between the child and his/her family and the 'readiness' of the classroom/school to teach that child" (p. 63). Conceptualizing young children's school readiness with such an ecological/transactional model shifts the focus from a discreet set of students' literacy skills at school entry to how students' skills grow and change and are a function of child, family, and school/classroom characteristics.

With respect to the transition to school, the ecological/transactional model of readiness would shift the focus of prior-to-school experiences and preparation from the child to the ecological system. Early childhood literacy education would not only focus on children's learning, but family characteristics and development, as well as school and classroom characteristics, including early literacy instruction. Stakeholders would likely focus on the transactions among these microsystems and exosystems (Bronfenbrenner, 1979; see Chapter 4), and how these systems influence students' development in concert. Thus, the transition to school is not an individual experience for the child, but rather a shared experience, involving a variety of individuals (Dockett & Perry, 2001).

A second implication for young students' transition to school is the importance of increased communication between preschool and kindergarten teachers. If stakeholders were to provide additional instances for preschool and kindergarten teacher collaboration, a more seamless transition to school might be facilitated for young children. For example, establishing communication between preschool and kindergarten teachers might allow teachers in both settings to align classroom expectations, procedures, and processes. With respect to early literacy instruction, preschool teachers could provide circle time in which emergent literacy skills and experiences (Sulzby, 1985) were provided. Kindergarten teachers could transform circle time into a shared reading experience for providing early literacy instruction for students. Through such alignment students would experience similar settings prior to kindergarten and upon kindergarten entry and the similarity across school cultures might facilitate an easier transition to school.

A third implication is earlier communication between kindergarten teachers and families new to elementary school. To accomplish such a goal, kindergarten teachers and school administrators would need to begin preparation for new kindergarten students much earlier to provide time for communication with new families. Earlier preparation, such as registration of new kindergarten students, creating class lists, and organizing meetings and/or orientations would not be easy tasks to undertake, but might be vital to improving young children's transitions to school. Through careful planning and evaluation of early preparation activities and communication efforts schools can facilitate successful transitions to school for young children entering kindergarten.

A final implication for young students' transition to school is parallel professional development in literacy for preschool and kindergarten teachers. If both preschool and kindergarten teachers were to receive access to the same professional development in early literacy instruction there might be greater continuity between instructional strategies and environments across the transition to school. Using the language of the "fit between the child and teacher" mentioned in first recommendation, it would seem important that teachers receive professional development in individualizing instruction for our most vulnerable children so that teachers learn to match their literacy instruction to the skill level of the child. This kind of instruction has recently been shown to be particularly effective in increasing early reading (Connor, Morrison, Fishman, Schatschneider, & Underwood, 2007; Morrison et al., 2005; Vernon-Feagans et al., in press). In addition, during communication with families (as suggested in the prior implication) teachers and schools could provide information to parents and guardians, as well as complementary strategies which could be used in the home. If preschool teachers, kindergarten teachers, and families were given complementary content/professional development, young children may enter "ready" schools, better equipped to meet young students' needs (Vernon-Feagans, 1996).

FUTURE DIRECTIONS

In the current chapter we have focused on selected aspects of the transition to school for young children in the United States. Although the transition to school has recently received increased attention (cf. Pianta & Cox, 1999), there is still work to be done. First, as discussed in the first implication, it is vital that the concept of readiness is embraced by stakeholders with an ecological/transactional theoretical frame. Research designs that test such a theory or model for explaining factors related to children's successful or unsuccessful transitions to school could provide vital information to inform teachers, school administrators, and families. Results might also inform creation of transition to school programs or processes which could facilitate successful transitions for children, families, and schools.

Second, the effects of peer relationships on the transition to school have not been deeply researched. As peers influence multiple systems in the ecological/transactional model, the effects of peer relationships are likely not insignificant. Future research should address the effect of peer relationships on the transition to school, including both positive and negative effects.

Third, based on the ecological/transactional model (Vernon-Feagans et al., 2008) practitioners and researchers could collaborate to create interventions or programs to be evaluated through research. Again, research and/or evaluation designs should address the specific aspects related to the ecological/transactional model. Of particular importance would be specific research questions that address how specific transition practices benefit particular groups of children, in particular which transition to school practices make the most difference for students who might be delayed in their literacy development.

CLOSURE

In this chapter we have discussed issues related to the transition to formal schooling for students in the United States. We have reviewed research related to the transition to school and child characteristics and skills, the role of the family, the role of the teacher, and school and community contexts and practices. We then presented implications of the research review as well as future directions for the field with respect to the transition to school. As increasingly diverse numbers of children enter formal schooling in the United States, it becomes increasingly important for all stakeholders to embrace the ecological/transactional model of readiness (Vernon-Feagans et al., 2008), and expand their understanding of the many contextual factors and systems which influence young children's transition to school. Such expanded understandings could provide a foundation for future research, program development, and professional development for early educators.

REFERENCES

Alexander, K. L., & Entwisle, D. R. (1988). Achievement in the first 2 years of school: Patterns and processes. *Monographs of the Society for Research in Child Development, 53*(2), 1–157.

Baker, J. A. (2006). Contributions of teacher–child relationships to positive school adjustment during elementary school. *Journal of School Psychology, 44,* 211–229.

Birch, S., & Ladd, G. W. (1997). The teacher–child relationship and children's early school adjustment. *Journal of School Psychology, 35*(1), 61–79.

Bohan-Baker, M., & Little, P. M. D. (2004). The transition to kindergarten: A review of current research and promising practices to involve families [Electronic version]. Retrieved March 30, 2009, from http://www.hfrp.org/publications-resources/browse-our-publications/the-transition-to-kindergarten-a-review-of-current-research-and-promising-practices-to-involve-families.

Brenitz, Z., & Teltsch, T. (1989). The effect of school entrance age on academic achievement and social–emotional adjustment of children: Follow-up study of fourth graders. *Psychology in the Schools, 26,* 62–68.

Bronfenbrenner, U. (1979). *The ecology of human development: Experiments by nature and design.* Cambridge, MA: Harvard University Press.

Burchinal, M. R., Vernon-Feagans, L., & Cox, M. (2008). Cumulative social risk and infant development in rural low-income communities. *Parenting: Science and Practice, 8,* 41–82.

Burkam, D. T., Michaels, D. L., & Lee, V. E. (2007). School grade span and kindergarten learning. *Elementary School Journal, 107*(3), 287–303.

Connor, C. M., Morrison, F. J., Fishman, B. J., Schatschneider, C., & Underwood, P. (2007). Algorithm-guided individualized reading instruction. *Science, 315,* 464–465.

Coyner, L., Reynolds, A., & Ou, S. (2003). The effect of early childhood interventions on subsequent special education services: Findings from the Chicago Child–Parent Centers. *Education Evaluation and Policy Analysis, 25*(1), 75–95.

Davis, B. G., Trimble, C. S., & Vincent, D. R. (1980). Does age of entrance affect school achievement? *The Elementary School Journal, 80,* 133–143.

Diamond, K., Reagan, A., & Bandyk, J. (2000). Parents' conceptions of kindergarten readiness: Relationships with race, ethnicity, and development. *Journal of Educational Research, 86*(1), 93–100.

Dockett, S., & Perry, B. (2001). Starting school: Effective transitions. *Early Childhood Research & Practice, 3*(2), 1–15.

Dunn, L. M., & Dunn, L. M. (1997). *Peabody picture vocabulary test iii.* Circle Pines, MN: American Guidance Services.

Evans, G. W. (2004). The environment of childhood poverty. *American Psychologist, 59,* 77–92.

Farver, J. M., Natera, L. X., & Frosch, D. L. (1999). Effects of community violence on inner-city preschoolers and their families. *Journal of Applied Developmental Psychology, 20,* 143–57.

Feagans, L., & Haskins, R. (1986). Neighborhood dialogues of black and white 5-year olds. *Journal of Applied Developmental Psychology, 20,* 143–58.

Graue, M. E. (1992). Social interpretations of readiness for kindergarten. *Early Childhood Research Quarterly, 7,* 225–243.

Gutman, L. M., Sameroff, A. J., & Cole, R. (2003). Academic growth curve trajectories from 1st to 12th grade: Effects of multiple social risk factors and preschool child factors. *Developmental Psychology, 39,* 777–790.

Han, W. (2005). Maternal non-standard work schedules and child cognitive outcomes. *Child Development, 76,* 137–154.

Hart, B., & Risley, T. R. (1995). *Meaningful differences in the everyday experience of young American children.* Baltimore: Paul H. Brookes.

Heath, S. B. (1983). *Ways with words: Language, life, and work in communities and classrooms.* New York: McGraw-Hill; Oxford University Press.

Heaviside, S., & Farris, E. (1993). *Public schools kindergarten teachers' views on children's readiness for school* (NCES No. 93–410). Washington, D.C.: U.S. Department of Education, Office of Educational Research and Improvement.

Howes, C., Phillipsen, L., & Peisner-Feinberg, E. S. (2000). The consistency of perceived teacher–child relationships between preschool and kindergarten. *Journal of School Psychology, 38*(2), 113–132.

Hughes, D., & Chen, L. (1997). When and what parents tell children about race: An examination of race-related socialization among African American families. *Applied Developmental Science, 1,* 200–214.

Jewett, J. (1998). Four early childhood teachers reflect on helping children with special needs make the transition to kindergarten. *The Elementary School Journal, 98,* 329–338.

Jones, D. J., Foster, S., Forehand, G., & O'Connell, C. (2005). Neighborhood violence and psychosocial adjustment in low-income urban African American children: Physical symptoms as a marker of child adjustment. *Journal of Child and Family Studies, 14,* 237–249.

Juel, C. (1988). Learning to read and write: A longitudinal study of fifty-four children from first through fourth grade. *Journal of Educational Psychology, 80*(4), 437–447.

Kagan, S. L., & Neuman, S. B. (1998). Lessons from three decades of transition research. *The Elementary School Journal, 98,* 365–379.

Kainz, K., & Vernon-Feagans, L. (2007). The ecology of early reading development for children in poverty. *The Elementary School Journal, 107,* 407–427.

Kraft-Sayre, M. E., & Pianta, R. C. (2000). *Enhancing the transition to kindergarten: Linking children, families, and schools.* Charlottesville, VA: University of Virginia.

Ladd, G. W. (1990). Having friends, keeping friends, making friends and being liked by peers in the classroom: Predictors of children's early school adjustment. *Child Development, 61,* 1081–1100.

Ladd, G. W., & Kochendorfer, B. J. (1996). Linkages between friendship and adjustment during early school transitions. In W. Bukowski, A. F. Newcomb, W. Hartup (Eds.), *The company they keep: Friendship in childhood and adolescence* (pp. 322–345). Cambridge: Cambridge University Press.

La Paro, K. M., Kraft-Sayre, M. E., & Pianta, R. C. (2003). Preschool to kindergarten transition practices: Involvement and satisfaction of families and teachers. *Journal of Research in Childhood Education, 17*(2), 147–158.

Ledger, E., Smith, A., & Rich, P. (1998). 'Do I go to school to get a brain?' The transition from kindergarten to school from the child's perspective. *Childrenz Issues, 2*(1), 7–11.

Lewitt, E. M., & Baker, L. S. (1995) School readiness. *The Future of Children: Critical Issues for Children and Youths, 5*(2), 128–139.

Lin, H. L., Lawrence, F. R., & Gorrell, J. (2003). Kindergarten teachers' view of children's readiness for school. *Early Childhood Research Quarterly, 18,* 225–237.

Love, J,. M., Logue, M. E., Trudeau, J. V., & Thayer, K. (1992). *Transitions to kindergarten in American schools: Final report of the national transition study.* Portsmouth, NH: U.S. Department of Education, Office of Policy and Planning.

Margetts, K. (2000). Indicators of children's adjustment to the first year of schooling. *Journal for Australian Research in Early Childhood Education, 7*(1), 20–30.

McClelland, M. M., Morrison, F. J., & Holmes, D. L. (2000). Children at risk for early academic problems: The role of learning related social skills. *Early Childhood Research Quarterly, 15*, 307–329.

Meisels, S. J. (1999). Assessing readiness. In R. C. Pianta & M. J. Cox (Eds.), *The transition to kindergarten* (pp. 39–66). Baltimore, MD: Paul H. Brookes Publishing.

Morrison, F. J., Bachman, H., & Connor, C. M. (2005). *Improving literacy in America: Guidelines from research.* New Haven: Yale University Press.

Morrison, F. J., Griffith, E. M., & Alberts, D. M. (1997). Nature–nurture in the classroom: Entrance age, school readiness, and learning in children. *Developmental Psychology, 33*(2), 254–262.

Murry, V. M., Brown, P. A., Brody, G. H., Cutrona, C. E., & Simons, R. L. (2001). Racial discrimination as a moderator of the links among stress maternal psychological functioning and family relationships. *Journal of Marriage and the Family, 63*, 915–926.

National Association of State Boards of Education. (1991). *Caring communities: Supporting young children and families* (Report of the National Task Force on School Readiness). Alexandria, VA: Author.

National Education Goals Panel. (1993). *Background on the National Education Goals Panel* [Electronic version]. Retrieved April 22, 2009, from http://www.eric.ed.gov:80/ERICDocs/data/ericdocs2sql/content_storage_010000019b/80/13/0f/80.pdf.

Neuman, S. B., & Celano, D. (2001). Access to print in low-income and middle-income communities: An ecological study of four neighborhoods. *Reading Research Quarterly, 36*, 8–26.

Pianta, R. C., & Cox, M. J. (Eds.). (1999). *The transition to kindergarten.* Baltimore, MD: Paul H. Brookes Publishing Co.

Pianta, R., Cox, M., & Snow, K. (2007). *School readiness and the transition to kindergarten in the era of accountability.* Baltimore: Paul H. Brookes Publishing Company.

Pianta, R. C., Cox, M. J., Taylor, L., & Early, D. (1999). Kindergarten teachers' practices related to the transition to school: Results of a national survey. *The Elementary School Journal, 100*(1), 71–86.

Pigott, T. D., & Israel, M. S. (2005). Head Start children's transition to kindergarten: Evidence from the Early Childhood Longitudinal Study. *Journal of Early Childhood Research, 3*, 77–104.

Piotrowski, C. S., Botsko, M., & Matthews, E. (2000). Parents and teachers beliefs about children's school readiness in a high-need community. *Early Childhood Research Quarterly, 15*(4) 537–558.

Ramey, S. L., Gaines, R., Phillips, M., & Ramey, C. T. (1998). Perspectives of former Head Start children and their parents on the transition to school. *Elementary School Journal, 98*, 311–328.

Ramey, S. L., & Ramey, C. T. (1994). The transition to school: Why the first few years matter for a lifetime. *Phi Delta Kappan, 76*, 194–198.

Ramey, S. L., & Ramey, C. T. (1999). *Going to school.* New York: Goddard Press.

Rimm-Kaufman, S. E., Pianta, R. C., & Cox, M. J. (2000). Teacher's judgments of problems in the transition to kindergarten. *Early Childhood Research Quarterly, 15*(2), 147–166.

Schoen, M. J., & Nagle, R. J. (1994). Prediction of school readiness from kindergarten temperament scores. *Journal of School Psychology, 32*, 135–137.

Schulting, A. B., Malone, P. S., & Dodge, K. A. (2005). The effect of school-based kindergarten transition policies and practices on child academic outcomes. *Developmental Psychology, 41*, 860–871.

Silver, R. B., Measelle, J. R., Armstrong, J. M., & Essex, M. J. (2005). Trajectories of classroom externalizing behavior: Contributions of child characteristics and the teacher–child relationships during the school transition. *Journal of School Psychology, 43*, 39–60.

Skinner, D., Bryant, D., Coffman, J., & Campbell, F. (1998). Creating risk and promise: Children's and teachers' co-constructions in the cultural world of kindergarten. *The Elementary School Journal, 95*(4), 297–310.

Sulzby, E. (1985). Children's emergent reading of favorite storybooks: A developmental study. *Reading Research Quarterly, 20*, 458–481.

U.S. Department of Education. National Center for Education Statistics. (2000). *America's Kindergartners*, NCES 2000–070, by Kristin Denton, Elvira Germino-Hausken. Project Officer, Jerry West, Washington, DC.

Vernon-Feagans, L. (1996). *Children's talk in communities and classrooms.* Cambridge, MA: Blackwell Publishers.

Vernon-Feagans, L. (in press). School readiness. In R. A. Shweder, T. R. Bidell, A. C. Dailey, S. D. Dixon, P. J. Miller & J. Modell (Eds.), *The child: An encyclopedic companion.* Chicago: University of Chicago Press.

Vernon-Feagans, L., & Blair, C. (2006). Measurement of school readiness: Introduction to a special issue of *Early Education and Development. Early Education and Development, 17*, 1–5.

Vernon-Feagans, L., Garrett-Peters, P., Willoughby, M., & Mills-Koonce, H. (under review). Chaos, poverty, and parenting: Predictors of toddler language development. *Child Development.*

Vernon-Feagans, L., Odom, E., Panscofar, N., & Kainz, K. (2008). Comments on Farkas and Hibel: A transactional/ecological model of readiness and inequality. In A. Booth & A. C. Crouter (Eds.), *Disparities in school readiness* (pp. 61–78). New York: Lawrence Erlbaum Associates.

Part III

Transition from Primary to Secondary School

7 Moving to Secondary School
What Do Pupils in England Say About the Experience?

Maurice Galton

This chapter looks at the impact on pupils when they first arrive at secondary school. Transition[1] is often described as an anxious time but it is more true to say that pupils generally feel excitement tinged with a touch of apprehension. The following pages explore what schools are doing to make transition a more satisfactory experience and the reactions of pupils to these initiatives. The data presented here are an amalgam of three transition studies conducted in England, that of Hargreaves and Galton (2002), Galton, Gray, and Rudduck (2003), and an unpublished study carried out as part of a policy review for a local authority in England. In Hargreaves and Galton (2002), the field work in six transition schools was carried out in 1996–1997, while Galton et al. (2003) involved some 20 schools situated mainly in 5 Local Authorities in the Midlands and East Anglia covering the period 2000–2002. The review for the Local Authority took place in 2005–2006 and involved three schools. In all cases, groups of pupils were interviewed during the last term at primary school[2] shortly after induction day, again at half-term following the move to secondary school and finally at the end of the year following transition. Throughout the chapter various suggestions are made concerning ways in which the transition process might be improved.

CHANGES IN TRANSITION PROCEDURES OVER TIME IN ENGLAND

Hargreaves and Galton's (2002) study attempted to replicate the original research carried out during the ORACLE (Observational Research and Classroom Learning Evaluation) project (Galton, Simon, & Croll, 1980; Galton & Willcocks, 1983) two decades earlier. This showed that a number of significant changes had taken place with regard to the administration of the transition process and that schools had moved to eliminate some of the immediate anxieties which earlier studies of transition had highlighted. Some of these changes were less the result of fresh thinking about transition and had more to do with the changed circumstances of schools, particularly the decline in the power of the Local Education Authorities and the 'market forces' approach to education with its emphasis on parental choice, which had been the flagship of the Conservative administration (Tomlinson, 2005). Thus in the late 1970s when the first ORACLE transition study was carried out the choice of secondary school was wholly, or in the case of voluntary aided schools, partially determined by the Local Authority, who allocated most pupils to the school catchment area in which they resided. In these circumstances, therefore, secondary schools gave little thought as to how to accommodate parents' and pupil's wishes so that a 'take it or leave it' attitude tended to dominate. Thus in most cases in the original 1975/80 ORACLE study children visited the school for one morning only as part of a transition program. There they were addressed by the coordinator/tutor responsible for transition, given a conducted tour of the school and then sent back to their primary feeder schools before lunch. The Year 7 coordinator might perhaps also pay a follow-up visit to the main primary feeder schools following the tour of the transition school. A Parents' Evening would also be arranged towards the end of the Summer Term prior to transition. Its main purpose would be to instruct the audience on the rules of the school and the clothing policy, particularly the required items for PE and various sports (Delamont & Galton, 1986; Galton & Willcocks, 1983).

By the 1990s, however, things had changed. Most schools now had Liaison Committees where the administrative issues of transition were considered. Unlike the 1970s these arrangements were less hierarchical in that the chairperson tended to rotate between the primary and secondary head teachers. Matters like the transition of children's records, the provision available for children with special needs, the sharing of curriculum issues now often featured on the agenda. In an effort to gain as many new pupils as possible, most transition schools now organized several Parents' Meetings one year prior to transition in the following mid-September. This involved opportunities to visit classrooms and see pupils (brought in especially for the evening) engaged in various curriculum activities. In some cases the transition school's facilities were available for use by the primary schools, particularly science laboratories, drama studios, and ICT suites. As suggested earlier, the reasons behind these moves often appeared to have less to do with the actual transition process and were more concerned to encourage pupils' parents and pupils to choose the particular school so that its numbers could be boosted and its finances increased. Hence these contacts were also supplemented by regular newsletters and other documents, designed to inform potential clients of the advantages of bringing their child to the particular institution.

INDUCTION DAYS

One major change, however, has been in the treatment of pupils prior to transition. Now almost every Local Authority organizes a special day toward the end of the summer term when all children whose parents had opted to send them to a particular school spend a whole Induction Day on the premises. In most schools the Induction Day follows a similar pattern. Pupils are initially divided into their tutor and form groups and spend some time getting to know each other through a series of ice-breaker activities. There will be an assembly at which the school Principal welcomes the new pupils followed by a conducted tour of the school. Whereas the tour in the 1970s was often superficial with a volunteer pupil briefly stopping outside a room to say, "This is where you do French," or "This is where you queue for snacks," these latter tours are generally conducted by the form tutors with frequent stops to allow question and answer sessions. In most schools the tour is followed by an early lunch to avoid the queues when the main body of pupils finish morning sessions. In between and during the afternoon there will be various lessons, a mix of core and other subjects. These lessons are generally made as exciting as possible so that for example in Science there will be plenty of explosions and lots of smoke accompanied by strange smells. The final session usually consists of questions and answers about any remaining issues that the pupils might have. Sometimes these are conducted by the Year 7 Coordinator but more often space is allowed for the visiting primary intake to question existing Year 7 pupils. At some point during the day there will be an early introduction into the school routines and rules, generally during a tutor meeting (Hargreaves & Galton, 2002).

Interviews with the pupils (Hargreaves & Galton, 2002) found that the response to these activities was generally positive. Pupils found that their immediate anxieties were dealt with. These usually consisted of whether they would make new friends and get on with pupils from other primary schools, getting to see what the new teachers were like, and working out practical arrangements such as how one paid for lunch, what one did in break time, and where to put one's bag. The conclusion of the Oracle Replication Transition Study was that, in respect of these activities designed to improve social adjustment, little more could be done. Indeed, to do more would be perhaps to tip the scales too far away from the direction of maintaining some degree of discontinuity; in this case slight apprehension on the parts of the pupils so that they would continue during the summer vacation to see the move to the new school as a significant change in their status.

Pupils, however, expressed reservations about the content of these induction days. In the 2005–2006 study pupils complained that many of the 'taster' sessions were too short so that it was impossible to finish off the picture in art or the experiment in science. They found that the guided tour of the school often served to confuse them more because they were not provided with a map and therefore had no understanding of their whereabouts (relative to their form room) or the permissible traffic routes. One group of pupils suggested that it would make a good exercise to provide a map and send them off in groups on a 'treasure hunt' to identify various parts of the school because:

Not only would we get to work it out for ourselves but we would have more time to get to know others in our form and make new friends.

Having sufficient time to meet in tutor groups and make new friends was deemed to be the most important part of the day. Next to this was the opportunity to meet with the present Year 7 away from the teacher's close supervision,

So we could get to know what it was really like.

In one school the dining room was sited on the edge of the area where pupils congregated during break times. Pupils complained that at lunch time it felt like being in a zoo because when the main school arrived they crowded around the windows, making faces while they watched them eat. While appreciating the chance to take an early lunch in order to work out the menu choices and payment methods most pupils felt the process was too rushed.

A bigger problem involved the organization of the day itself. Because teachers who take part (as form tutors, providing lessons, etc.) have other teaching commitments throughout the day it is inevitable that timings will slip because classes sometimes over-run. This resulted in pupils having to stand around waiting to be collected. Often they were told to remain silent while waiting and when talking began teachers would attempt to re-impose control, often by shouting so that they were seen by many pupils as 'stressy' because,

They shout and get mad when someone speaks when they're speaking and take it out on the rest of us.

It was also often the case that in arranging these activities the Year 7 coordinator required pupils to return to some familiar central point, such as the Assembly Hall, so that the new teacher could collect his/her charges from the previous one. Sometimes this led to pupils returning from a teaching block only to then set out for another classroom in the same location with the new teacher. One solution is to use older pupils to act as guides and mentors throughout the day, thereby allowing the newcomers to be moved directly to their next location to await the teacher's arrival.

IMMEDIATE POST-TRANSITION IMPRESSIONS

For the majority of pupils the immediate anxieties associated with transition appear relatively short lived. There is remarkable agreement on this point when studies spanning four decades are compared. Youngman (1978) and Youngman and Lunzer (1977) found only 20% of pupils in England retained negative feelings after one term in the transition school, a conclusion supported by Spelman (1979) in Northern Ireland and by Dutch and McCall (1974) in Scotland. More recently, Evangelou et al. (2008) have reported that 75% of pupils said they had adjusted well by the end of their first term in the transition school. Among the pupils who failed to adjust within a short period, between 6 and 10% have reported persistent problems (Chedzoy & Burden, 2005; ILEA, 1986). Galton and Willcocks (1983) found that with only about 12% of pupils were the dips in attainment sustained and relatively serious (i.e., >2 standard deviations).

A recent search of the literature[3] found 24 UK studies in which pupils' pre- and post-transition concerns were identified covering the four decades since 1968. Most of these concerns could be classified under six distinct headings:

   i. Personal adaptability: Mainly concerns about being the youngest and smallest and about fitting in with older pupils;
  ii. Work: Coping with different subjects and doing homework on time;
 iii. Size: Getting lost, not using the authorized routes, etc.;
  iv. Teachers: Adjusting to several teachers (particularly how strict they were);
   v. Friendships: Making new friends and keeping old ones; and
  vi. Moving: Getting to school on time, learning the rules, bringing the right books and equipment, buying school dinners, getting a locker.

In Figures 7.1 the relative frequencies of these various concerns are portrayed prior to transition. The most frequent concerns are related to making new friends and retaining old ones from the primary school. This emphasis is reflected in the earlier comments on induction days. The second most commonly expressed concern relates to the size of the secondary school and of getting lost. Concerns about harder work and coping with homework, the next highest category, are balanced by looking forward to having better

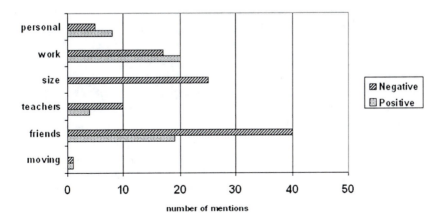

Figure 7.1   Pre-transfer concerns.

facilities such as laboratories for science, a proper drama studio and a dedicated gymnasium for PE.

In Figure 7.2 the post-transition perceptions are displayed. Issues relating to the move are now the most frequently mentioned aspect of the transition but these references are mostly positive. Pupils have learned to find the way around the various buildings, are coping with the school dinner queue, the vagaries of the timetable and getting themselves to school on time. On the negative side, peer relationships and issues to do with work still get most mentions but this is now closely followed by concerns about various teachers, particularly the way that they apply school rules, including the tendency of some teachers to punish the whole class for an individual's misdemeanor. The following are taken from the 2005–2006 study.

> *Good teachers explain things and don't accuse you of not listening, can have a laugh, listen to your reasons when you're late and don't pick on the whole class when just one or two are fooling about.*

> *It's weird sometimes because if another teacher comes into the class they act a lot different to when the other teacher isn't there. They're really jolly and nice but when the other teacher goes out they're back to shut up and shouting like normal.*

Supply (or cover) teachers appear to present particular difficulties:

> *Sometimes they can't control the class so they get another teacher. I think they kind of exaggerate the story so the teacher thinks we've been worse than we have. That way they don't look so hopeless but we get told off more for it.*

> *Basically, the substitute doesn't teach. Most of the work set is written, out of books. Like they tell us to do a page and write out the questions and answer them. That's when people start misbehaving because they're bored.*

Not having sufficient friends remains a particular cause of concern, not least because there is security in numbers and a person with friends is less likely to be bullied. Break times, particularly lunch were a constant worry for the 2005–2006 sample.

> *The older years act as if you're really tiny. They push your sandwich in your mouth. In the lunch queue I stood by my cousin who's Year 9 and these two girls were mouthing off at me.*

> *When you're in the dinner line they push you out of the way. It's like we're ghosts, they ignore us and act as if we're not there.*

On work related issues the emphasis tends to have shifted since before transition. There are now fewer concerns about coping and more expressions of disappointment about the repetitive nature of activities which were already covered at primary school and on the emphasis on writing in subjects such as science and mathematics. Foreign Language lessons also involve lots of copying and are disliked mainly for that reason.

It's [maths] the same here [as at primary school] but more complex. . . . We just do bigger numbers.

We write more in maths than we do in English. She writes on the board and then says, "Here you go. Open your books and do questions 1, 2 and 3" so we just write.

We hardly do any practical. If we do it, doesn't last long and we have to write it up from the board.

We couldn't understand our teacher's French. Then we had a supply and we couldn't understand her English. So we just copy from the book.

For these reasons it is the subjects where there is less writing and more active participation which receive greater acclaim. Art gets most positive mentions with Physical Education next followed by Humanities.

I used to hate art in primary but here it's unbelievable. You've got so much information, lots of equipment and so much you can do.

I like the athletics, sprinting, hurdles and things. I now go to a real gym on Friday nights and go on treadmills and stuff.

History is fun. We make things like a modern roundhouse out of straw and I've tried it at home.

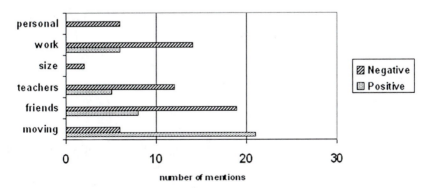

Figure 7.2 Post-transfer concerns.

In the final interviews, which took place one year after transition, pupils are already looking forward to moving to the second year of secondary school in the hope that some of these concerns about teachers, work and bullying will no longer apply or if they do to a lesser degree.

> *In Year 8 the teachers will trust you more and we'll hopefully get fewer supply teachers.*

> *We will mix up classes so I can make a fresh start with new teachers and avoid some of the teachers I didn't get on with this past year.*

> *We will get to use computers more.*

> *We will not be the youngest so won't be picked upon so often.*

And, finally reflecting on their Year 7 experience pupils offered the following advice to their Year 6 peers who would be joining the school after the summer holiday:

> *Don't cry in front of people or they'll take the mick.*

> *Keep yourself to yourself.*

> *Don't go around telling kids you don't like to shut up.*

> *Don't say personal stuff out in class or you'll get laughed at. Don't give cheek to older pupils or they'll have a go at you.*

However, there were also some positive words of encouragement:

> *Don't worry. All big people won't bully you. Come here and settle in—it's just like your old school but bigger so don't be scared.*

> *Respect the teacher, respect your friends and you'll be proud of yourself. Respect, like react to people how you want them to react to you.*

BRIDGING UNITS AS AN AID TO CURRICULUM CONTINUITY

A continuing problem with regard to transition has been the failure of many secondary schools to take account of what has been taught in primary school. The so-called 'fresh start' approach is epitomized in Galton and Willcocks (1983, p. 114) where the art master told the new pupils that "instead of a bit of splash and fun we are really going to think about drawing . . . about the basic elements of design; color, shape and form."

In Galton, Gray and Rudduck (1999) many of the science teachers interviewed had never examined a primary school science syllabus and were therefore unaware that some of the topics they intended to teach Year 7 had been covered during the primary years. As discussed earlier in the chapter, pupils enter the secondary school looking forward to more difficult work tempered with concerns about their ability to cope. When they find that much of the Year 7 work replicates that of Year 6 they easily become disillusioned and their attitudes toward these subjects dip (Galton et al., 2003).

One particular strategy for overcoming this problem has been to develop what have become known as "Bridging Units." These consisted of a series of exercises, mainly in English, mathematics, and science, which pupils start in the last few weeks of their primary school. The books containing the pupils' work then move with them to the secondary school where further exercises, building on the earlier work, are continued during the first month in Year 7. Besides ensuring a degree of continuity the associated aim of these bridging units is to enable teachers to gain insights to the capabilities of their new pupils and to use this knowledge in their planning of activities once the units are completed.

However, the first of these units, developed by the Qualification and Curriculum Authority (QCA, 2002) in English and mathematics met with partial success. Galton et al. (2003) found that these units were received with mixed feelings by both primary and secondary teachers. Teachers at primary level said that the need to devote each morning to literacy and numeracy activities in the period up to the national tests meant that the rest of the curriculum was squeezed so that children missed out on subjects like art, drama, and physical education. There was also little time available for extended investigation. Primary teachers therefore tended to use the time after the National Tests to do more imaginative and creative activities. Consequently, there was a certain degree of resentment at having to devote more time to the core subjects, particularly since some of the topics chosen by the QCA had been "done to death" during Year 6 as part of the National Curriculum. Where primary teachers did do the units, therefore, they tended not to follow their logical order but to pick and choose from various sections which they thought would be more interesting to the pupils. This made a mockery of the idea of continuity.

For the secondary teachers there were also problems. To begin with, not all transition schools had distinct catchment areas; some took pupils from up to 15 primary feeder schools. While in this situation, the main proportion of pupils might come from three or four schools others might contribute as few as half a dozen pupils. Liaison with these latter primary schools would be poor so that pupils might arrive for the first term after the move to secondary school having not done any of the bridging units. This presented problems to the teachers who then had to have some pupils doing extra work that others had already done in the main feeder schools.

Moreover there appeared to be uncertainties among teachers as to the purpose of the units. Many teachers saw them as yet another element in the process of social adjustment by giving pupils work with which they would have been familiar from primary school, thus providing an easy introduction into academic life in the secondary school. Where this view prevailed certain consequences followed. First, secondary teachers spent less effort reviewing the work done before transition, since they did not see the curriculum continuity issue as of vital importance. This in turn produced indifference on the part of the pupils who thought that the teachers were not interested in the work and therefore did not take the tasks set at secondary level seriously. More importantly, because teachers did not see the purpose was to promote curriculum continuity they tended to see the units as a finite piece of work and therefore did not associate what was undertaken with what was to follow subsequently. As one pupil interviewed by Galton et al. (2003) responded in relation to a locally-produced Science bridging unit on the life cycle of the moth:

> *Once we'd finished it the teacher put on his white coat and we did the Bunsen burner.*

Nevertheless, there have been more favorable reports of the use of bridging units, particularly when they are jointly constructed within a pyramid and take account of local factors (Suffolk, 2001). This approach has several advantages compared to the weaknesses of the QCA units. First, such units are more likely to provide a meaningful context so that the pupils can study recognizable topics with which they are familiar and which hopefully are of interest to them. Investigating the canals in a Midland town, the characteristics of a coastal region in a school on the Norfolk/Suffolk border, solving a murder mystery entitled 'Who killed the Chef?' based on a famous city hotel which had been the subject of a TV program are all such examples. In the latter case pupils in the primary school used microscopes to identify materials found at the murder scene in order to deduce from the evidence the most likely guilty person. On coming to the secondary school they were introduced to further ideas about chromatography and on then re-testing various samples were able to arrive at a new suspect. This is the kind of unit recommended by both Davis and McMahon (2004) and Braund and Driver (2005). According to these latter authors 'too many introductory topics in Year 7 still begin with training in basic laboratory skills' and fail to recognize the previous levels of competence and experience gained at primary school as one Year 7 pupil explained:

> You are always experimenting, testing and investigating about the same things [*as in primary school*] only in secondary school you just have better equipment. (Braund & Driver, 2005, p. 88)

These authors therefore argue that a crucial factor in designing effective bridging units is to ensure that the levels of practical skills and the concepts used are an advance of what was done at primary school thus building in an element of discontinuity but also of progression as in the 'Who killed the Chef?' unit described previously. In their own work based on these ideas they report around 87% pupil satisfaction. It is also noticeable that in the best examples schools have tended to use an integrated approach which combines some work in Science with different forms of writing and some mathematics calculations. This has the advantage that pupils do not have to do too many units thus making them feel that they are still doing primary school work. This approach only appears to work however, if there is active cooperation between the various departments within the secondary school and it is not just part of an induction program mainly handled through the Personal, Social and Health Education (PSHE) program. Braund (2007) offers a more ambitious alternative in seeking to identify common topics taught in the final 2 years in primary school and the first 2 years after transition so that teachers at each level can make explicit links both forwards and backwards in terms of the concepts taught and the experimental techniques used. Built into these teaching units are pupil self-assessment activities designed to ensure smoother progression.

Bridging units work best therefore when there are clearly defined local pyramids so that most of the teachers in the feeder and transition schools can play a part in their production. An added advantage of developing locally based units is that the discussions will involve not only the curriculum content but also the pedagogy to be used in order to deliver the materials.

SHARING PEDAGOGY ACROSS TRANSITION

More recently, schools have also attempted to become more aware of each other's teaching approaches. In the 1970s there were the occasional attempts by secondary teachers to visit primary schools and to observe lessons. By the new millennium these visits had become something of a regular occurrence and, moreover, some of these exchanges were two-way so that primary teachers were also able to come and see what was taking place in Year 7 classes. These reciprocal visits have been well received by teachers who during interview often spoke of the interesting things that were going on in the primary school compared to the rather restricted approaches used at Year 7 and Year 8.

However, the research based on observation seems to challenge these claims. In Figure 7.3 the overall teacher pupil interactions recorded during the Oracle Replication (Hargreaves & Galton, 2002) are shown. In the Oracle approach interactions are divided into different types of questions, different types of statements, silent interactions (mainly when teachers are listening to pupils report or explain or read), and periods where there are

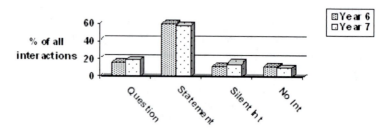

Figure 7.3   Percentage of interactions; pre- and post- transfer.

no interactions because teachers are housekeeping (giving out books) or monitoring what is happening. As Figure 7.3 shows, the patterns are almost identical in both the Year 6 and the Year 7 classes. Classroom talk is dominated by teachers making statements.

Figure 7.4 shows a breakdown of class questions. In the Oracle observation schedule these can be either to do with seeking facts, obtaining a single answer (closed), or more challenging in that they allow for possible alternative answers (open). These latter so-called challenging questions were a central feature in New Labour's (ruling party in the UK at that time) push for 'interactive whole class teaching.' At both primary and secondary level the proportions of the different type of questions are approximately the same with open questions constituting the smallest percentage overall at around 5% of the total number.

In Figure 7.5, where the proportions of statements used are analyzed, there are some minor variations (in the order of 5%) between Year 6 and Year 7. Secondary teachers make more factual statements and give more directions overall while primary teachers appear to be concerned more often with routine. This is fairly easily explained in terms of the classroom situation where a primary teacher will have what has been called 'periods of evaporated time' when the class or a group of children in a class switch from one curriculum area to another. These switches often require pupils to change places or move in and out of groups and teachers to collect in old and hand out new books or to return homework. In relation to making statements of ideas, again associated with problem-solving, exploration, and higher order thinking, Year 6 and Year 7 classes show both the lowest

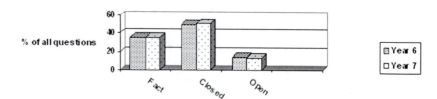

Figure 7.4   Percentage of questions before and after transfer.

percentage and also equal amounts of activity. Overall, therefore, despite the claims of teachers who visit each other's classroom that there are major differences in the ways that pupils are taught, the patterns of interaction suggest that the classroom pedagogy in both Year 6 and Year 7 classes is remarkably similar and that the main differences concern seating arrangements (in groups at primary; rows or pairs in secondary).

How then to account for the fact that the perceptions of teachers differ from this research evidence? Two factors provide possible explanations. The first of these concerns the timing of these exchange visits. Typically, when teachers were questioned about timing they said that the visits took place in June and July. This was because it was convenient for the secondary teachers since they had more free time, having 'got rid of Year 11 classes,' while the primary teachers were concerned that the visits should not take place until after they 'had finished with the SATS (Standard Assessment Tasks).' But, as has been seen in the account of the use of bridging units, the period after the National Curriculum tests is just the time when teachers in primary schools are likely to engage in more creative problem-solving activities. Thus what the secondary teachers see on these visits is not typical of what takes place during the rest of the year when as other studies have shown, there is a considerable amount of coaching and direct instruction (Alexander, 2000; Smith, Hardman, Wall, & Mroz, 2004).

A second factor which may explain the discrepancy is that the visits of teachers tend to be largely unstructured. It may be, for example, that when the teachers see pupils in the primary school sitting in groups, they make the assumption that they are cooperating whereas the research evidence (Kutnick, Blatchford, & Baines, 2002) suggests that often this may not be the case. Indeed more recent studies have suggested that there has been a reversal in trends in primary schools toward even more direct teaching. Commenting on a series of studies stretching from 1976 to 2005, Galton (2007) has shown that the patterns of interaction (questions and statements) have been remarkably stable or had regressed. In another study by Webb and Vulliamy (2006), 18 out of the 45 primary classrooms visited now had desks or tables arranged in rows. The shift to whole-class pedagogy therefore seems to have promoted a dominance of teaching as transmission. A similar conclusion was reached by Smith et al. (2004) whose analysis suggests that questioning was now conducted at a rapid pace using predictable

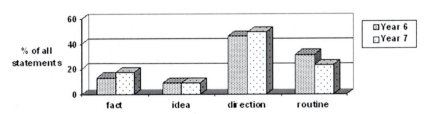

Figure 7.5 Percentage of statements before and after transfer.

sequences of teacher-led recitation and that much of the teaching in the primary classroom was interrogative and directive in nature.

Thus the wheel appears to have come full circle in that the changes mandated by governments have promoted a high degree of continuity in the pedagogy used by teachers in the final year of primary and first year of secondary school. However, whereas the starting point of those concerned in the 1970s was to make secondary teaching more like primary teaching (albeit as we have seen primary teaching was not as exciting as was often claimed) legislators have now succeeded in making primary teaching much more like typical secondary teaching with the consequences that the dips in attainment, attitude and motivation continue because pupils expect things to be more interesting and varied, when they move to the secondary school and quickly find out, that very little has changed.

RECENT TRANSITION INITIATIVES

Table 7.1 summarizes the main changes observed during the last 30 years using what has become known as the *five bridges of transition*. It can be seen that in the administrative sphere there is greater use of computers for data transition and packages such as SIMS are now more widely available. In the social awareness area there is increasing use of e-mail and the Internet to link primary and secondary pupils so that before transition it is possible for those in primary school to quiz their peers in the secondary school concerning their anxieties. Some schools organize pupil exchanges so that when the Year 7 coordinators go to a primary school they take Year 7 pupils with them to answer the Year 6 pupils' questions. Some schools have adopted a buddying system whereby on arrival at the secondary school the new Year 7 pupil is allocated a particular individual who will help and support him during the year. More often these buddies are taken from Year 9 whereas, since one of the main complaints of Year 7 pupils is that they resent reverting after transition to the most junior status, the use of the current Year 7 in relation to the Year 6 intake would at least give them a certain degree of responsibility for which they appear to yearn. If this arrangement was developed then the buddying system could go right through the school so that new Year 7 pupils retained their buddy in Year 8 and Year 9.

As discussed earlier in the chapter, the biggest change has been in the use of bridging units as a means of improving curriculum continuity although there is little evidence that the official recognized units that replaced those of the QCA's as part of the Key Stage 3 strategy have been taken up by a large number of schools. Instead, as described earlier, the preference seems to be for schools to develop their own units.

The evidence would suggest that much of the transition school's efforts are still concentrated on overcoming the short-term concerns of pupils. Pre- and post-induction sessions, the use of 'bridging units' where work started

Table 7.1 The 5 Transition Bridges (1997—present)

Transition bridges	Practice in 1977	Practice in 1997	Practice now
1. Administrative (designed to smooth the process of transition)	*Occasional meetings of headteachers. Transition of pupil records, pre-transition tests.*	*Headteachers meet regularly. Fewer records exchanged. Visits to Y6 classes by Y7 coordinator & Senco.*	*As in 1997 but with computerized data transition. Some subject specialists now also visit primary feeders.*
2. Social/User Friendly (measures to ease pupil's anxieties)	*Brief visit to transition school followed by parent evening.*	*Summer induction days. Several parents' evenings. Use of transition school facilities (ICT, PE, drama).*	*As in 1997 but more pupil exchanges, buddy schemes, e-mail exchange. More reliance on pupil voice.*
3. Curriculum (seeking to maintain continuity and progression)	*No activity*	*Bridging Units (QCA) Summer School (Gifted in art/drama; less able in maths and literacy).*	*More use of locally constructed bridging units, fewer summer schools. Using Y7 as a motivating year (more active curriculum. etc.).*
4. Teaching & Learning	*No activity*	*Little activity*	*More 2-way teacher exchanges involving peer observation sometimes structured.*
5. Managing Learning (helping pupils become 'professional learners')	*No activity*	*Little activity*	*Some post-induction programs but mostly excluding core subjects.*

in the primary school carries on during the first three weeks after transition, are all designed to provide improved continuity during the settling-in period rather than promote a series of graduated changes to the pupils' circumstances which are in accord with stage-environment fit theory. The need for schools to think longer term in relation to transition is supported by work in other disciplines. For example, in the field of occupational psychology Nicholson (1987) has proposed that work-role transitions consist of four phases. Phase 1, described as *preparation*, parallels the kinds of program most secondary schools now offer with induction days, visits of the Year 7 tutor to the primary feeder schools, and parents' evenings. This might be extended, as some schools are doing, by increasing the number of induction days to include more experience of typical teaching and by extending the buddy system whereby Year 7 pupils exchange information with their Year 6 peers on a regular basis using electronic forms of communication.

Nicholson's Phase 2 consists of initial *encounters* and would correspond to a post-induction program which would extend beyond the existing use of activities, such as bridging units, aimed at improved continuity, and include various activities that build on the idea of *'learning to be a professional pupil'* (Lahelma & Gordon, 1997). Only a few schools in England appear to have developed such programs which include the development of study and thinking skills designed to support independent working, together with the introduction of more cooperative forms of learning and familiarization and sensitivity exercises which build on the experiences of earlier schooling. Galton et al. (2003) however found that even where these programs existed they tended to be undertaken in PSHE time and as a result the skills learned were not applied in subjects such as mathematics and science where attitudes and motivation are poorest.

Nicholson's final two phases consist of *adjustment* and *stabilisation*, respectively. At the adjustment phase normal working conditions pertain but there is frequent and immediate feedback provided on both success and failure. While teachers will provide feedback it tends to be *corrective* by pointing out errors, demonstrating the correct procedures, etc. rather than *informing* whereby pupils' reasoning is explored and strategies for identifying and correcting mistakes identified (Hattie & Timperley, 2007). Neither is the overall picture of the pupil's progress coordinated other than at parents' evenings and in end-of-term reports. For Nicholson, stabilisation involves future goal setting and appraisal of what is termed 'role evolution.' This should concentrate on addressing those aspects of the pupil's adjustment (whether social, personal, or academic) where improvement is required and setting future goals for the following year. Thus attention to the issues surrounding adjustment at transition needs to extend beyond the present relatively short periods of concern. This would be in accord with the findings of West, Sweeting, and Young (2008) who collected pupils' retrospective views of the transition experience and found that higher levels of concern at transition were positively correlated with various measures of wellbeing such as depression and self esteem at two later age points (13 and 15). This is likely to have come about because pupils who have concerns at transition about making friends, getting on with teachers and so on are likely to experience similar difficulties in the following years.

In deriving and sustaining such transition initiatives it seems clear that schools need to pay more attention to the voices of their pupils. They are the ones who have first-hand knowledge of what it is like to make the transition from primary to secondary school, as many of their comments demonstrate. They are thus in the best position to offer relevant and useful suggestions in helping to reduce some of the tensions associated with the move to the new school.

NOTES

1. In the UK transition is often also referred to as transfer.
2. In England the last year in the primary school is Year 6 so the first year at secondary school is Year 7. Most transitions take place at this stage when pupils are aged between 10–11 years.
3. I am grateful for the help of my colleague, Ms. Jenny Symonds, who has carried out an extensive review of transition studies on which the two figures are based.

REFERENCES

Alexander, R. (2000). *Culture & pedagogy: International comparisons in primary education.* Oxford: Blackwell.

Braund, M. (2007). Bridging work and its role in improving progression and continuity: An example from science education. *British Educational Research Journal, 33*(6), 905–926.

Braund, M., & Driver, M. (2005). Pupils' perception of practical science in primary and secondary school: Implications for improving progression and continuity of learning. *Educational Research, 47*(1), 77–91.

Chedzoy, S. M., & Burden, R. L. (2005). Making the move: Assessing student attitudes to primary–secondary transition. *Research in Education, 74,* 22–35.

Davis, D., & McMahon, K. (2004). A smooth trajectory: Developing continuity and progression between primary and secondary science education through a jointly planned projectile project. *International Journal of Science Education, 26*(8), 1009–1021.

Delamont, S., & Galton, M. (1986). *Inside the secondary classroom.* London: Routledge.

Dutch, R., & McCall, J. (1974). Transition to secondary—An experiment in a Scottish comprehensive school. *British Journal of Educational Psychology, 44*(3), 282–289.

Evangelou, M., Taggart, B., Sylva, K., Melhuish, E., Sammons, P., & Siraj-Blatchford, I. (2008). *What makes a successful transition from primary to secondary school?* Effective Preschool, Primary and Secondary Education 3–14 Project (EPPSE 3–14) Research Report DCSF-RR019. Annersley, Notts: Department for Children, Schools and Families.

Galton, M. (2007). *Learning and teaching in the primary classroom.* London: Sage Publications.

Galton, M., Gray, J., & Ruddock, J. (1999). *The impact of school transitions and transfers on pupil progress and attainment.* Research Report RR131. Nottingham: DfEE Publications.

Galton, M., Gray, J., & Ruddock, J. (2003). *Transfer and transitions in the middle years of schooling (7–14): Continuities and discontinuities in learning.* Research Report RR443. Nottingham: DfEE Publications.

Galton, M., Simon, B., & Croll, P. (1980). *Inside the primary classroom.* London: Routledge & Kegan Paul.

Galton, M., & Willcocks, J. (Eds.). (1983). *Moving from the primary school*. London: Routledge and Kegan Paul.

Hargreaves, L., & Galton, M. (2002). *Moving from the primary classroom: 20 years on*. London: Routledge.

Hattie, J., & Timperley, H. (2007). The power of feedback. *Review of Educational Research, 77*(1), 81–112.

ILEA. (1986). *ILEA transition project*. London: Inner London Education Authority.

Kutnick, P., Blatchford, P., & Baines, E. (2002). Pupil groupings in primary school classrooms: Sites for learning and social pedagogy? *British Educational Research Journal, 28*(2), 189–208.

Lahelma, E., & Gordon, T. (1997). First day in the secondary school: Learning to be a 'professional pupil.' *Educational Research and Evaluation, 3*(2), 119–139. doi:10.1080/1380361970030202.

Nicholson, N. (1987). The transition cycle: A conceptual framework for the analysis of change and human resources management. *Research in Personnel and Human Resources Management, 5*, 167–222.

QCA. (2002). *Transition units (English and mathematics)*. London: Qualifications and Curriculum Authority.

Smith, F., Hardman, F., Wall, K., & Mroz, M. (2004). Interactive whole class teaching in the national literacy and numeracy strategies. *British Educational Research Journal, 30*(3), 395–412.

Spelman, B. (1979). *Pupil adaptation to secondary school*. Publication No. 18, Belfast: Northern Ireland Council for Educational Research.

Suffolk. (2001). *Transition review*. Ipswich: Suffolk LEA. Retrieved April 20, 2009, from www.slamnet.org/transition.

Tomlinson, S. (2005). *Education in a post-welfare society*, 2nd ed. Maidenhead: Open University Press.

Webb, R., & Vulliamy, G. (2006). *Coming full circle? The impact of New Labour's education policies on primary school teachers' work*. London: Association of Teachers and Lecturers (ATL).

West, P., Sweeting, H., & Young, R. (2008). Transition matters: Pupils' experiences of the primary–secondary school transition in the West of Scotland and consequences for well-being and attainment. *Research Papers in Education*, 1–29, first article retrieved on 26th March 2009 from http://pdfserve.informaworld.com/238792_731526789_902379213.pdf.

Youngman, M. (1978). Six reactions to school transition. *British Journal of Educational Psychology, 48*(4), 280–289.

Youngman, M., & Lunzer, E. (1977). *Adjustment to secondary school*. Nottingham: School of Education.

8   Moving Through Elementary, Middle, and High Schools

The Primary to Secondary Shifts in the United States

Patrick Akos

In the United States, public school configurations vary significantly based on a variety of factors. From the genesis of a one-room school house where all students are educated together, primary and secondary schools emerged. Around the turn of the century, junior highs (age 11–14) were created and the contemporary shift in the last 30 years is the move to the developmentally responsive middle school concept (age 10–13). The ideal school configuration has been a recurrent question that still lacks conclusive research evidence, and seemingly is influenced by geography, enrollment, financial considerations, and district consolidation among other factors, more so than what is best for students. While many diverse configurations still exist (e.g., K–12 schools, single grade schools, K–8) and shifts in configurations seem to ebb and flow, the predominant structure in the US today includes the elementary, middle, and high school.

To date, the practice and research literature suggests that transitions between school levels may be risky for students as negative outcomes have been prevalent but not conclusive. Each of the three school contexts is vastly different, and the negotiation of movement between these levels during significant development change presents challenges for students and schools. This chapter will highlight literature on each transition and outline what schools can generally do to support successful transitions.

THE TRANSITION FROM ELEMENTARY TO MIDDLE SCHOOL

Typically, the transition from elementary to middle school occurs between fifth and sixth grade. There are many changes that take place both within the individual and the school environment that complicate this transition. The dual timing of personal and ecological transitions, the magnitude in change from elementary to middle school, and the mismatch between developmental needs and school ecology have been offered as explanations for transition difficulties.

Developmental Shifts

Aside from infancy, no other phase of life is characterized by greater, more rapid, and diverse development than early adolescence. Early adolescence is a qualitatively distinct developmental phase. Students experience a wave of new hormones, brain development, and other physiological and pubertal changes. For example, classic cognitive development theory (Piaget) suggests students shift from concrete operational thought to formal operational thought, where students are able to think in more abstract and logical terms (Broderick & Blewitt, 2006). With these new cognitive abilities, early adolescents begin to challenge authority, investigate and entertain possibilities for the future.

Students also may negotiate critical psychosocial transitions concurrent with the school transition. Most students in elementary school have developed a sense of industry and begin to make decisions around identity (Erikson, 1968). With intense self comparison, early adolescents make judgments about their competence and use these assessments to inform who they are. Feeling as though they are on the world's stage constantly being scrutinized by peers, an "imaginary audience" thought process places a great burden of stress on youth (Elkind, 1988). The state of flux and self consciousness can be debilitating, as peer comparison and acceptance, fads, and group belonging contribute to feelings of inferiority or role strain. Additionally, because these changes are occurring at different times and at different rates for early adolescents, there is a vast range of "normal" development during middle school (Akos, 2005).

Although contemporary research has viewed pubertal changes as more an opportunity rather than a crisis (Papalia, Olds, & Feldman, 2001), the varied timing of early adolescent development is still difficult for students and the adults who work with them. These rapid and intense developmental changes occur in interaction with multiple systems. Family, peers, and the classroom and school environment are all a part of the microsystem which directly influences development (Bronfenbrenner, 1979; Newman, Lohman, Newman, Myers, & Smith, 2000). Early adolescents play an active role in these relationships as they differentiate from family. Early adolescents question parental authority and often distance parents with assertive or aggressive attempts at independence. Inconsistent behavior and variation in mood often lead to some rejection of rules and authority of their parents and peers may take on increased importance for daily decisions. While both family and peer groups are influential, the transition from the elementary to middle school environment is another significant systemic influence.

Contextual Shifts

Concurrent with the significant developmental change, the elementary to middle school context represents a major ecological shift. The neighborhood elementary school environment becomes very familiar to students after typically spending 6 years at the school. The elementary school becomes almost like a family or home environment for many children due to the long term relationships with school staff and continuity built with one class-room teacher annually. Elementary school teachers tend to be nurturing and attend to relationships with students and families.

In contrast, the middle school environment is typically much larger, less personal, more controlling, and more focused on academics (Anderman, Maehr, & Midgley, 1999). Research has demonstrated greater teacher control and discipline, and fewer opportunities for student decision making, choice, and self-management in junior high as compared to elementary school (Midgley, Feldlaufer, & Eccles, 1989). Wigfield, Eccles, Mac Iver, Reuman, and Midgley (1991) and others report stricter evaluation practices and that teachers feel less efficacious in middle school. There also seems to be a greater emphasis on social comparison, relative ability, and competition (Eccles & Midgley, 1989; Schumacher, 1998). For example, student identities are especially vulnerable when students move from heterogeneous ability groupings in elementary school to homogenous ability levels in junior high. This emphasis on relative ability and comparative performance may be particularly debilitating for minority and poor students who are more likely to be placed in lower academic tracks (Oakes, 1985).

Students entering any new environment must learn new school rules and routines. In middle school, students must accomplish this while learning to function more independently (Perkins & Gelfer, 1995). Students face challenges including finding their way around a larger, new, and different environment, learning and negotiating the new expectations of multiple teachers, finding and connecting to a changing peer group, and learning to interact with older students (Elias et al., 1992). "Two critical factors of the school setting that affect the difficulty students have in mastering the essential transitional tasks are the complexity of the school environment and the setting's capacity to respond to students' needs" (Felner et al., 1993, p. 113).

Outcomes Related to the Transition to Middle School

Academic Motivation and Achievement

Simmons, Rosenberg and Rosenberg's (1973) initial outcome study alerted school personnel to potential risk in the transition from elementary school to junior high. They determined that students experience declines in academic achievement and self-esteem due to the transition. Since then, studies have shown that achievement, student motivation, and attitudes toward school tend to decline during the transition to middle school (Alspaugh, 1998; Anderman et al., 1999; Crockett, Peterson, Graber, Schulenberg, & Ebata, 1989; Gutman & Midgley, 2000; Seidman, Allen, Aber, Mitchell, &

Feinman, 1994; Simmons & Blyth, 1987). Academic declines following the transition into middle school may result from a poor person environment fit (Eccles et al., 1993). For example, motivational declines seen among early adolescents may relate to decreases in personal and positive relationships with teachers, increases in ability grouping, lack of focus on higher level thinking skills, and limited opportunity for autonomy and self-determination in the classroom. Anderman et al. (1999) demonstrated that students who moved to a school that was primarily task focused (rather than performance focused) exhibited fewer negative shifts in motivation after a transition. In fact, the way information is presented in the classroom within the middle school environment appears significant. Reis, Trockel, and Mulhall (2007) found that instruction focused on understanding (rather than memorization), student inclusion in policy and rule process, and cultural sensitivity all correlated with decreased student aggression toward other students during middle school years.

Others (Furrer & Skinner, 2003) have also reported on the influence of positive attachments on academic motivation and performance during transition. There appears to be a significant drop in relatedness to teachers between fifth grade and sixth grade, which correlates to declining school engagement over the sixth grade year. Marchand and Skinner's (2003) longitudinal study on motivation and coping suggests that decreases in students' help-seeking behavior between fifth and sixth grade is related to the change in motivational resources associated with the middle school environment. They argue that help-seeking behavior is an adaptive coping strategy that can benefit students socially and academically in difficult school situations, and that is significantly affected by teacher support and social environment changes.

Several other factors may influence the academic trajectory associated with transition. Perceptions of competence decline between the fifth and sixth grade for many students (Anderman et al., 1999). Rudolph, Lambert, Clark, and Kurlakowsky (2001) suggest that students with pre-existing maladaptive beliefs about their personal control over school success may experience an even more difficult transition to middle school. Students who are part of a transition involving several elementary schools into a single middle school may experience more significant achievement loss than those in a system where a single elementary feeds into a single middle school (Alspaugh, 1998). In fact, Simmons and Blyth (1987) and others (e.g., Alspaugh, 1998), found more negative consequences for students in the transition from elementary to middle school as compared to students making the same grade transition in K–8 schools.

Social Relationships

In addition to the academic changes that can occur as a result of the transition, peer relationships also seem to play a key role in outcomes. Aikins,

Bierman, and Parker (2005) suggest that transition experiences can be predicted by students' social skills and self-expectations. Through interviews with 123 sixth-grade students, they found that higher levels of social skills were associated with better friendship qualities both before and after transition. They also found that negative expectations about the self and the middle school setting actually impeded adaptation to the transition. Kingery and Erdley (2007) assessed peer acceptance, number of friends, and friendship quality among 146 students during elementary school and then again in middle school to see if these factors played a role in easing the transition experience. When children experience low peer acceptance and poor friendship quality before the transition, they often have a harder time coping with the move to middle school.

Finally, through questionnaires given to fifth- and sixth-grade students, Fenzel (2000) examined the relationships between peer relationships, school demands, social support, feelings of self-worth, and academic and social competence as perceived by the student in relation to transition into middle school. The research suggests that students who perceive themselves as more capable of making friends prior to moving into middle school are less likely to experience significant strain on peer relationships upon entering into transition. Overall, these data suggest that the middle school transition disrupts social networks and higher levels of social skills and strong peer relationships or acceptance can be a protective factor or keeps students more resilient during the transition into middle school.

Individual Differences

There has been mixed speculation on which students struggle most with school transitions. Anderson, Jacobs, Schramm, and Splittgerber (2000) suggest that four factors, including gender, prior problem behavior, low academic achievement, and a combination of socioeconomic status and race, all lead to differences in transition experience. It is suggested that females, students with behavior problems in elementary school, students who are not academically prepared, and students living in poverty (often African Americans and Hispanic students) all experience a more difficult transition.

Early research (Blyth, Simmons, & Carlton-Ford, 1983; Crockett et al., 1989; Eccles et al., 1993) demonstrated higher self-esteem declines in girls, perhaps due to the salience of peer networks (Mizelle & Mullins, 1997) or the physical impact of puberty in the dual timing of the transition. Research has also demonstrated that girls experience more depression than boys over the elementary to middle school transition (Blyth et al., 1983; Hirsch & Rapkin, 1987). Based on assessments of students in the fifth and sixth grade, Chung, Elias, and Schneider (1998) suggested that while both boys and girls demonstrated a significant rise in psychological stress across the transition period the form of stress experienced varied by gender. Boys showed decreased academic achievement during the first year of middle school, while girls expressed their psychological distress through physical symptoms. This implies that females are more likely to internalize stress while boys are more likely to express stress through externalized behavior problems. Chung et al. also suggest that students who show high levels of psychological distress before a transition period may be at a higher risk of experiencing a stressful transition, regardless of gender.

Finally, some research has also speculated that the African-American students, especially those in poverty, also have more difficulty. Grade declines seem to be more severe for African-American students than for European-American students (Simmons, Black, & Zhou, 1991), as African-American students showed greater decreases in Grade Point Average (GPA) and more dislike for school after the elementary to middle school transition. Two additional studies focused on African-American students making the transition to middle school found similar results. Burchinal, Roberts, Zeisel, and Rowley (2008) followed 74 African American children from birth and assessed how risk factors played into their lives. They suggest that the association between risk factors and externalizing problems increased during the middle school transition. Similarly, Gutman and Midgley (2000) studied 62 African-American families living in poverty and suggested a drop in academic performance during the transition. Some research has demonstrated that Latino students may view the transition as more difficult (Akos & Galassi, 2004) and Latinos have demonstrated a distinct drop in grades due to the transition (Wampler, Munsch, & Adams, 2002). These data remain inconclusive, as findings have varied depending on sample, design, and context of the research study.

Positive Outcomes

While the elementary to middle school transition has demonstrated risk, not all research has replicated the negative outcomes (Proctor & Choi, 1994). Students also report increases in freedom and friendships as aspects they most look forward to in the middle school transition (Akos & Galassi, 2004). Further, Barber and Olsen (2004) found several positive changes including more support from teachers, more hours spent on homework, higher self-esteem, lower depression, and less loneliness after the middle school transition.

This suggests that some students remain resilient and cope with change and/or have ecological supports that may serve as protective factors (see Chapter 2 for details). In fact, Felner et al. (1993) suggest that the transition is an opportunity to enhance developmental outcomes and build coping skills. The conversion from the junior high model to the middle school concept may be one mitigating factor in the diverse research results. Eccles and Midgley (1989) found that many characteristics of the middle school philosophy (e.g., small house programs, team teaching, and advisory sessions) outlined by Turning Points (Carnegie Council on

Adolescent Development, 1989) help facilitate successful student transitions into middle school. For example, Ruble and Seidman (1996) found that when "true" middle school pedagogy was practiced, self-esteem declines across the transition were not found. According to Feldlaufer, Midgley, and Eccles (1988, p. 152), "The transition to a facilitative educational environment, even at this vulnerable stage of life, could result in more positive self- and achievement-related beliefs."

THE TRANSITION FROM MIDDLE TO HIGH SCHOOL

Even though the transition to high school is receiving increased attention, partly due to the fact that ninth-grade failures, dropout rates, and suspension/expulsion rates are often higher than all other high school grade levels (Hertzog & Morgan, 1998), less conclusive conceptual and outcome research is available. Mac Iver and Epstein (1991) suggested that most middle schools provide four to five bridge activities between the elementary and middle school, yet in the transition to high school, only two to three bridge activities were reported. The data that are available suggest the transition from middle to high school similarly provides challenges for students and schools.

Again developmental and contextual challenges are pervasive. Like early adolescence, pubertal changes continue to occur and high school includes some novel independence, risk taking, and developmental tasks often with more severe consequences (Kerr, 2002). For many, the passage into this adolescence stage of development is one of heightened responsibility as well as new awareness of the self. Rather than the stage of life itself being an issue, some suggest that normative feelings of anxiety and anticipation accompany major educational transitions such as the transition from middle school to high school (Mizelle & Irvin, 2000).

The new and complex school environment of the high schools is often difficult for students to navigate (Kerr, 2002). The physical, support, and accountability structures of high school are often vastly different than those of the traditional middle school. Changes in physical school size, faculty and staff, and rules and expectations are very common during the transition from middle school to high school (Letrillo & Miles, 2003). Many middle schools operate under the teaming structure, where students are taught by a team of teachers who meet and share concerns and strategies about specific students. Usually, these teams are located in the same area of the school and are year-long classes. Traditionally in high school, students will have four to eight different teachers in a departmental, rather than team structure that are scattered throughout a school that may or may not consult with each other at all. Students report that new relationships with teachers as well as adjusting to the physical setting of high school, and adapting to new academic challenges (e.g., homework that counts toward grades) all intertwine to make the transition to high school more difficult (Newman et al., 2000).

Although the contextual differences between middle and high school are less than those from elementary and middle school, seemingly more is at stake upon moving to high school. The distinctive aspects of the transition from middle to high school involve the academic transition and the heightened implications of unsuccessful transitions. Students often choose academic tracks that impact not only the next 4 years of high school, but also their future post-secondary and work options.

Outcomes Related to the Transition to High School

Research suggests that the transition from middle school to high school has generally been perceived as a time of overall achievement loss. The concerns of both students and parents are mostly academic in nature (Akos & Galassi, 2004; Newman et al., 2000). Some of these concerns include homework, pressure to do well, difficult class work, and an increase in homework, note-taking, and study time (Akos & Galassi; Newman et al.). Similar to the transition to middle school, some reports have demonstrated declines in grades and attendance (Alspaugh, 1998; Mizelle & Irvin, 2000; Reyes, Gillock, & Kobus, 1994) with the transition to high school.

Like the middle school transition, achievement has been linked to a student's self perceptions. Silverthorn, DuBois, and Crombie (2005) found that self-perceptions in eighth grade were predictive of achievement loss or gain in ninth grade. These findings were most significant in areas of math and English, and Silverthorn et al. noted that self perceptions become increasingly important during periods of academic stress and demand, such as the middle to high school transition. Gillock and Reyes (1996) reported similar results in a study they performed on self-perceptions with racial minority youth and transitions suggesting that self-perceptions and social connectedness had a great impact on success during the transition to high school.

As students continue through adolescence, they continue to rely heavily on their peers (Fuligni, Eccles, Barber, & Clements, 2001). Many students in this developmental period often go to their friends for advice and support and depend on them more than their parents. However, extreme attachment to peers may relate to increases in problem behaviors and low academic performance during the high school years (Fuligni et al., 2001). Students report that peers are both a challenge and a support system during the transition (Newman et al., 2000). Students report that part of the strain of adjusting to high school comes with making friends, resisting peer pressure, and getting used to all the new people (Newman et al.). Students also worry about getting involved in the school community (such as sports teams) (Chapman & Sawyer, 2001) showing that students are concerned about finding the right peer group and being able to fit in their new environment. Chapman and Sawyer suggest that students are concerned about being in a school with students who are older and physically bigger than they are and are worried about fights that may take place.

Less inquiry into individual differences and positive aspects of the high school transition is available. Similar to the middle school transition, some differential outcomes have been noted by gender and race. Akos and Galassi (2004) found that boys reported feeling significantly more connected to high school than girls in ninth grade (which was opposite to the gender difference in the connection to middle school). Additionally, Akos and Galassi reported that Latino students found this transition significantly more difficult than others in a suburban high school. Finally, even though students report worries prior to attending high school, their perceptions of the difficulty is less than that reported by teachers and parents (Akos & Galassi, 2004).

SCHOOL TRANSITION PROGRAMMING

As evident in the research and practice literature, school transitions need attention by schools through policy, system level intervention or reform, and programming for students. The following recommendations are informed by research and contemporary school programming efforts (Akos, 2005; Anderson et al., 2000).

Conduct a Needs Assessment and Examine School/District Level Data

On a policy level, school districts must first examine school level data to determine if and what transition needs exist. Data from sixth and ninth grade are not sufficient in this analysis as patterns of achievement and behavior (e.g., attendance, behavior referrals, counseling referrals) should be examined longitudinally or at least across transition years (fifth to sixth grade, eighth to ninth grade). Poor behavior or academic performance that *persists across* the transition is not necessarily a transition issue. It is the outcomes that *emerge or change as a result of* the transition that should be the focus of school transition policy and programming.

Research has also demonstrated that different school cultures and contexts relate to distinct transitional needs. For example, outcome data differs between a transition from one elementary to one middle school as compared to a transition from three elementary schools to one middle school (Alspaugh, 1998). Students moving with an intact peer group may be less concerned about new social structures at the new school than students being combined with multiple elementary schools. Further, the change in the size of the school may impact peer networks significantly. As another example, students from a high performing district may be most concerned about the academic demands of the new school, whereas a school district with high levels of violence may be more concerned about safety than academic demands in the new school.

Create Transition Teams in the District and the School

Using data to inform action, effective efforts that support school transitions must include multiple stakeholders and requires interdisciplinary work. Team composition should include, at minimum, teachers and school counselors at both feeder and receiving schools. It would also be useful to include administrators at each level, special needs instructors (e.g., special education, English as a Second Language), club and extracurricular coordinators, parents of students in transition, and even students from transition year grades.

Vertical teaming is a term often used to describe teacher collaboration between levels. For example, vertical teams of teachers can focus on curriculum articulation, task/mastery versus performance goals, classroom management and discipline, homework and grading procedures, parent-teacher meetings, and a variety of topics related to the classroom. Outcome data is clear on the impact of classroom practices (task versus performance focus) on motivation across the transition. Discussions about ideal person environment fit, differentiation rather than ability grouping, and relationship building all could help mitigate transition problems. This would mirror processes between school counselors where special student needs and scheduling may be discussed. It would also be essential for teachers to help plan and implement orientation programs—as the majority of orientation programming would involve teachers, directly effect teachers, and be more effective with teacher delivery. This sense of collaboration begins a process of information exchange—one of the most important assets for students making a transition.

Prepare and Document a Year Long Transition Plan

Once data and a team is in place, a documented yet flexible plan can be drafted. Mac Iver and Epstein (1991) found that an extensive articulation program (using three or more transition activities) increases the likelihood that students will succeed in the first year of school. Research suggests the most common transition activities include students visiting the next level of schooling (e.g., tours), administrators meeting on articulation and programs, and school counselors meeting across levels (Mac Iver & Epstein, 1991). This research also discovered that high socioeconomic status and high achieving schools have more extensive articulation programs and that extensive articulation programs increase the likelihood of student success in the first year.

It may be most useful to conceive the transition as a year-long process. Even though the traditional school calendar starts in mid-August and concludes in mid-June, the transition calendar should run on a different schedule to bridge the transition. Beginning in January of the fifth- or eighth-grade year and ending in December of the sixth- or ninth-grade year, a comprehensive program for the transition can be cultivated based on national research, local needs, and school resources. A transition year helps scaffold contextual change across schools, giving the feeder schools responsibility to prepare students for transition and receiving schools responsibility to help students connect and adjust to the new school.

In feeder schools, a number of interventions can target preparedness (Anderson et al., 2000) of students. Academic preparedness, social skills, and coping abilities are all important dimensions. Common pre-transition (January–mid-June) interventions may include:

- Presentations by middle/high school staff for student and parents at elementary/middle schools;
- Clear information and parent involvement on course choices and academic tracks near the end of elementary and middle school;
- Transition group counseling (Akos & Martin, 2003);
- Coping skills curriculum (Hellem, 1990; Snow, Gilchrist, Schilling, & Schinke, 1986);
- Academic and course scheduling;
- Social skills training;
- School tours (fifth- or eighth-grade students and parents);
- Vertical teaming and curriculum articulation;
- Teacher and student "shadow" programs (Ferguson & Bulach, 1994);
- Fifth- or eighth-grade student and parent participation in extracurricular events at the middle/high school (e.g., PTA/PTO, plays, sporting events); and
- Aggressive dissemination of information to fifth- and eighth-grade students and parents about the new school.

In the fall (post-transition), the concept of adjustment and support (Anderson et al., 2000) becomes more relevant. Orientation programs are the most common intervention choice in the later summer (before school starts) or early fall (at the start of school). Presumably, orientation programs are offered to all students and focus most of the organizational or procedural changes in the transition. Orientation programs can be one day events or last 3–4 weeks at the end of summer and start of the school year. Orientation activities may include introduction of staff and school rules/policies, team building, social activities to increase connectedness, and orientation to school events and extracurricular opportunities. Orientation is important to build a sense of community and belonging (Anderson et al.) that should lead to more and persistent student engagement in school. Additional fall activities can include:

- Peer ambassador or mentor programs;
- Peer counseling/tutoring (Leland-Jones, 1998);
- Group counseling with teacher and parent support;

- Social skills and drama curriculum (Walsh-Bowers, 1992);
- Ninth-grade academies or school reform;
- Events and programs to connect students to the new school (e.g., extracurricular programs like sports, drama, or other clubs; social events such as school dances); and
- After orientation and periodically throughout the fall, identification of students who are struggling specifically due to the transition. These students can then receive additional help from school counselors in individual or group counseling, or a variety of programs that promote school adjustment.

This list is not exhaustive nor inclusive of every intervention that may be useful for the transition. For example, many schools have included a new student web link or portal that organizes information (e.g., contacts, policies, virtual tour, clubs and organizations, registration forms) particularly for new students.

One of the most prominent examples of school reform for transition needs are ninth-grade academies in high schools. These types of reforms are evident in the movement to smaller learning communities, with academy, schools within a school, and house structures for ninth grade (Paige, Neuman, & D'Amico, 2001). Most freshman academies offer academic and emotional support beyond the regular classroom setting (Holland & Mazzoli, 2001). Some of these programs are offered for the entire entering ninth-grade student body and others are targeted for students who are more at risk. Ninth-grade academies vary considerably by school; however some common strategies seem to mirror structures related to the middle school concept including the physical separation and clustering of ninth graders from other high school students, teacher teams, advisory periods, common planning time for teachers, intentional parental involvement, frequent progress reports, and heterogeneous grouping. Earlier conceptions of this type of school reform (e.g., School Transition Environment Project; Felner et al., 2001) designed to reduce the flux in social and physical environments have demonstrated positive outcomes (e.g., lower dropout rate, higher grades, lower absenteeism, and greater teacher satisfaction).

It seems a balance of preparation and support to scaffold ecological changes would be most useful in promoting a successful transition (Anderson et al., 2000). Preparing students for the changing structure, rules, and organization of the middle school and providing information and teacher or staff support at the start of middle school are both important.

While the transition program is created and revised, it is essential that the program be clear, replicable, and documented. The document should propose the specific activities, responsibilities of people involved, provide dates and sequence of activities, and evaluation plans for each activity. The transition plan should be approved at the central office level and be disseminated among all schools and school staff. The dissemination across schools is especially necessary in larger school districts with multiple feeder and receiving schools. It would also be useful for transition plans to coordinate and build from elementary to middle to high school when appropriate. With consensus and a clearly articulated transition plan; students, parents, teachers, and school staff have reduced anxiety and clear focus on using the transition as an opportunity to promote success. This level of structure is also salient as leadership and delivery of transition programming is often diffuse among staff between levels and in the schools.

Facilitate and sequence organizational, personal/social, and academic needs

There also is emerging evidence that transition needs are temporal (Akos & Galassi, 2004), or that there may be an appropriate sequence to addressing these needs. For example, organizational or procedural needs relate to topics like schedules, lockers, navigating the school building, where and how to see the school nurse, and school rules. These needs are mentioned by nearly all students and are most intense right before a transition and at the start of a new school year. It is also possible that these data reflect not only a major concern (e.g., larger buildings), but significant positive aspects (e.g., lockers, multiple teachers, moving between classes, lunch, athletics) found in previous student perception research (Akos, 2002; Odegaard & Heath, 1992). It is also possible that organizational advice in the transition is most concrete and tangible for students and parents.

In contrast, not all student express particular academic or personal/social difficulties related to the transition, and these needs often emerge after the transition occurs. Academic concerns focus on coping with increased homework and more difficult courses, while social concerns include fitting in and making new friends, getting along with peers, and coping with bullies or older students. Most students will probably adjust much more quickly to the procedural aspects (e.g., finding their away around the more complex physical environment of the new school) of a school transition than to its academic (e.g., more homework and greater academic pressure) or social aspects (e.g., fitting in or making new friends).

These core areas provide another template to conceive or organize transition programming. They are not dichotomous areas, as they often overlap, but may be another useful way to organize program resources or assign school personnel. For example:

- Procedural/Organization Programming (administrator, teacher, and counselors)—scheduling, tours, orientation to using lockers and locks, rules and procedures at the new school (e.g., where and how to see the school counselor, bus routes, and rules), website links, information dissemination;

- Personal/Social Programming (primarily counselors)—student shadowing, school dances and extracurricular programs, ambassador or peer mentor programs, increased opportunities for social support and coping skills; and
- Academic Programming (primarily teachers and counselors)—enrichment activities, schedule adjustments, study skills, organizational skills, vertical teaming.

Special Needs and Multiple System Programming

While transition programming should be universal for all students, these programs are not often tailored to special needs students or to parents. Intuitively, low-achieving students may need summer enrichment or more intensive academic intervention (e.g., tutoring, mentoring) to help with adjustment to the new school. Academic struggles can be intensified by increased and new demands in the transition. Similarly, special education students require individual transition plans, where special education teachers discuss useful techniques and revisions to Individual Education Plans for the new school. Another example of special consideration includes Limited English Proficient (LEP) students. It may be useful to include Latino nights, where extended family and bilingual presentations help prepare students for the transition prior to coming to middle school. While not all are inclusive of students with special needs, these are but a few examples of programs that might exist in a school district.

Although students are often the main focus, it is well documented that parent participation both positively influences student achievement and that it drops off significantly as students move beyond elementary school. Students do report parents as significant sources of help in the transition, although the same research suggests parents most often provide warnings (or negative information) about middle and high school (Akos, 2002). Parent newsletters and Parent Teacher Associations (PTA) meetings that originate at middle and high school should include parents of feeder schools in the spring prior to the transition year. By engaging parents prior to the transition, parents will have more open communication and feel more invested in the receiving school. Additional parent programming may include parent mentors for new sixth- and ninth-grade parents, additional orientation to procedures and policies at the receiving schools, and increased parent outreach (e.g., positive calls or emails, invite to school events).

Research, Evaluate, and Document Transition Program Effectiveness

As with any school intervention or reform, it is important to collect data and determine the effectiveness of transition programs. Determining the 'right' amount of transition programming and what is most cost-effective are difficult questions. The answers depend on district configurations, feeder systems, particular needs of students and parents, school culture and climate, and a variety of other factors. While existing and emerging research will help answer these questions, the only way to know for sure is to design evaluation and research on local transition program efforts. Once data is analyzed, it is also important to revise programming and publicize transition program results.

CONCLUSIONS

Research has demonstrated potential risk in the transition from elementary to middle school and the transition from middle to high school in the United States. The concurrent developmental and ecological change requires attention from school staff in order to scaffold learning experiences and to promote optimal developmental paths for all students. Several options exist for schools to intervene, however, local school data and distinct district and school culture and context require tailored reform or intervention to optimize efforts.

REFERENCES

Aikins, J., Bierman, K., & Parker, J. (2005). Navigating the transition to junior high school: The influence of pre-transition friendship and self-system characteristics. *Social Development, 14*(1), 42–60.

Akos, P. (2002). Student perceptions of the transition from elementary to middle school. *Professional School Counseling, 5(5)*, 339–345.

Akos, P. (2005). The unique nature of middle school counseling. *Professional School Counseling, 9*(2), 95–103.

Akos, P., & Galassi, J. (2004). Middle and high school transitions as viewed by students, parents, and teachers. *Professional School Counseling, 7(4)*, 212–221.

Akos, P., & Martin, M. (2003). Transition groups for preparing students for middle school. *The Journal for Specialists in Group Work, 28*(2), 139–154.

Alspaugh, J. W. (1998). Achievement loss associated with the transition to middle school and high school. *Journal of Educational Research, 92*, 20–25.

Anderman, E., Maehr, M., & Midgley, C. (1999). Declining motivation after the transition to middle school: Schools can make a difference. *Journal of Research and Development in Education, 32*, 131–147.

Anderson, L. W., Jacobs, J., Schramm, S., & Splittgerber, F. (2000). School transitions: Beginning of the end or a new beginning? *International Journal of Educational Research, 33*(1), 325–339.

Barber, B. K., & Olsen, J. A. (2004). Assessing the transitions to middle and high school. *Journal of Adolescent Research, 19*, 3–30.

Blyth, D., Simmons, R., & Carlton-Ford, S. (1983). The adjustment of early adolescents to school transitions. *Journal of Early Adolescence, 3*,105–120.

Broderick, P. C., & Blewitt, P. (2006). *The life span: Human development for helping professionals.* Upper Saddle River, NJ: Pearson Education, Inc.

Bronfenbrenner, U. (1979). *The ecology of human development: Experiments by nature and design.* Cambridge, MA: Harvard University Press.

Burchinal, M., Roberts, J., Zeisel, S., & Rowley, S. (2008). Social risk and protective factors for African American children's academic achievement and adjustment during the transition to middle school. *Developmental Psychology, 44*(1), 286–292.

Carnegie Council on Adolescent Development. (1989). *Turning points: Preparing American youth for the 21st century: The report of the Task Force on Education of Young Adolescents.* Washington, DC: Author.

Chapman, M., & Sawyer, J. (2001). Bridging the gap for students at risk of school failure: A social work-initiated middle to high school transition program. *Children & Schools, 23*(4), 235–240.

Chung, H., Elias, M., & Schneider, K. (1998). Patterns of individual adjustment changes during middle school transition. *Journal of School Psychology, 36,* 83–101.

Crockett, L., Peterson, A., Graber, J., Schulenberg, J., & Ebata, A. (1989). School transitions and adjustment during early adolescence. *Journal of Early Adolescence, 9(3),* 181–210.

Eccles, J. S., & Midgley, C. (1989). Stage–environment fit: Developmentally appropriate classrooms for young adolescents. In C. Ames & R. Ames (Eds.), *Research on motivation in education: Vol. 3. Goals and cognitions* (pp. 13–44). New York: Academic Press.

Eccles, J. S., Wigfield, A., Midgley, C., Reuman, D., Mac Iver, D. J., & Feldlaufer, H. (1993). Negative effects of traditional middle schools on students' motivation. *The Elementary School Journal, 93,* 1553–1574.

Elias, M., Ubriaco, M., Reese, A., Gara, M., Rothbaum, P., & Haviland, M. (1992). A measure of adaptation to problematic academic and interpersonal tasks of middle school. *Journal of School Psychology, 30,* 41–57.

Elkind, D. (Winter 1988). Disappearing markers and deviant behavior. *School Safety,* 16–19.

Erikson, E. (1968). *Identity: Youth and crisis.* New York: W. W. Norton & Co.

Feldlaufer, H., Midgley, C., & Eccles, J. (1988). Student, teacher, and observer perceptions of classroom environments before and after the transition to junior high school. *Journal of Early Adolescence, 8,* 133–156.

Felner, R., Brand, S., Adan, A., Mulhall, P., Flowers, N. Sartain, B., et al. (1993). Restructuring the ecology of the school as an approach to prevention during school transitions: Longitudinal follow-ups and extensions of the School Transition Environment Project (STEP). *Prevention in Human Services, 10*(2), 103–136.

Fenzel, L. (2000). Prospective study of changes in global self-worth and strain during the transition to middle school. *Journal of Early Adolescence, 20,* 93–116.

Ferguson, J., & Bulach, C. (1994). *The effect of the shadow transition program on the social adjustment of Whitewater Middle School students.* (ERIC Document Reproduction Service No. ED 380 878)

Fuligni, A. J., Eccles, J. S., Barber, B. L., & Clements, P. (2001). Early adolescent peer orientation and adjustment during high school. *Developmental Psychology, 37*(1), 28–36.

Furrer, C., & Skinner, E. (2003). Sense of relatedness as a factor in children's academic engagement and performance. *Journal of Educational Psychology, 95,* 148–162.

Gillock, K., & Reyes, O. (1996). High school transition-related changes in urban minority students' academic performance and perceptions of self and school environment. *Journal of Community Psychology, 24*(3), 245–261.

Gutman, L. M., & Midgley, C. (2000). The role of protective factors in supporting the academic achievement of poor African American students during the middle school transition. *Journal of Youth and Adolescence, 29*(2), 223–248.

Hellem, D. (1990). Sixth grade transition groups: An approach to primary prevention. *The Journal of Primary Prevention, 10*(4), 303–311.

Hertzog, C. J., & Morgan, P. L. (1998). Breaking the barriers between middle school and high school: Developing a transition team for student success. *NASSP Bulletin, 82*(597), 94–98.

Hirsch, B., & Rapkin, B. (1987). The transition to junior high school: A longitudinal study of self-esteem, psychological symptomology, school life, and social support. *Child Development, 58,* 1235–1243.

Holland, H., & Mazzoli, K. (2001). Where everybody knows your name. *Phi Delta Kappan, 83*(4), 294–303.

Kerr, K. A. (2002). *An examination of approaches to promote ninth-grade success in Maryland public high schools.* Educational Research Service, Summer 2002. Retrieved March 20, 2009, from http://www.ers.org/spectrum/sum02a.htm.

Kingery, J., & Erdley, C. (2007). Peer experiences as predictors of adjustment across the middle school transition. *Education and Treatment of Children, 30*(2), 73–88.

Leland-Jones, P. (1998). *Improving the transition of sixth-grade students during the first year of middle school through a peer counselor mentor and tutoring program.* (ERIC Document Reproduction Service No. ED 424 911)

Letrillo, T., & Miles, D. D. (2003). The transition from middle school to high school: Students with and without learning disabilities share their perceptions. *The Clearing House, 76,* 212–214.

Mac Iver, D. J., & Epstein, J. L. (1991). Responsive practices in the middle grades: Teacher teams, advisory groups, remedial instruction, and school transition programs. *American Journal of Education, 99,* 587–622.

Marchand, G., & Skinner, E. (2003). Motivational dynamics of children's academic help-seeking and concealment. *Journal of Educational Psychology, 99*(1), 65–82.

Midgley, C., Feldlaufer, H., & Eccles, J. (1989). Change in teacher efficacy and student self and task related beliefs during the transition to junior high. *Journal of Educational Psychology, 81,* 247–258.

Mizelle, N. B., & Irvin, J. L. (2000). Transition from middle school to high school. *Middle School Journal, 31,* 57–61.

Mizelle, N. B., & Mullins, E. (1997). Transition into and out of middle school. In J. Irving (Ed.), *What current research says to middle level practitioners* (pp. 303–313). Columbus, OH: National Middle School Association.

Newman, B. M., Lohman, B. J., Newman, P. R., Myers, M. C., & Smith, V. L. (2000). Experiences of urban youth navigating the transition to ninth grade. *Youth & Society, 31*(4), 387–416.

Oakes, J. (1985). *Keeping track: How schools structure inequality.* Yale University Press.

Odegaard, S., & Heath, J. (1992). Assisting the elementary school student in the transition to a middle level school. *Middle School Journal, 24,* 21–25.

Paige, R., Neuman, S. B., & D'Amico, C. (2001). An overview of smaller learning communities in high school. *U.S. Department of Education.*

Papalia, D. E., Olds, S. W., & Feldman, R. D. (2001). *Human development, 8th edition.* New York: McGraw-Hill.

Perkins, P., & Gelfer, J. (1995). Elementary to middle school: Planning for transition. *The Clearing House, 68,* 171–173.

Proctor, T., & Choi, H. (1994). Effects of transition from elementary school to junior high on early adolescents' self-esteem and perceived competence. *Psychology in the Schools, 31,* 319–329.

Reis, J., Trockel, M., & Mulhall, P. (2007). Individual and school predictors of middle school aggression. *Youth & Society, 38,* 322–347.

142   *Patrick Akos*

Reyes, O., Gillock, K., & Kobus, K. (1994). A longitudinal study of school adjustment in urban, minority adolescents: Effects of a high school transition program. *American Journal of Community Psychology, 22*, 341–369.

Ruble, D. A., & Seidman, E. (1996). Social transition: Windows into social psychological processes. In E. T. Higgins & A. W. Kruglanski (Eds.), *Social psychology: Handbook of basic principles* (pp. 830–856). New York: The Guilford Press.

Rudolph, K. D., Lambert, S. F., Clark, A. G., & Kurlakowsky, K. D. (2001). Negotiating the transition to middle school: The role of self-regulatory processes. *Child Development, 72*, 929–946.

Schumacher, D. (1998). *The transition to middle school* (Report No. EDO-PS-98-6). Washington, DC: Clearinghouse on Elementary and Early Childhood Education. (ERIC Document Reproduction Service No. ED 422 119)

Seidman, E., Allen, L., Aber, J., Mitchell, C., & Feinman, J. (1994). The impact of school transitions in early adolescence on the self-system and perceived social context of poor urban youth. *Child Development, 65*, 507–522.

Silverthorn, N., DuBois, D., & Crombie, G. (2005). Self-perceptions of ability and achievement across the high school transition: Investigation of a state-trait model. *Journal of Experimental Education, 73*(3), 191–218.

Simmons, R., Black, A., & Zhou, Y. (1991). African American versus white children and the transition into junior high school. *American Journal of Education, 99*, 481–520.

Simmons, R., & Blyth, D. (1987). Moving into adolescence: The *impact of pubertal change and school* context. Hawthorne, NY: Aldine de Gruyter.

Simmons, R., Rosenberg, F., & Rosenberg, M. (1973). Disturbance in the self-image at adolescence. *American Sociological Review, 38*, 553–568.

Snow, W., Gilchrist, L., Schilling, R., & Schinke, S. (1986). Preparing for junior high school: A transition training program. *Social Work in Education, 9*(1), 33–43.

Walsh-Bowers, R. (1992). A creative drama prevention program for easing early adolescents' adjustment to school transitions. *The Journal of Primary Prevention, 13*, 131–147.

Wampler, R., Munsch, J., & Adams, M. (2002). Ethnic differences in grade trajectories during the transition to junior high. *Journal of School Psychology, 40*, 213–237.

Wigfield, A., Eccles, J., Mac Iver, D., Reuman, D. A., & Midgley, C. (1991). Transitions during early adolescence: Changes in children's domain specific self-perceptions and general self-esteem across the transition to junior high school. *Developmental Psychology, 27*, 552–565.

9 Learning and Well-Being in Transitions
How to Promote Pupils' Active Learning Agency?

Janne Pietarinen, Tiina Soini, and Kirsi Pyhältö

INTRODUCTION

Comprehensive schools around Europe are currently faced with a diversity of multidimensional educational reforms. In Finland, the most recent of the pedagogical school reforms is the implementation of undivided basic education (UBE). The current reform is based on the Finnish school legislation and regulations emphasizing constructivist views of learning which emphasize an active and collaborative nature of learning. The aim of the reform is to support pupils in their learning path through the various transitions of their school careers and guarantee everybody equal opportunities to get a basic education (Basic Education Act, 628/1998; National Core Curriculum for Basic Education, 2004). More specifically, the reform aims to ensure a consistent, coherent, and understandable comprehensive school education for all pupils, both in terms of learning different subjects in meaningful continuums, and in terms of safe and supportive everyday learning environments.

The Finnish children's school career will typically start with pre-primary school (not compulsory) at the age of 6. After 1 year they move to the comprehensive school which includes traditionally the primary (grades 1–6) and secondary school (grades 7–9) phases. Therefore, the reform also includes developing inner coherence of schools by showing curricular consistency from preschool to ninth grade and even upper secondary school or vocational education.

However, there is still a challenge in bridging the gap between primary and secondary schools. This is shown in the school culture as a lack of collaboration between the pupils as well as class, subject, and special education teachers and other staff, and also as a fragmentation of school-based curricula between primary and secondary schools. Furthermore, the pupils have been found to have problems in transferring from primary to secondary school in many European countries, including Finland (Anderson, Jacobs, Schramm, & Splittgerber, 2000; Davies & McMahon, 2004; Galton & Hargreaves, 2002; Kvalsund, 2000; Muschamp, Stoll, & Nausheem, 2001; Ward, 2000). Moreover despite Finland's success with regard to pupils' learning outcome comparisons, for example, in PISA (Program for International Student Assessment), there are some indications of problems with the well-being of pupils in Finland. For example, signs of earlier social exclusion and a rise in depressive symptoms among girls, and an increase in negative attitudes toward school among boys have been identified in national surveys of school health issues (Rimpelä, Kuusela, Rigoff, Saaristo, & Wiss, 2008; Rimpelä, Rigoff, Kuusela, & Peltonen, 2007).

From the perspective of developing undivided basic education, various school transitions provide both challenges and opportunities. Transitions may lead to gaps and pitfalls that can eventually lead a pupil to be excluded from school activities. On the other hand, they can also provide opportunities for learning and personal growth. From this perspective transitions can be understood as a learning process in which pupils negotiate their learning agency in relation to the school environment. Pupils' learning agency can be considered as a capacity for intentional and responsible management of new learning within and between school transitions. However, very little is known about how pupils' themselves perceive their school path and various transitions in terms of this entwined relationship between learning and well-being. In this chapter, we look at the case of Finnish comprehensive schools as an example of the complexity in pupils' school career.

Research Project and Instrument

This chapter is based on the findings of research project: "Learning and development in comprehensive school" (2004–2009), which focuses on undivided basic education (UBE) in Finland (Huusko, Pietarinen, Pyhältö, & Soini, 2007). The project aims to identify and understand preconditions for successful school reforms. Altogether 87 municipalities and 237 schools around Finland participated in the first phase of the research project (2005–2007). The project was carried out using a systemic design research approach (Brown, 1992; Collins, Joseph, & Bielaczyc, 2004; De Corte, 2000; Salomon, 1996). It included data collection from four different levels of the schooling system: (a) heads of school districts; (b) principals; (c) teachers; and (d) pupils (ninth graders). To capture the views of different actors, the data was collected through mixed methods such as inquiries and interviews, reflective discussions, and interventions in selected case school communities (n = 9).

The empirical findings reflected in this chapter focus on lessons we have learned from pupils' reflections on their school careers. The data was collected through retrospective essays from ninth graders (n = 518) from six comprehensive schools around Finland. The essays embodied questions on four themes: significant (negative and positive) school experiences throughout the school career, interactions with teachers, school development, and the problems pupils have faced in their school path.

School transitions have often been studied with longitudinal research designs (Jindal-Snape & Foggie, 2008; Muschamp et al., 2001; Salmela-Aro, Kiuru, & Nurmi, 2008; Gillison, Standage, & Skevington, 2008) which make it possible to reveal social, cognitive, behavioral, or emotional changes perceived by pupils before and after a certain transition. In our research pupils were encouraged to identify gaps and pitfalls more openly from their learning path. The aim was to identify and describe critical incidents and transitional processes that construct discontinuities for the pupils' school career and challenge their learning and well-being in a comprehensive school.

SCHOOL AND TRANSITIONS

In order to understand pupils' learning path and transitions within this path, some features of the school as a distinctive social, cultural, and psychological environment, need to be discussed. It could be argued that learning environments provided by the comprehensive school as well as pupils' individual learning paths are transformative by nature, always introducing a certain amount of challenges. During their school careers pupils are exposed to various pedagogical subcultures and expectations, participate in different kinds of peer groups and adopt various roles in school's dynamic and complex multilayered community of practice.

Teachers and pupils are the core of the school community. However, teachers' and pupils' intentions, orientations, and perceptions toward school activities have been found to differ fundamentally. For instance, teachers tend to perceive the classroom environment more positively and more favorably than pupils do (e.g., Hofman, Hofman, & Guldemond, 2001; Zimmer-Gembeck, Chipuer, Hanisch, Creed, & McGregor, 2006). There is also an interrelation between teachers' and pupils' orientations toward school work: for example, if a teacher perceives her work as primarily regulated by demands coming from different stakeholders outside the school community (such as politicians and school administrators), she is likely to use more external control and this results in more external strategies of learning for the pupils. Moreover, teachers' and pupils' learning and well-being can be seen as complementary processes. They are closely intertwined in the complexity of pedagogical contexts in schools. Substantial amounts of research have shown, for instance, that teachers' self-efficacy, emotional involvement, motivational structure, and work engagement are linked together and affect the instructional practices they adopt. This in turn affects the goals and strategies adopted by the pupils, for example the use of social self-regulation strategies such as help seeking (Butler & Shibaz, 2008; Pelletier, Legault, & Séguin-Lévesque, 2002; Ryan, Gheen, & Midgley, 1998). Accordingly a modern school provides a context of continuing negotiations of authority and meaning making between pupils and teachers. Both the ambiance of the school community and the achievement of pedagogical goals are to a great extent dependent on the success of these negotiations (Gregory & Ripski, 2008; Schweinle, Turner, & Meyer, 2008; Van Petegem, Aelterman, Rosseel, & Creemers, 2006). Especially in school transitions the significance of negotiations and meaning making is crucial for the pupils (Anderson et al., 2000).

In addition to the pupil–teacher interaction in schools, pupils' peer interaction is another essential element of the school as a social environment. Pupil peer interaction is often seen as something superfluous, just a potential source of disorder distracting from the formal pedagogical goals and activities of school. This is for instance reflected in public debate about bullying among pupils. At the same time, there has been a growing interest among researchers in the impact of peer interaction on the entire school life, including pedagogical intentions (Boekaerts, De Koning, & Vedder, 2006; Giota, 2006; Hofer, 2007; Tuominen-Soini, Salmela-Aro, & Niemivirta, 2008). Informal interactions and the forming and maintaining of friendships are crucial elements of personal growth and feelings of meaningfulness and belonging, especially for young people. Consequently peer interaction may significantly facilitate not just personal well-being but also a motivation toward school work.

During their school career pupils face contextual changes and developmental transitions (e.g., adolescence) which are intertwined with the expression of physical, psychological, social, and emotional changes and challenges (Anderson et al., 2000; Ellonen, Kääriäinen, & Autio, 2008; Gillison et al., 2008). They also face several normative, predictable, and structural changes such as entering school or moving to the secondary school. Hence research on transitions has focused on significant events, time period and change faced by pupils in their school career. Research demonstrates significant positive as well as negative changes in terms of pupils' academic achievement, learning motivation, well-being (e.g., school burnout or aggression) or interpersonal relations (e.g., peer group status or teacher–student relationship) during these normative transitions (Cillesen & Mayeux, 2007; Galton & Morrison, 2000; Hofer et al., 2007; Kiuru, 2008; Midgley & Edelin, 1998; Salmela-Aro et al., 2008; Zimmer-Gembeck et al., 2006). However, at the same time little is known about the 'transition process' in which pupils are continuously defining their individual role as a learner and a member of the school community in interaction with teachers and the peer group.

VERTICAL AND HORIZONTAL TRANSITIONS

Our results concur with previous research and indicate that normative transitions within the pupils' school careers are significant phases and as such provide both positive resource and challenge for pupils. We refer to these normative changes in pupils' school career as *vertical* transitions. In practice vertical transition often means moving from lower grades to upper grades or in a more abstract sense advancing in learning and knowledge construction or becoming more accountable, more "grown-up" in the social structure of school.

However, in our study, pupils also identified and described more unpredictable and non-normative transitions in their everyday school life. These transitions described by the pupils were often related to the variety of social and cultural contexts of the school community that they participated in. The events reported by the pupils challenged them to negotiate their position as a member of the school community. It appeared that pupils' experiences were primarily regulated by the quality of interaction with peers, teachers, and the school community as perceived by the pupils. These kind of everyday practices could be seen as another dimension of school's learning environment that is here referred to as *horizontal*. Especially changes in pupils' peer relationships seemed to challenge them to reflect their emotional and behavioral engagement in pedagogical activities in school. In pupils' experiences, expected learning outcomes and personal goals such as the need to gain social approval from the peer group may even appear to be in conflict, and this might constitute a paradox to school work. Pupils might underachieve in some or all school subjects due to a strong social pressure from the peer group having negative attitudes/intentions toward schooling. Moreover, the pupils experienced that the emphasis on learning outcomes often override the social aims of school education, for example, if a teacher ignores or fails to recognize problems such as bullying within the pupils' peer group interaction. These unpredictable transitions perceived by pupils can also cause gaps and pitfalls in pupils' learning path both in vertical and horizontal directions and simultaneously regulate pupils' meaningful learning. Hence, in order to support pupils' learning and development in their school path effort from the school community is required in coherence making, both in vertical and horizontal directions.

Our results suggested that quality of interactions in pedagogical situations is the key regulator for pupils' experienced horizontal and vertical coherence within their school path. Especially the conflict situations and the way they were resolved were considered to play a key role, both in hindering and enabling pupils' active and meaningful learning, as perceived by them. Processing the social conflicts both in (a) the pupil–teacher interaction; and (b) within the peer group was considered a crucial precondition for learning and well-being in school by the pupils. At its worst, problems and conflicts in the interaction with teachers and peers may lead to exclusion from the educational and social aims of the school. Due to these social conflicts, the pupil's connection to the school community and possibilities to participate actively in the process of meaningful learning are weakened. The risk of exclusion introduces different kinds of challenges in supporting pupil learning and well-being in the school context, and especially in transition processes.

PUPILS' LEARNING AND WELL-BEING IN TRANSITIONS

School transition studies have shown that ensuring a consistent, coherent, and understandable learning path for pupils, both in terms of learning different subjects, and in terms of safe and supportive everyday learning environment that promotes pupils' well-being is a real challenge (Galton & Morrison, 2000; Midgley & Edelin, 1998; see also Boekaerts, 1993; Boekaerts et al., 2006). Transitions are processes in which learning and well-being are closely intertwined. Hence it is essential to consider learning and well-being in relation to each other. They are regulated at least partly by similar preconditions.

Research on both learning and well-being has lately been developing in similar directions. Both have adopted holistic and systemic aspects, moving toward an increasingly multidimensional, process-oriented, and interactive view of human action. In both research fields there has also been a shift toward a more positive orientation that focuses on human potential and resources (e.g., Hakanen, Bakker, & Schaufeli, 2005; Hakkarainen, Palonen, Paavola, & Lehtinen, 2004; Krapp, 2005; Lazarus & Lazarus, 1994; Seligman & Csikszentmihalyi, 2000; Sheldon & King, 2001). In this chapter we argue that construction of well-being can be understood as a learning process, particularly from the social-psychological point of view. In turn, experienced well-being regulates new learning. Learning of well-being can be seen as an active, collaborative, and situated process in which the relationship between individuals and their environment is constantly constructed and modified. This means that experienced well-being is affected by learners' prior positive and negative learning experiences and by learners' strategies or approaches. Perceptions and strategies are constructed and re-constructed in everyday interactions, so the quality of these interactions becomes a key regulator for meaningful learning. It is understood that well-being as learning is not only about acquisition of knowledge and skills, but about an ongoing, interactive process of sense making and development in which motives and emotions play an important part (e.g., Lasky, 2005; Lonka, Hakkarainen, & Sintonen, 2000; Nonaka & Nishiguchi, 2001; Paavola & Hakkarainen, 2005; Wenger, 1998; Wertsch, 1993).

It appears that perceived well-being regulates learning in many ways, for example, it can affect the ability to concentrate and observe the environment, perceive affordances, and interpret received feedback. The core criteria for experienced well-being that are reflected in learning outcomes are relatedness, competence, and autonomy (Deci & Ryan, 2002). The crucial preconditions for both overall well-being and meaningful learning are postulated to be belonging, meaningfulness, success in one's intentions, and a sense of coherence and agency (Antonovsky, 1987, 1993; Deci & Ryan, 2002; Ryan & Deci, 2001). Consequently, the quality and coherence of pedagogical processes in school could be assessed by examining to what extent they facilitate these preconditions for learning and well-being for pupils.

The interrelated nature of learning and well-being suggests that in addition to the intended learning outcomes, the pedagogical processes within school communities can generate either feelings of engagement and empowerment, and a sense of satisfaction, or feelings of stress and anxiety for the participants of the process (Boekaerts, 1993; Konu, Lintonen, & Autio,

2002; Krapp, 2005; Pelletier et al., 2002; Silins & Mulford, 2002; Tarter & Hoy, 2004; Van Houtte, 2006). Pupils' sense of academic mastery is entwined with success in studying, which in turn is linked with the pupil's ability to participate in the learning community and school activities. The ability and will to promote and develop one's capacity to participate in pedagogical practices is centrally regulated by the pupil's learning agency in the school community (see also Midgley & Edelin, 1998).

TOWARD AN ACTIVE LEARNING AGENCY

Pupil's learning agency can be considered as a capacity for intentional and responsible management of new learning, both at an individual and community level. Pupil's sense of learning agency is regulated by one's perceptions of the objects of activities in school, for example how they perceive pedagogical goals, processes, or school community. Coherent, systemic, and functional perceptions of school's pedagogical and social activities are likely to facilitate pupil's attainment of active learning agency. Respectively, fragmented, dogmatic, and narrow perceptions are likely to result more in a passive agency in terms of one's learning and participation in school community. Moreover, learning agency is relational in the sense that it incorporates the capacity to offer and to ask for support from others and align one's thoughts and actions with those of others in order to interpret problems and negotiate the object of the activity (Bandura, 2001; Edwards, 2005; Evers, Brouwers, & Tomic, 2002). Therefore, pupils' learning agency is embedded in interactions with teachers, with peers, and with other members of the school community. Experienced learning agency affects the approaches pupils assume in their school work and in their interactions with peers and teachers, which in turn play a significant part in the construction of meaningful learning path for the pupils.

Pupils' experienced learning agency is generated in different contexts of interactions in school. Consequently, the quality of interactions both in the informal (e.g., peer interaction during breaks) and in the formal (e.g., instruction for the learning task) contexts of school are important (Lahelma, 2002). Characteristics of the type of pedagogical interactions that promote learning agency (by facilitating satisfaction, engagement, and empowerment) are that participants' perceive themselves as active learners and they experience a sense of coherence, meaningfulness, and belonging (Antonovsky, 1987, 1993; Bowen, Richman, Brewster, & Bowen, 1998; Deci & Ryan, 2002; Kristersson & Öhlund, 2005; Pallant & Lae, 2002; Ryan & Deci, 2001; Torsheim, Aarø, & Wold, 2001). Hence, a precondition for a pupil to be able to understand the learning goals is that one perceives oneself as an active member of the school community. In contrast, unsolved disagreements and perceived detachment are likely to cause frictions, feelings of alienation, and inequality and hence undermine the pupil's active learning agency.

Adopting active learning agency is likely to support pupils' overall well-being. At its best, the pupils' active learning agency generated in classrooms, for example, may function as a buffer against the negative effects on pupil's well-being produced by other elements of one's life. Accordingly it could be seen as a crucial asset of resilience (e.g., Jindal-Snape & Miller, 2008; Masten & Reed, 2005). On the other hand at its worst the action orientation and coping strategies adopted by the pupil, such as avoidance or defensive strategies, may gradually cause an inability to connect with the school community, resulting in exclusion from the learning processes. This could have a severe negative impact on all aspects of pupils' life. The processes leading to exclusion from the school community may be embedded so deeply in everyday practices and interactions that members of the community are not even aware of them. Moreover, pupil's experiences of well-being and learning agency may differ between interaction contexts within the school community. Thus, a pupil may simultaneously experience empowerment, joy, and satisfaction in their classroom interactions with peers along with feelings of fear, anxiety, and stress caused by problems with teachers.

Our results suggested that pupils continuously evaluate and monitor their social, cognitive, and emotional capacity to cope with various challenges set by a school system (see also Anderson et al., 2000). Especially the pupils who feel that they do not have enough support from members of the school community or experience their needs overlooked in transition processes may adopt rather passive strategies of participation and study. For instance if a pupil perceives that in the decisions related to transition she is not appreciated or listened to the pupil may stop investing in studies or transfer her focus of attention to activities outside school. In practice this may reflect on pupils' unwillingness to ask for help during the transition process, which in turn is likely to lead to further decrease in support provided by the school system (see also Butler & Shibaz, 2008; Pelletier et al., 2002; Ryan et al., 1998). This may further weaken their sense of agency and may affect both learning and well-being in the school path in future. On the other hand a prerequisite to successful coping with transition processes seems to be a high capacity for intentional and responsible management of new learning. Active learning agency anticipates functional self-regulation such as help seeking, and thereby increases potential for support from the social environment in transitions. Accordingly pedagogical practices that simultaneously presuppose and emphasize the significance of pupils' active learning agency and the complementary contexts of interaction in school provide both challenges and opportunities for it.

Constructing an Active Learning Agency in the School Path

Pupil's active learning agency can be seen as an essential ingredient in sustaining both meaningful learning orientation and elements of well-being, such as a sense of belonging in transition processes, and thus in developing more coherent learning path for pupils. Hence facilitating collaboration in peer groups within the single teaching lesson or coherent continuum of a certain subject is essential, but not sufficient condition to support pupils' meaningful learning and belonging in transformative context of school. Therefore, in order to succeed in development work, more careful analysis of a continuum of school career needs to be done.

Our results showed that pupils' learning agency is constructed both in schools' everyday practices (horizontal dimension) and in continuum of learning path (vertical dimension). On the other hand, agency is manifested in pupils' ability to cope successfully with various transitions. To be able to actively regulate their action in transitions, pupils should have learned strategies to analyze and anticipate the forthcoming challenges in their school career and simultaneously regulate their own intentions and actions in relation to challenges present in the school. This suggests that promoting pupils' active learning agency should be a key objective in schools' pedagogical processes, especially in terms of facilitating successful school transitions. This is a challenging task because of the contextual and dynamic nature of learning agency. Pupils' capacity to construct a sense of coherence or meaningfulness for their studies may vary significantly in different phases within a learning path—and even in different situations during the school day. This suggests that coherence making and promotion of learning agency should be ongoing processes that take place in shared continuous negotiations between pupils and teachers in everyday practices of school. The negotiations and re-negotiations on how to advance both vertical and horizontal dimensions of coherence in schools' pedagogical practices provide activating and collaborative learning process for pupils. Within this process pupils' readiness to regulate their learning and studying activities in relation to challenges and goals set by the school environment can develop. This promotes adopting active agency over their learning. The process can be supported by the teachers who can provide spaces for constructing both personal and shared learning paths. Next we will introduce a research based instrument for designing the research and interventions in schools' pedagogical processes from the perspective of adopting active learning agency in school path (see Figure 9.1).

The vertical dimension in Figure 9.1 refers to a pupil's capacity to analyze and anticipate the future challenges in one's learning path. The horizontal dimension refers to a pupil's capacity to regulate her/his own intentions and actions in relation to challenges present when attending school. Figure 9.1 shows preconditions that empower pupils to construct the coherence in both vertical and horizontal dimensions (++), and hence promote adopting active learning agency. Respectively, the lack of coherence making or failure in negotiating meaning may result in low capacity to analyze and anticipate the challenges of future learning path. Furthermore this is likely to reflect on pupil's intentions and actions in relation to present challenges (--), which in turn hinders agency in terms of learning.

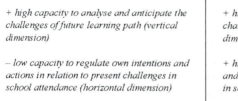

Vertical coherence

+ *high capacity to analyse and anticipate the challenges of future learning path (vertical dimension)*	+ *high capacity to analyse and anticipate the challenges of future learning path (vertical dimension)*
− *low capacity to regulate own intentions and actions in relation to present challenges in school attendance (horizontal dimension)*	+ *high capacity to regulate own intentions and actions in relation to present challenges in school attendance (horizontal dimension)*
	Horizontal coherence
− *low capacity to analyse and anticipate the challenges of future learning path (vertical dimension)*	− *low capacity to analyse and anticipate the challenges of future learning path (vertical dimension)*
− *low capacity to regulate own intentions and actions in relation to present challenges in school attendance (horizontal dimension)*	+ *high capacity to regulate own intentions and actions in relation to present challenges in school attendance (horizontal dimension)*

Figure 9.1   Coherence making enabling pupils' active learning agency.

However, it is also possible that strong horizontal coherence leads to self-regulation in relation to present challenges while at the same time there is a lack of future perspective due to poor vertical coherence (-+). This may be the case, for example, when functional interaction between teachers and pupil creates a good ambiance and supports pupil's sense of belonging, but at the same time a failure in negotiating meaningful learning goals for the future is causing the low capacity to self-regulate and anticipate challenges ahead. This may be manifested in lack of views in terms of life after basic education. Further, it is possible that strong vertical coherence leads to high hopes for future but at the same time failure in negotiating meaningful strategies to carry out the aims (+-). This may manifest itself in unrealistic goals compared to performance at the moment or in incapability to reflect and choose the line of action in present learning situation. Hence opportunity to construct an active learning agency through personal learning path and school career is essential in terms of both learning and well-being. Accordingly coherence making can be seen as an ongoing process that often becomes more explicit in the processes of transitions where the learning agency is constructed and re-constructed. Therefore, it is suggested that pupils should not only cope with gaps or pitfalls encountered in their school career, rather they should be encouraged to be active participants and take part also in school development by identifying discontinuities in school career and constructing a more coherent learning path for themselves in collaboration with teachers.

DISCUSSION

In this chapter we argue that in order to support pupils in the various transitions of the school path more effort should be put on constructing the school culture that promotes pupils' empowerment, learning agency, and active collaboration (e.g., buffering the perceived stress or solving the social conflicts) both within and between transitions. The concept of learning agency is used here to refer to the complex entity of pupils' self-regulation and perceived control in terms of their learning and experienced well-being as members of learning community. We argue that the concept of learning agency offers a new approach for reflecting on school transitions from pupil's perspective by emphasizing the importance of active coherence and meaning making and the entwined relationship between learning and well-being at the same time, as a precondition for successful transitions within the comprehensive school path.

Facilitating pupils' active learning agency requires that teachers have identified both challenges and resources they have within their school community to promote horizontal and vertical coherence making. However, attaining holistic and shared understanding about the resources, problems, and optimal course of pupils' learning, within the school's professional community is not easy. Teachers, for example, seem to be increasingly overwhelmed in pedagogical situations where their didactic intentions and subject specific expertise do not provide them with functional tools to cope with the social aims and challenges of school education. Consequently, there appears to be an abiding demand for more resources to hire specialized experts in schools to deal with the problems of well-being, and disturbing behavior, and to guide pupils through transitions. From teachers' perspectives, learning outcomes and the more general social goals of education may even appear to be in conflict. Accordingly, instead of attaining a more holistic approach to pupils' learning and growth, there is a danger that teachers along with other professionals in the school adopt more segregated and segmented approach on school activities. Moreover, the responsibility of guiding these processes may be divided between professionals instead of collaborative problem solving. This can be considered problematic because fragmentation of both school community and pedagogical activities are not likely to result in long lasting and functional solutions for the challenges that are holistic and dynamic in nature.

The undivided basic education reform is an attempt to answer this question not by segmentation but by introducing the goal of curricular and community level coherence making. However, success in the reform, as school reforms worldwide, is not self-evident. Sustainable development in school organization provides a systemic approach; conceptualizing, analyzing, and changing the school practices at different levels of the whole system. In the context of school transitions this means that more profound understanding not only regarding normative transitions and their effects, but also about the unpredictable and non-normative transitions need to be constructed to promote school development. This requires creating new insights and complementary perspectives on research on school transitions, for example by focusing on exploring how these changes take place and what is the nature of the transitions processes pupils face during their comprehensive school path.

Moreover moving research on transitions from "vitro" to "vivo" requires the collaboration of educational researchers and professionals (McLaughlin & Mitra, 2001). Successful collaboration prerequisites novel instruments to be developed that promote shared meaning making between researchers and other educational professionals. We have suggested one conceptual instrument in this chapter. At the general level it means creating more open and reciprocal dialogue between researchers and the practitioners to overcome the problems partly caused by focusing on parts while disregarding the way the whole structure of basic education and school as a learning environment hangs together. Especially, complex composites such as learning environments need to be studied as designed composites, not as separate units reduced to their basic ingredients. This does not mean that the basic ingredient studies should be replaced by composite studies, but rather that the latter should complement the former (Salomon, 1996; Vygotsky, 1978). We should also be able to explore which factors and parallel processes regulate the transition process and how the process is affected by pupil's own actions of learning environment.

Note: The authors wish to thank the Finnish Ministry of Education and Finnish Work Environment Fund for funding the research project Learning and Development in Comprehensive School.

REFERENCES

Anderson, L. W., Jacobs, J., Schramm, S., & Splittgerber, F. (2000). School transitions: Beginning of the end or a new beginning? *International Journal of Educational Research, 33*(4), 325–339.

Antonovsky, A. (1987). *Unraveling the mystery: How people manage stress and stay well.* San Francisco: Jossey-Bass.

Antonovsky, A. (1993). The structure and properties of the sense of coherence scale. *Social Science Medicine, 36*, 725–734.

Bandura, A. (2001). Social-cognitive theory: An agentic perspective. *Annual Review of Psychology, 52*, 1–26.

Basic Education Act. (628/1998). Finnish Act of Parliament. Retrieved May 18, 2009, from http://www.finlex.fi/en/laki/kaannokset/1998/en19980628.

Boekaerts, M. (1993). Being concerned with well-being and with learning. *Educational Psychologist, 28*(2), 149–167.

Boekaerts, M., De Koning, E., & Vedder, P. (2006). Goal-directed behaviour and contextual factors in the classroom: An innovative approach to the study of multiple goals. *Educational Psychologist, 41*(1), 33–51.

Bowen, G. L., Richman, J. M., Brewster, A., & Bowen, N. (1998). Sense of school coherence, perceptions of danger at school, and teacher support among youth at risk of school failure. *Child and Adolescent Social Work Journal, 15,* 273–286.

Brown, A. (1992). Design experiments: Theoretical and methodological challenges in creating complex interventions in classroom setting. *The Journal of the Learning Sciences, 2*(2), 141–178.

Butler, R., & Shibaz, L. (2008). Achievement goals for teaching as predictors of students' perceptions of instructional practices and students' help seeking and cheating. *Learning and Instruction, 18*(5), 453–467.

Cillesen, A. H. N., & Mayeux, L. (2007). Expectations and perceptions at school transitions: The role of peer status and aggression. *Journal of School Psychology, 45,* 567–585.

Collins, A., Joseph, D., & Bielaczyc, K. (2004). Design research: Theoretical and methodological issues. *The Journal of the Learning Sciences, 13*(1), 15–42.

Davies, D., & McMahon, K. (2004). A smooth trajectory: Developing continuity and progression between primary and secondary science education through a joint-planned projectiles project. *International Journal of Science Education, 26*(8), 1009–1021.

Deci, E. L., & Ryan, R. M. (2002). *Handbook of self-determination research.* Rochester, NY: The University of Rochester Press.

De Corte, E. (2000). *High-powered learning communities: A European perspective.* Keynote address presented at the first Conference of the Economic and Social Research Council's Research Programme on Teaching and Learning, Leicester, UK.

Edwards, A. (2005). Relational agency: Learning to be a resourceful practitioner. *International Journal of Educational Research, 43*(3), 168–182.

Ellonen, N., Kääriäinen, J., & Autio, V. (2008). Adolescent depression and school support: A multilevel analysis of a Finnish sample. *Journal of Community Psychology, 36*(4), 552–567.

Evers, W. J. G., Brouwers, A., & Tomic, W. (2002). Burnout and self-efficacy: A study on teachers' beliefs when implementing an innovative educational system in the Netherlands. *British Journal of Educational Psychology, 72*(2), 227–243.

Galton, M., & Hargreaves, L. (2002). Transfer a future agenda. In M. Galton, & L. Hargreaves (Eds.), *Transfer from primary classroom: 20 years on* (pp. 185–208). London: Routledge Falmer.

Galton, M., & Morrison, I. (2000). Concluding comments. Transfer and transition: The next steps. *International Journal of Educational Research, 33*(4), 443–449.

Gillison, F., Standage, M., & Skevington, S. (2008). Changes in quality of life and psychological need satisfaction following the transition to secondary school. *British Journal of Educational Psychology, 78,* 149–162.

Giota, J. (2006). Why am I in school? Relationships between adolescents' goal orientation, academic achievement and self-evaluation. *Scandinavian Journal of Educational Research, 50*(4), 441–461.

Gregory, A., & Ripski, M. B. (2008). Adolescent trust in teachers: Implications for behaviour in the high school classroom. *School Psychology Review, 37*(3), 337–353.

Hakanen, J. J., Bakker, A. B., & Schaufeli, W. B. (2005). Burnout and work engagement among teachers. *Journal of School Psychology, 43*(6), 495–513.

Hakkarainen, K., Palonen, T., Paavola, S., & Lehtinen, E. (2004). *Communities of networked expertise. Professional and educational perspectives.* Oxford: Elsevier.

Hofer, M. (2007). Goal conflicts and self-regulation: A new look at pupils' off-task behaviour in the classroom. *Educational Research Review, 2*(1), 28–38.

Hofer, M., Schmid, S., Fries, S., Dietz, F., Clausen, M., & Reinders, H. (2007). Individual values, motivational conflicts, and learning for school. *Learning and Instruction, 17*(1), 17–28.

Hofman, R. H., Hofman, A., & Guldemond, H. (2001). Social context effects on pupils' perception of school. *Learning and Instruction, 11*(3), 171–194.

Huusko, J., Pietarinen, J., Pyhältö, K., & Soini, T. (2007). *Yhtenäisyyttä rakentava peruskoulu. Yhtenäisen perusopetuksen ehdot ja mahdollisuudet* [*The preconditions for undivided basic education in comprehensive school*]. Research in Educational Sciences 34. Turku: Finnish Educational Research Association.

Jindal-Snape D., & Foggie, J. (2008). A holistic approach to primary–secondary transitions. *Improving Schools, 11*(1), 5–18.

Jindal-Snape, D., & Miller, D. J. (2008). A challenge of living? Understanding the psycho-social processes of the child during primary–secondary transition through resilience and self-esteem theories. *Educational Psychology Review, 20*, 217–236.

Kiuru, N. (2008). *The role of adolescents' peer groups in the school context. Jyväskylä Studies in Education, Psychology and Social Research, 331.* Jyväskylä: Jyväskylä University Printing House.

Konu, A. I., Lintonen, T. P., & Autio, V. J. (2002). Evaluation of well-being in schools—A multilevel analysis of general subjective well-being. *School Effectiveness and School Improvement, 13*, 187–200.

Krapp, A. (2005). Basic needs and the development of interest and intrinsic motivational orientations. *Learning and Instruction, 15*(5), 381–395.

Kristersson, P., & Öhlund, L. S. (2005). Swedish upper secondary school pupils' sense of coherence, coping resources and aggressiveness in relation to educational track and performance. *Scandinavian Journal of Caring Science, 19*, 77–84.

Kvalsund, R. (2000). The transition from primary to secondary school level in smaller and larger rural schools in Norway: Comparing differences in context and social meaning. *International Journal of Educational Research, 33*(4), 401–423.

Lahelma, E. (2002). School is for meeting friends: Secondary school as lived and remembered. *British Journal of Sociology of Education, 23*(3), 367–381.

Lasky, S. (2005). A sociocultural approach to understanding teacher identity, agency and professional vulnerability in a context of secondary school reform. *Teaching and Teacher Education, 21*(8), 899–916.

Lazarus R. S., & Lazarus, B. N. (1994). *Passion and reason: Making sense of our emotions.* New York: Oxford University Press.

Lonka, K., Hakkarainen, K., & Sintonen, M. (2000). Progressive inquiry learning for children—Experiences, possibilities, limitations. *European Early Childhood Education Association Journal, 8*(1), 7–23.

Masten, A. S., & Reed, M.-G. J. (2005). Resilience in development. In C. R. Snyder & S. J. Lopez (Eds.), *Handbook of positive psychology* (pp. 74–88). New York: Oxford University Press.

McLaughlin, M. W., & Mitra, D. (2001). Theory-based change and change-based theory: Going deeper, going broader. *Journal of Educational Change, 2*(4), 301–323.

Midgley, C., & Edelin, K.C. (1998). Middle school reform and early adolescent well-being: The good news and the bad. *Educational Psychologist, 33*(4), 195–206.

Muschamp, Y., Stoll, L., & Nausheem, M. (2001). Learning in the middle years. In C. W. Day & D. Van Veen (Eds.), *Educational Research in Europe Yearbook 2001* (pp. 323–350). Belgium: Garant Publisher.

National Core Curriculum for Basic Education. (2004). The Finnish National
   Board of Education. Retrieved May 11, 2009, from http://www.oph.fi/english/
   page.asp?path=447,88611,27598,37840,72101,72106.
Nonaka, I., & Nishiguchi, T. (Eds.). (2001). *Knowledge emergence: Social, techni-
   cal and evolutionary dimensions of knowledge creation.* New York: Oxford
   Press.
Paavola, S., & Hakkarainen, K. (2005). The knowledge creation metaphor—An
   emergent epistemological approach to learning. *Science & Education, 14*(6),
   535–557.
Pallant, J. F., & Lae, L. (2002). Sense of coherence, well-being, coping and personality factors: Further evaluation of the sense of coherence scale. *Personality and
   Individual Differences, 33,* 39–48.
Pelletier, L. G., Legault, L., & Séguin-Lévesque, C. (2002). Pressure from above
   and from below as determinants of teachers' motivation and teaching behav-
   iours. *Journal of Educational Psychology, 94,* 186–196.
PISA, Program for International Student Assessment. Retrieved September 1, 2008,
   from http://www.oecd.org/document/2/0,3343,en_32252351_32236191_3971
   8850_1_1_1_1,00.html.
Rimpelä, M., Kuusela, J., Rigoff, A.-M., Saaristo, V., & Wiss, K. (2008). *Hyvinvoinnin ja terveyden edistäminen peruskoulussa 2. Perusraportti kyselystä
   1.–6. vuosiluokkien kouluille. [School Health Promotion Study. Grades 1.–6.]*
   Helsinki: Ministry of Education, National Research and Development Center
   for Welfare and Health.
Rimpelä M., Rigoff A.-M., Kuusela J., & Peltonen H. (Eds.). (2007). *Hyvinvoinnin
   ja terveyden edistäminen peruskouluissa—perusraportti kyselystä 7.–9. vuosiluokkien kouluille. [School Health Promotion Study. Grades 7.–9.]* Helsinki:
   Ministry of Education & National Research and Development Center for Welfare and Health.
Ryan, A. M., Gheen, M. H., & Midgley, C. (1998). Why do some students avoid
   asking for help? An examination of the interplay among students' academic efficacy, teachers' social-emotional role, and the classroom goal structure. *Journal
   of Educational Psychology, 90*(3), 528–535.
Ryan, R. M., & Deci, E. L. (2001). Intrinsic and extrinsic motivations: Classic definitions and new directions. *Contemporary Educational Psychology, 25,* 68–81.
Salmela-Aro, K., Kiuru, N., & Nurmi, J.-E. (2008). The role of educational track
   in adolescents' school burnout: A longitudinal study. *British Journal of Educational Psychology, 78,* 663–689.
Salomon, G. (1996). Unorthodox thoughts on the nature and mission of contemporary educational psychology. *Educational Psychology Review, 8*(4), 397–417.
Schweinle, A., Turner, J. C., & Meyer, D. K. (2008). Understanding young adolescents' optimal experiences in academic settings. *The Journal of Experimental
   Education, 77*(2), 125–143.
Seligman, M. E. P., & Csikszentmihalyi M. (2000). Positive psychology. An introduction. *American Psychologist, 55*(1), 5–14.
Sheldon, K. M., & King, L. (2001). Why positive psychology is necessary. *American Psychologist, 56*(3), 216–217.
Silins, H., & Mulford, B. (2002). Schools as learning organisations. The case for
   system, teacher and student learning. *Journal of Educational Administration,
   40,* 425–446.
Tarter, C. J., & Hoy, W. K. (2004). A systems approach to quality in elementary
   schools. A theoretical and empirical analysis. *Journal of Educational Administration, 42,* 539–554.
Torsheim, T., Aarø, L. E., & Wold, B. (2001). Sense of coherence and school-
   related stress as predictors of subjective health complaints in early adolescence:

Interactive, indirect or direct relationships. *Social Science and Medicine, 53*, 603–614.

Tuominen-Soini, H., Salmela-Aro, K., & Niemivirta, M. (2008). Achievement goal orientations and subjective well-being: A person-centred analysis. *Learning and Instruction, 18*(3), 251–266.

Van Houtte, M. (2006). Tracking and teacher satisfaction: Role of study culture and trust. *The Journal of Educational Research, 99*(4), 247–254.

Van Petegem, K., Aelterman, A., Rosseel, Y., & Creemers, B. (2006). Student perception as moderator for student wellbeing. *Social Indicators Research, 83*, 447–463.

Vygotsky, L. S. (1978). *Mind in society: The development of higher psychological processes.* Cambridge, MA: Harvard University Press.

Ward, R. (2000). Transfer from middle to secondary school: A New Zealand study. *International Journal of Educational Research, 33*(4), 365–374.

Wenger, E. (1998). *Communities of practice. Learning, meaning and identity.* Cambridge: Cambridge University Press.

Wertsch, J. V. (1993). *Voices of the mind: A sociocultural approach to mediated action.* Cambridge, MA: Harvard University Press.

Zimmer-Gembeck, M., Chipuer, H. M., Hanisch, M., Creed, P. A., & McGregor, L. (2006). Relationships at school and stage-environment fit as resources for adolescent engagement and achievement. *Journal of Adolescence, 29*, 911–933.

Part IV
Transition to Post-School

10 Interactive Behaviors for Building Independence in Exceptional Youth

Keith J. Topping and Jocelyn Foggie

INTRODUCTION

UK government policy and legislation has been especially concerned with young people at risk of social exclusion sometimes known as the NEET group (Not in Education, Employment, or Training; e.g., Berthoud, 2003; Gilligan, 2000; Raffe, Brannen, & Croxford, 2001). This chapter reports on a project in Scotland which deployed key workers to support young people who had recently left school and were at risk of social exclusion, aiming to enhance independence, self-sufficiency, and employability. The youngsters were exceptional and vulnerable in the sense that many had a variety of special needs, while others were involved with drugs or the criminal justice system.

On the surface, the project appeared to be generally successful. However, the study went on to unpack the interactive behaviors the key workers used to develop transferable skills and build active independence in the young people—in the perceptions of the key workers and as directly observed during interactions with young people. The research explored whether the professionals did what they thought they did, and what opportunities for enhanced effectiveness could be discerned.

PREVIOUS RESEARCH

Much of the previous literature has concentrated on broad policy issues, descriptions and epidemiological surveys of problems, young person views of what they would like, or evaluations of multiple-component programs (often with scant regard to implementation fidelity or variability; Smokowski, 1998). The literature includes little detail about how specific interventions might be effectively structured. Furlong, Cartmel, Biggart, Sweeting, and West (2003) found that most young people overcame difficult or unexpected situations through determination and persistence combined with family support, and the majority eventually secured jobs without external intervention. This finding of spontaneous remission without intervention sets a comparative benchmark for the effect sizes that might be expected from active intervention.

Lent, Hackett, and Brown (1999) suggested that in order to achieve a successful adjustment to life after school, children and young people needed to develop: positive and realistic self-efficacy and outcome expectations; academic and career interests; career goals and aspirations; the ability to turn their goals into actions; high or adequate academic and employment skills and the ability to correct problems which affect performance; and an understanding of the supports and barriers that may help or hinder progress. Young people with special needs might be disadvantaged in all of these, but all are potentially amenable to outside intervention. All might be notionally addressed in "transition planning" prior to leaving school, but in what depth and to what effect? (Ward, Mallett, Heslop, & Simons, 2003).

The Education (Additional Support for Learning) (Scotland) Act 2004 (Her Majesty's Stationery Office, 2004) signaled a range of changes for the whole Scottish Education System. In particular, it called for improved organizational planning for post-school transition. This Act emerged in light of the authoritative Beattie Committee Report, "Implementing Inclusiveness, Realising Potential" (Scottish Executive, 1999) which focused on post-school education and training for young people with additional support needs. These young people face multiple barriers in accessing and sustaining further education, employment, and training as a result of the diverse and complex nature of their needs, and they are at the greatest risk of social exclusion.

The Beattie report made many recommendations for improving the transition, employability, and employment of vulnerable young people at risk of social exclusion. One important recommendation related to the involvement of key workers to support the young people throughout the transition from school to post-school learning or employment. The key feature of the key worker is to ensure that there is one consistent person supporting the young person through the transition process. This key worker is in the unique position of being a sole point of contact for the young person, who can provide support and guidance to help the young person access and make use of the various agencies; advocate and negotiate on behalf of the young person in order to secure the most appropriate provision to meet their needs; and act as the primary source for all agencies in the event of any problems.

There are reports of multiple component interventions with exceptional youth in the literature. For example, an intervention from England is the Connexions Service which oversees the Transition Plan delivery and supports young people aged 13–19, or up to 25 for those with learning difficulties. It amalgamates the careers service with features from youth services and aims to decrease the NEET cohort. For those with disabilities, a Social Worker or Care Manager will be best placed to ensure the coordination of services during the transition out of school. Similarly, Transition Workers are available in some localities. They support the transition, offer advice and liaise between the Child and Adult teams within Social Work. A voluntary organization, Fairbridge in Scotland provides personal and social development for the hardest to reach young people and those who disengage from formal education and learning. They offer a long-term development program for 13–25-year-olds to build the skills, confidence, and motivation they need to reach their potential and ease their transition into post-school opportunities.

The effectiveness of these interventions will not be reviewed here. Instead we focus upon the question of what are the effective behavioral features of interventions by key workers with such young people. The literature here is sparse, however, with many reports focusing upon the behavior of the young person rather than the key worker. Thus, Riffel et al. (2005) studied four transition-age students with cognitive disabilities, using a palmtop computer running a software program to increase independence on vocational and independent living tasks. The palmtop decreased the need for prompts from the instructor and increased the number of steps completed in a given task without external prompts. However, independence skills were observed in the clients, not prompts among the key workers.

Brown, Clopton, and Tusler (1991) advocated a "Student Development Model" (SDM) which intended to help students move from dependence to independence. They claimed that the "traditional service delivery model" promoted dependence rather than independence. The professional did everything for the young person, thereby failing to develop the skills the student would require in their life. By contrast, the SDM involved the professional encouraging the student to take on many of the responsibilities themselves, developing the skills necessary to become independent. Similarly, Ackerman (2006) asserted that children and youth with disabilities perform more poorly in transitional outcomes than their non-disabled peers owing to limitations in self-determination—which can and should be taught (although Ackerman is somewhat light on exactly how). In a survey by Carter, Lane, Pierson, and Glaeser (2006), disabled students identified infrequent opportunities at school and home for engaging in self-determined behavior, whereas educators and parents differed in their assessments of opportunities in each setting.

Healy and Rigby (1999) interviewed 10 young people with physical disabilities (aged 17–21 years) at the start of The Independence Programme (TIP), after participation and at a four month follow-up. TIP was a multi-component 20-day residential program. It aimed to help the young people to develop basic independent living skills and engage in opportunities which would lead to them believing in their own abilities and potential. It addressed the barriers facing these young people in their daily lives in areas such as personal care, household tasks, community living, and leisure by steadily developing the necessary skills for gaining some autonomy in dealing with these experiences.

Healy and Rigby (1999) found that every young person had benefits in terms of performance and satisfaction with that performance, and that these benefits remained to some extent at follow-up. However, these young people were selected as motivated to develop independent living skills; they were able to evaluate their own needs and abilities, and able to establish realistic goals. Additionally, precise key worker behaviors were not specified.

Heslop, Mallett, Simons, and Ward (2002) studied young people aged 13–25. From interviews with these young people and their parents, the authors identified issues which limited the young person's independence. Many of the young people and their parents were anxious about personal safety. Some young people had already suffered bullying and assault, while others worried about being attacked or about road safety. Some parents recognized that they were often over-protective. The authors noted that these fears impeded the young person's progression to independence and there was a lack of support to help them deal with this issue. Heslop et al. (2002) also found that sufficient information was not provided about benefits issues, and some parents acknowledged that their child's independence could be increased if they managed their own money and developed budgeting skills. The ability to use public transport enhances a young person's independence by enabling them to access recreational pursuits when and where they want, without having to rely on their parents/carers to give them a lift. Heslop et al. (2002) found that a gradual supportive introduction to public transport increased the young people's confidence and flexibility. However, many of the parents were concerned about their child's ability to travel independently, or about their safety in doing so. The tension between parental over-protectiveness and the young person's need for self-determination was highlighted. Again, no precise key worker behaviors were specified.

King-Sears (2006) designed self-management instruction for middle-school students with different disabilities. However, no participant's self-management increased unless their teachers specifically followed up with them. Thus the importance of follow-up by adults was highlighted. Most relevantly, Hoggarth and Smith (2004) found that the effective behavioral features of interventions included:

- a trusting relationship between the young person and his/her key worker;
- commitment and flexibility from the key worker;
- maintaining frequent and regular contact;
- listening;
- responding accurately;
- realistic negotiating;
- delivering on promises;
- having available a range of intervention tools and strategies for referral;

- negotiating and advocating appropriately for opportunities and provision;
- accessing young people variously through drop-in surgeries, outreach, and voluntary and youth organizations; and
- joint partnership protocols and service agreements which were understood and valued by all involved.

However, some of these features are vague, and detail on how to establish these desiderata in practice was not given.

Thus there are difficulties with precise identification of the critical attributes of effective key worker practice in promoting independence, the extent to which these are measured by the observation instrument, and in the relationship between use of the interactive behaviors by transition personnel and greater independence by young adults with disabilities.

SCOTTISH CASE STUDY

The current study refers to an evaluation of a multiple-component program, but goes beyond this to investigate the use by professionals of specific behaviors likely to develop adaptive transferable skills, personal resilience and meta-transitional skills in young people—three of the six requisites for successful transition outlined previously by the authors. The research question was to what extent key workers reported that they used, and actually used during observation, interactive behaviors which seem likely to promote independence.

Methodology

The Intervention

The present study was of a single project based in a city in Eastern Scotland. The diverse Key Workers (KWs) in this project aimed to support the transition from school to employment, training, or college and independent living for exceptional and vulnerable young people (YPs) at risk of social exclusion. In line with the Beattie Committee report, they were expected to act as a readily available and central point for help and to guide the YPs through the complexities of contacts with many other agencies. The KWs were from various backgrounds (social work, community education, careers, higher education, and the voluntary sector). Movement from passive recipient to active learner was seen as crucial, hopefully resulting in independence, self-sufficiency, and employability. However, for the young people served by the project, these outcomes were difficult to achieve due to the complexity of their problems. They faced multiple barriers and often had more pressing needs to be addressed before any developments in employment, education or training could be made. These young people faced barriers such as being looked after or leaving care, homelessness, physical or learning disabilities, behavioral or emotional difficulties, mental health issues, addictions, offending, autistic spectrum disorders, and other learning difficulties.

As individuals move toward independence it should be possible to see a reduction in the amount of expert intervention, direction, and scaffolding, and an increase in the learner's discriminating and conditional use of skills and knowledge, coupled with enhanced self-awareness, self-efficacy, self-regulation, and resilience. These principles were intended to guide key worker behavior, and all KWs had received some training in their use.

Participant Sampling and Procedure

A total of approximately 800 YPs had been served to some degree by the project. They had been referred by other agencies, and many but not all were accepted. Their special needs or other issues were varied, and many experienced more than one problem. Their ages ranged from 15 to 24; the older ones having been involved with the project for some time. About 24 KWs had been involved. All project KWs not randomly selected to participate in a national evaluation were selected for this study (50% of the total)—consequently these participants were also random. This project focused upon all currently open cases. From these, the researchers randomly selected cases to make up the sample.

Data gathering methods chosen were:

(i)   KW Interview—a random sample of 12 from 24 KWs, each interviewed with regard to three specific YPs chosen at random from their caseload, known for 3–6 months, 6–12 months, and 12+ months respectively, and also interviewed about the typicality of those YPs;

(ii) KW/YP Observation—of interactions between the KW and the one specific YP known for 6–12 months (this period chosen as mid-point in the intervention and least susceptible to biasing factors). The observation instrument was based on the principles of the intervention as outlined in the guidance for KWs, and the behaviors reported to be used in the interviews with KWs, but its psychometric properties were unknown. Broader psychometric scales of independence are targeted on a normal population. Assessment of "independence" can be one feature of functional assessments of those with disabilities (e.g., Jeffree & Cheseldine, 1998). However, both of these describe the behavior of the client, not of the key worker; and

(iii) YP interview of the specific YP known for 6–12 months.

In every case the informed written consent of the KW and YP was obtained. The intention was to complete 12 KW interviews (each about three separate YP cases), 12 6–12 KW–YP interaction observations, and 12 6–12 YP interviews. The YP about whom the KWs were interviewed were to represent a cross section of engagement with YPs over time. Time did not allow for further KW/YP Observation or YP Interviews.

Ten different referral problems were identified, many YPs manifesting more than one, the most common being behavioral/emotional difficulties, learning difficulties, and mental health problems. Many had been in residential care ("looked after") during their adolescence, and some were homeless. For about half the YPs physical disability, autistic spectrum disorder, juvenile justice entanglements, or drug/alcohol problems were mentioned at referral.

Instrumentation and Time Sampling

Interview Schedules for both KWs and YPs and Observation Schedules for KW/YP interaction were developed and piloted by the researchers. This raises questions about reliability and validity, but no previously existing measures of known and adequate reliability and validity appeared to focus on the research questions for this study. The researchers drafted and piloted the KW interview schedule with two KWs not participating in the main study. These KWs also gave feedback on the draft YP interview schedule. The researchers also produced the KW/YP interaction observation schedule (Appendix Table 10.8). The observations were to take place in an informal natural setting, during a regular meeting between the KW and their client YP. In order to minimize contamination and interference, the observation was carried out first; then the client interview; and then the KW interview, all on the same day. The time window for completion of all this data-gathering was 2 months.

For the observations, the method of time sampling used was 5-second interval sampling, 2 minutes on 2 minutes off for first 16 minutes (50%), then 2 minutes on 6 minutes off (25%) for the remainder of interaction session. For each KW, the number of occurrences of each observed behavior was noted during the first time sampling period (agg1), the second time sampling period (agg2; where the observations continued into the second time sampling period, which they did not always do), and the total of both (aggtot; which of course should be interpreted with caution). To equalize the sampling frames, the observations from different periods were reduced to a base statistic of the mean number of occurrences per 2 minute sampling period. These means were calculated for period 1 (mean1), period 2 (mean2) and the whole observation period (meantot).

Results

The main focus of this chapter is the relationship between KW perceptions of their interactive behaviors and the observations of those behaviors, and this is reported in some detail. Other results which help to describe the context are reported in summary only. The interview data are the self-reported perceptions of participants, and as such are subjective. Many of the data are descriptive, but some inferential statistical analysis has been carried out. It was decided to utilize parametric statistical analysis for inferential comparisons, albeit with appropriate caution in subsequent interpretation. However, sample size renders further such analysis of limited value.

Interviews with Young People

Many of the young people could not or did not give elaborated responses in individual interview, but were generally very positive about the project, with virtually no complaints about their KWs. YPs were upbeat about developing and following action plans (more so than KWs—see next section)—70% of 6–12 month YPs reported that action plans were developed and followed. Similarly, all YPs reported that requested services were delivered, and 70% reported that these services were consistently effective (compared to 50% of KWs). All but one of the YPs felt more independent and active/initiating, and all reported improved or sustained self-confidence, self-esteem, and self-care skills. Seventy percent of YPs reported improved self-assessment skills and 50% improved planning skills. Regarding employability, YPs were again more optimistic than KWs (see following section). YPs identified exit strategies more frequently than KWs.

Interviews with Key Workers

KWs' original professional training, relevant prior field experience and host employing organizations were very diverse. KWs were predominantly full-time, with 2 years project experience, and female, while YPs were predominantly male. These gender biases might have affected interaction style. The considerable variation in active KW caseload size was statistically significant, averaging 27 YPs. On average, half the KW's time was spent with the YP, the rest divided between other agencies, administration and the YP's family (the last only 10%). Considerable variation was evident in the reported number of contacts per month with YPs, ranging from 1–30, average 4.5 (this was lower for 12+ month cases). The most frequent means of contact with YPs were face-to-face meetings, the second most frequent telephone. The reported length of KW contacts with YPs was very diverse (range 5–180 minutes, average 75 minutes). Face-to-face meetings with YPs were likely to be at the YP's home, in the community or at the KW's premises. Two-thirds of YPs had missed no contact appointments, irrespective of case engagement period. YPs with offending or drug/alcohol problems were particularly likely to fail contacts. KWs strongly endorsed the value of face-to-face meetings with YPs.

KWs perceived low social skills, lack of access to transport, limited family support, and low literacy and math skills as by far the most common barriers to YP progress. The percentage of action plans said to be followed averaged 75%; half of the KWs said all of their action plans were followed. There was a significant inverse correlation between failed contacts and the proportion of action plans followed. KWs expressed diverse views about the effectiveness of services delivered, but half (significant $p<0.001$) were of the opinion that most requested project services were delivered, accepted and effective. More than two-thirds of YPs were perceived by KWs to have developed or maintained adequate independence and active initiation, self-confidence, and self-esteem. Slightly less than two-thirds had developed or maintained adequate persistence and resilience, self-care skills and life/transferable skills. More than half had developed or maintained adequate self-organizational and self-planning skills. Slightly less than half had developed or maintained adequate self-assessment and self-evaluating skills.

However, KWs appeared to have no exit strategy in place for almost two-thirds of the YPs. No relationship between exit strategy and engagement period was evident. Exit strategies mentioned were extremely various, and quite frequently involved referral to yet another agency. Exit strategies seemed particularly uncommon with YPs with behavioral/emotional difficulties, learning disability/difficulties, or mental health challenges.

KW perceptions of personal skills and qualities important for their project work particularly included: awareness of resources/outside agencies/options, listening, disability awareness/knowledge, empathy, social skills, client-centeredness, and patience. KWs also reported their perceptions of the interactive behaviors they felt important for their project work, and their estimates of how frequently they used these behaviors. These covered a very wide range, but the most frequently named were: listening, questioning, empathy, and enthusiasm (see Table 10.1).

Interactive behaviors felt to have been most successful included: developing trust, listening, self-disclosure/humor/irony, enthusiasm/optimism/envisaging goal-state, and encouraging/confidence-building (see Table 10.2).

Observation of KW–YP Interactions

The perceptions of the KWs and the YPs as expressed in interviews were extremely valuable, but people embedded in situations are not always completely aware of the complexities of their interactive behavior. The observations were undertaken to offer some triangulation with the perceptions of the participants. However, the observational data were not necessarily any more "objective," since they were subject to different forms of bias. For instance, the presence of the observer might have affected the responses of both KW and YP, or the meetings might have been partially arranged to meet the purposes of the research and thereby not have been truly "naturalistic" or representative. Additionally, the presence of an observer might have constrained or inhibited the meeting into a form it might not otherwise

Table 10.1   KW Quantitative Perceptions of Interactive Behaviors Used

KW perceptions of interactions	Frequency no typicality
Listening	33
Questioning (closed, open?)	33
Verbal/visual/activity/other - balance	29
Use of self-disclosure, humor, irony, etc.	31
Empathy	33
Enthusiasm, optimism, envisage goal state	33
Calm / aroused balance?	27
Developing trust - how?	32
Caring / challenging balance?	28
Encourage client to think aloud/brainstorm	25
Eliciting client questions	27
Informing (too much?)	29.5
Explaining (simple, clear?)	32
Do you give examples to client?	32
Suggesting, Proposing	32
Agree/Disagree	31
Build on client proposals	32
Modeling	27.5
Scaffolding	30
Encouraging, Confidence-building (realistic?)	31
Praising (appropriate?)	32
Feedback - gentle, appropriate, friendly?	30
Negotiation, Compromise	31

Table 10.1   continued

KW perceptions of interactions	Frequency no typicality
Directing	28
Checking understanding	32
Problem defining	29
Resources/strengths/opportunities listing	28
Barriers/weakness/threats listing	23.5
Objective setting (agreed, verbal, written?)	32
Action planning (time scales) (agreed, verbal, written?)	26
Prediction/rehearsal	18.5
Review/monitor/evaluate action - debrief	27.5
Update action plan (agreed, verbal, written?)	20.5
Summarise progress & feedback (+/-)	27
Consider where else skills useful	25
Record progress (agreed, verbal, written?)	29.5

maximum frequency = 33 (each question asked of each KW about 3 of their clients)

have taken. Furthermore, relevant incidents might have occurred outside the time sampling frame. Time only allowed the direct observation of KW behavior for the 6–12 engagement period group. This might have affected the pattern of observations—for example, might trust-building already be complete by 6–12 months?

Another issue is the reliability of the observer. To explore this latter issue, inter-rater reliability was established on an additional meeting with an additional case which was not part of the main study (but conducted by a KW who was part of the main study). Inter-rater reliability could be established on only one case, as ethical concerns inhibited further intrusion into sensitive interactions between KWs and YPs who were unlikely to benefit from such data-gathering. The parallel rater was a researcher familiar with observation but not with the specific scale used here. During the reliability observation, 120 observations were identical between raters, while 18 were made by only one rater. The proportion of inter-rater agreement was thus 87%, adequate to assure confidence in the remainder of the observational data.

Table 10.2   KW Perceptions of Most Successful Behaviors Used

KW - most successful interactions	Frequency typicality	Frequency no typicality
Listening	22	18
Questioning (closed, open?)	5	5
Activity	2	1
Self-disclosure, humor, irony, etc..	20	14
Empathy	8	5
Enthusiasm, optimism, envisage goal state	17	13
Developing trust	25	19
Caring / challenging balance?	8	7
Informing	7	6
Explaining	7	6
Give examples to client	4	3
Suggesting, Proposing	4	4
Build on client proposals	6	3
Scaffolding	5	4
Encouraging, Confidence-building	16	12
Praising	6	4
Feedback	2	4
Negotiation, Compromise	8	19
Directing	4	4
Checking understanding	9	8
Resources/strengths/opportunities	5	4
Barriers/weakness/threats listing	2	3
Objective setting	2	1

Table 10.2 continued

KW - most successful interactions	Frequency typicality	Frequency no typicality
Action planning (time scales)	4	3
Prediction/rehearsal	1	1
Review/monitor/evaluate action - debrief	3	3
Update action plan	2	2
Summarize progress & feed back (+/-)	4	4
Consider where else skills useful	2	2
Record progress	2	2

The observations were particularly intended to explore the interactive behaviors used by KWs with YPs which seemed most successful, and which seemed most likely to promote the project objectives. However, no observational data were gathered on client response to KW behaviors, so there was no direct measure of impact of interactive behaviors. Even had such data been gathered, they would only be cross-sectional at one time and give no evidence of development, as well as being context-specific.

The observational data are summarized in Table 10.3, which gives (for each observed behavior with a substantial number of observations over all KWs) the aggregated frequency count over both observation periods (aggtot) and adjusted mean frequency count over both observation periods (meantot).

At first sight, there is evidence of a good deal of questioning, listening, information-giving, and explaining, coupled with a moderate amount of action planning and making suggestions. These were present across all KWs to some extent. Encouragement and praise were present but only in very modest quantity. Observations of other behaviors were few or zero. Considerable variation between KWs was evident, as the standard deviations in Table 10.3 demonstrate, even in the most frequently used behaviors. By way of example, details for each KW are given in Table 10.4 for the Listening behavior.

A large number of behaviors which might have been expected were observed very rarely or not at all: Verbal/visual/activity/other—balance; Empathy; Calm/aroused balance; Encourage client to think-aloud/brainstorm; Eliciting client questions; Examples given; Build on client proposals; Modeling; Scaffolding; Negotiation, Compromise; No utterances—period of silence; Problem defining; Resources/strengths/opportunities listing; Barriers/weaknesses/threats listing; Prediction/rehearsal; Review/monitor/

Table 10.3   Observed Interactive Behaviors

Behavior	Aggregate Frequency (aggtot)	s.d.	Adjusted Mean Frequency (meantot)	s.d.
Listening	321	26.15	63.72	4.01
Questioning	165	10.27	34.32	2.11
Self-disclosure, humor, irony, etc.	78	10.91	15.84	1.35
Enthusiasm, optimism, envisage goal state	9	1.10	2.17	0.32
Developing trust	30	6.75	11.25	3.14
Caring/challenging balance	12	2.10	1.75	0.27
Informing	118	6.76	28.71	1.93
Explaining	72	5.09	15.39	1.05
Suggesting, proposing	43	4.03	8.72	0.64
Agree/disagree	16	2.12	3.80	0.53
Encouraging, confidence-building	20	2.11	6.38	0.89
Praising	13	2.26	3.33	0.47
Feedback	9	1.37	2.05	0.35
Directing	9	1.37	2.83	0.46
Checking understanding	12	2.49	2.71	0.62
Small talk not for building trust	11	3.14	1.75	0.41
Objective settings	9	1.37	3.00	0.45
Action planning (with time scales)	25	3.66	4.38	0.53
Summarize progress & feed back (+/-)	8	1.62	2.30	0.53

n = 10 cases observed throughout
AF and AMF are frequencies; standard deviation of these frequencies given

Table 10.4   Observed Listening Behavior Across Key Workers

Keyworker	agg1	agg2	aggtot	mean1	mean2	meantot.
1	20	.	20	6.67	.	6.67
2	12	20	32	3.00	6.67	4.84
3	3	.	3	1.50	.	1.50
4	48	11	59	12.00	11.00	11.50
5	42	13	55	10.50	13.00	11.75
6	22	36	58	5.50	9.00	7.25
7	.	.	.	.	.	.
8	37	33	70	9.25	11.00	10.13
9	3	.	3	0.75	.	0.75
9	14	.	14	7.00	.	7.00
10	.	.	.	.	.	.
11	7	.	7	2.33	.	2.33

agg1 = aggregate observed frequency for observation period 1
agg2 = aggregate observed frequency for observation period 2
aggtot = aggregate observed frequency for total obervation period
mean1 = adjusted mean for observation period 1
mean2 = adjusted mean for observation period 2
meantot = adjusted mean for total obervation period

evaluate action—debrief; Update action plan; Consider where else skills useful; and Record progress.

Onward analysis compared KW reported interactions with observed interactions. As was evident from Table 10.1, most KWs reported they used virtually all the interactive behaviors. Substantial variation in reported interactive behaviors among KWs (at least 45% of KWs not reporting using) was noted only for: Brainstorming, Eliciting Questions, Barrier Listing, Action Planning, Prediction, Review, Update Action Plan, Consider Where Else Skills Useful. This contrasted with the observational data, which suggested a few behavior were used frequently, but most very rarely (although of course this could reflect sampling or other effects). KW reported frequencies of behaviors (excluding typicality) were compared with observed means and aggregates for both periods and in total, by behaviors (Table 10.5).

It is evident from Table 10.5 that even some behaviors that KWs identified as some of the most successful were actually observed to occur very little (e.g., Negotiating, Showing Enthusiasm, Encouraging), while others

Table 10.5 Comparison Between Reported and Observed Behaviors by Behavior

Behavior	cat	kwerp ac.	kwerp 6-12	mean1	mean2	mean tot	agg1	agg2	agg tot	most succ	succ 6-12
Listening	3	33.0	11.0	58.50	50.67	63.72	208	113	321	18	4
Question	3	33.0	11.0	37.92	12.25	34.32	131	34	165	5	1
Verbal/vi.	3	29.0	9.0	0	4.33	2.17	0	13	13	1	0
Self-disc	1	31.0	10.0	14.17	9.08	15.84	48	30	78	14	6
Empathy	1	33.0	11.0	0	0	0	0	0	0	5	1
Enthusias	2	33.0	11.0	2.50	0.33	2.17	8	1	9	13	6
Calm / ar	3	27.0	8.0	0	0	0	0	0	0	0	0
Deveopin	1	32.0	11.0	12.00	0.50	11.25	28	2	30	19	8
Caring /	5	28.0	11.0	2.83	0.33	1.75	11	1	12	7	2
Encourage	5	25.0	9.0	1.17	0	0.93	4	0	4	0	0
Eliciting	5	27.0	7.0	1.50	0	1.25	5	0	5	0	0
Informing	4	29.5	10.5	29.00	10.42	28.71	100	18	118	6	1
Explainin	4	32.0	11.0	17.50	3.50	15.39	62	10	72	6	1

Table 10.5 continued

Giving ex	4	32.0	11.0	0.83	0	0.59	3	0	3	3	1
Suggestin	4	32.0	11.0	8.17	6.33	8.72	29	14	43	4	0
Agree / Dis	4	31.0	11.0	3.25	3.33	3.80	12	4	16	0	0
Build on	5	32.0	11.0	0.33	1.00	0.83	1	1	2	3	1
Modeling	4	27.5	10.0	0	0	0	0	0	0	0	0
Scaffoldi	5	30.0	11.0	0	0	0	0	0	0	4	2
Encourag	2	31.0	11.0	6.25	1.00	6.38	17	3	20	12	5
Praising	2	32.0	11.0	3.33	1.00	3.33	10	3	13	4	2
Feedback	2	30.0	11.0	2.42	0	2.05	9	0	9	4	1
Negotiati	4	31.0	11.0	0.33	0	0.33	1	0	1	19	2
Directing	4	28.0	9.0	2.33	2.00	2.83	7	2	9	4	0
Checking	4	32.0	11.0	2.83	0.25	2.71	11	1	12	8	2
Problem d	5	29.0	11.0	0.58	0	0.58	2	0	2	0	0
Res / opps	5	28.0	10.0	0	0	0	0	0	0	4	1
Barriers	5	23.5	8.5	0	0	0	0	0	0	3	0

Continued

Table 10.5   continued

	cat	kwrepac	kwrep6-12	mean1	mean2	meantot	agg1	agg2	aggtot	mostsucc	succ6-12
Objective	5	32.0	11.0	3.00	0	3.00	9	0	9	1	1
Action pl	5	26.0	10.0	4.58	2.33	4.38	17	8	25	3	0
Predictio	5	18.5	8.5	0	0	0	0	0	0	1	0
Review/mo	5	27.5	10.0	0.75	1.00	0.88	3	3	6	3	0
Update ac	5	20.5	8.5	0	0	0	0	0	0	2	0
Summarize	5	27.0	11.0	2.42	0	2.30	8	0	8	4	1
Consider	2	25.0	9.0	0	0	0	0	0	0	2	0
Record pr	5	29.5	10.5	0	0	0	0	0	0	2	0
Small tal	5	.	.	2.25	0.75	1.75	8	3	11	.	.
No uttera	.	.	.	2.75	0.25	2.50	7	1	8	.	.

cat = category of behavior; discussed in more detail later
kwrepac = KW reported frequency for all cases
kwrep6–12 = KW reported frequency for 6–12 cases (arguably more comparable with the observational data, which were for 6–12 engagement period cases)
mean1 = adjusted mean for observation period 1
mean2 = adjusted mean for observation period 2
meantot = adjusted mean for total observation period
agg1 = aggregate observed frequency for observation period 1
agg2 = aggregate observed frequency for observation period 2
aggtot = aggregate observed frequency for total observation period
mostsucc = behaviors reported most successful by KWs for all cases
succ6–12 = behaviors reported most successful by KWs for 6–12 cases

Table 10.6 Interactive Behaviors Categorized by Type

INTERACTIONS CATEGORIZED

1 Building Trusts & Relationship

Developing trust—how?

Empathy?

Use of self-disclosure, humor, irony, etc.

2 Building Self-esteem / Self-confidence

Enthusiasm, optimism, envisage goal state

Encouraging, confidence-building (realistic?)

Summarize progress & feedback (+/-)

Feedback-gentle, appropriate, friendly?

Praising (appropriate)

3 Eliciting

Listening

Questioning (closed, open?)

Verbal/visual/activity/other-balance?

Calm/aroused balance?

4 Directing

Informing (too much?)

Explaining (simple, clear?)

Do you give examples to client?

Suggesting, proposing

Directing

Modeling

Checking understandings

Agree/disagree

Negotiation, compromise continued

Table 10.6   continued

INTERACTIONS CATEGORIZED
5   Building Active Independence

Eliciting client questions

Encouraging client to think aloud/brainstorm

Scaffolding

Build on client proposals

Caring/challenging balance?

Problem defining

Objective setting (agreed, verbal, written?)

Resources/strengths/opportunities listings

Barriers/weaknesses/threats listings

Action planning (time scales) (agreed, verbal, written?)

Prediction/rehearsals

Review/monitor/evaluate action-debrief

Update action plan (agreed, verbal, written?)

Consider where else skills useful

Record progress (agreed, verbal, written?)

were not observed as frequently as might be expected (e.g., Developing Trust, Self-disclosure). Correlation analysis between reported and observed behavior by behavior in 6–12 cases was carried out. There were no statistically significant correlations.

The project aim was movement from passive recipient to active learner, resulting in independence, self-sufficiency, and employability. To what extent did KWs report that they used, and actually used during observation, interactive behaviors which seem theoretically likely to promote these objectives? To pursue this question, the interactive behaviors were divided into five categories (see Table 10.6).

As individuals move toward independence, theoretically it should be possible to see a reduction in the amount of KW interactive behavior in

Table 10.7   Observed Frequencies of Independence Promoting Behaviors

Independence Promoting Behavior	Observed Frequency
Scaffolding	0
Resources/strengths/threats listing	0
Barriers/weaknesses/threats listing	0
Prediction/rehearsal	0
Update action plan	0
Consider where else skills useful	0
Record progress	2
Build on client proposals	2
Problem defining	4
Encouraging client to think aloud/brainstorm	5
Eliciting client questions	6
Review/monitor/evaluate action-debrief	9
Caring/challenging balance	12
Action planning	25

subcategories 1 and 4 (Building Trust and Directing; and maybe 3—Eliciting), and an increase in behavior in subcategory 5 (Building Active Independence). Correlations between reported interactive behaviors and observed interactive behaviors within the five categories of behavior were computed (in each category separately). The only statistically significant correlations found were for directing behaviors (subcategory 4), but these were negative, that is, there was an inverse relationship between what the KWs perceived they did and what they had been observed to do. Some category 5 (Building Active Independence) behaviors were used, others not at all. Table 10.7 shows the overall Observed Frequencies of Independence Promoting Behaviors.

Further analysis then explored variation across KWs in the reported use of behaviors within the categories. The statistical significance of any variation was calculated using the chi-square test. No significant differences were found for any category (values of chi-square were quite high, but n was small, and the amount of data in frequency tables small).

CONCLUSION

An evaluation was conducted of a project which deployed key workers (KWs) to support the post-school transition of exceptional and vulnerable young people (YPs) at risk of social exclusion, seeking to enhance independence, self-sufficiency, and employability. KWs and client YPs were interviewed, and KWs were observed in interaction with client YPs. The project was generally reported to be highly valued by the YPs who were the primary clients. All reported improved or sustained self-confidence, self-esteem, and self-care skills, and almost all reported feeling more independent and initiating. The KWs delivering the service also perceived and reported generally effective service delivery and wide-ranging improvements in the functioning of their clients. The overall picture was of an effective and worthwhile project. Most KWs reported they used a wide range of interactive behaviors with YPs. However, the correlation between KW perceptions and the observations of behaviors used was weak. Observation suggested a few behaviors were used frequently, but most very rarely. Specifically, no significant positive correlations between reported and observed Building Active Independence behaviors were evident, and actually observed Building Active Independence behaviors were very few.

IMPLICATIONS FOR FUTURE RESEARCH,
POLICY AND PRACTICE

The subjective perceptions of stakeholder participants do not provide the strongest outcome data. Future research should seek evidence of more tangible outcomes (e.g., employment successfully sustained, college awards achieved, measurable improvements in literacy or math skills), in research designs which more effectively control so far as possible for the effects of spontaneous maturation and interventions from other agencies, among other factors. Additional measures of "soft" outcomes such as self-esteem and transferable social/communication skills might also be employed, triangulated among a wider range of relevant client contacts. In this study, the real costs of providing project services were not known—future studies should also assay cost-effectiveness.

The implication of the positive evaluation findings would appear to be that such projects are worth extending and replicating. However, some areas for improvement were identified, which might be relevant to the current project KWs, new generations of KWs, or new projects on the same key working model (that is, supporting transitions by enhancing independence, self-sufficiency, and employability) starting elsewhere. KW perceptions of interactive behaviors used diverged considerably from behaviors actually observed in use. This is not to suggest that the KWs did not possess a wide repertoire of relevant behaviors, merely that it might be beguilingly easy to assume that the full range of such behaviors are therefore necessarily actually used. A clearer specification of relevant behaviors (informed by this study) might provide a clearer framework for reflection and self-assessment by KWs. Indeed, KWs might choose to video record interactive sessions (with client permission, of course) and subsequently analyze and reflect upon the interactions in the light of such a framework. This is not of course to suggest that all YPs would benefit from the same interactive style, or that all KWs should interact in the same way. Different interactive styles are likely to be differentially effective at different points of the casework engagement period.

The current study has implications for the content of pre-service training and continuing professional development; training, self-assessment and peer assessment in the active use of a wide range of interactive behaviors; and casework management and recording protocols. Specifically, Building Active Independence behaviors should be emphasized, and built into casework management.

This research was funded by Careers Scotland. The basis for this chapter is a paper which appeared in the Journal of Research in Special Educational Needs, 8(2), 57–67. The editor and publishers of this journal are thanked for allowing it to be used here.

REFERENCES

Ackerman, B. (2006). Learning self-determination: Lessons from the literature for work with children and youth with emotional and behavioral disabilities. *Child and Youth Care Forum, 35*(4), 327–337.

Berthoud, R. (2003). *Multiple disadvantage in employment: A quantitative analysis.* York: Joseph Rowntree Foundation. Retrieved December 1, 2006, from www.jrf.org.uk.

Brown, D., Clopton, C., & Tusler, A. (1991). Access in education: Assisting students from dependence to independence. *Journal of Postsecondary Education and Disability, 9*(3), 264–268.

Carter, E. W., Lane, K. L., Pierson, M. R., & Glaeser, B. (2006). Self-determination skills and opportunities of transition-age youth with emotional disturbance and learning disabilities. *Exceptional Children, 72*(3), 333–346.

Furlong, A., Cartmel, F., Biggart, A., Sweeting, H., & West, P. (2003). *Youth transitions: Patterns of vulnerability and processes of social inclusion.* Edinburgh: Scottish Executive. Retrieved December 1, 2006, from www.scotland.gov.uk/socialresearch.

Gilligan, R. (2000). Adversity, resilience and young people: The protective value of positive school and spare time experiences. *Children and Society, 14,* 37–47.

Healy, H., & Rigby, P. (1999). Promoting independence for teens and young adults with physical disabilities. *Canadian Journal of Occupational Therapy, 66*(5), 240–249.

Her Majesty's Stationery Office. (2004). *Education (Additional Support for Learning) (Scotland) Act 2004.* Edinburgh: HMSO.

Heslop, P., Mallett, R., Simons, K., & Ward, L. (2002). *Bridging the divide at transition: What happens for young people with learning difficulties and their families?* Kidderminster: British Institute of Learning Disabilities Publications.

Hoggarth, L., & Smith, D. (2004). *Understanding the impact of connexions on young people at risk*. London: Department for Education and Skills. Retrieved December 1, 2006, from www.dfes.gov.uk/research/data/uploadfiles/RR607.pdf.

Jeffree, D. M., & Cheseldine, S. (1998). *Pathways to independence, 2nd edition*. London: Hodder & Stoughton Educational.

King-Sears, M. E. (2006). Self-management for students with disabilities: The importance of teacher follow-up. *International Journal of Special Education, 21*(2), 94–108.

Lent, R. W., Hackett, G., & Brown, S. D. (1999). A social cognitive view of school-to-work transition. *Career Development Quarterly, 47,* 297–311.

Raffe, D., Brannen, K., & Croxford, L. (2001). The transition from school to work in the early 1990s: A comparison of England, Wales and Scotland. *Journal of Education and Work, 14*(3), 293–313.

Riffel, L. A., Wehmeyer, M. L., Turnbull, A. P., Lattimore, J., Davies, D., Stock, S., et al. (2005). Promoting independent performance of transition-related tasks using a palmtop PC-based self-directed visual and auditory prompting system. *Journal of Special Education Technology, 20*(2), 5–14.

Scottish Executive. (1999). *Implementing inclusiveness realising potential. The Beattie Committee Report*. Retrieved March 1, 2009, from *http://www.scotland.gov.uk/library2/doc04/bere-00.htm*.

Smokowski, P. R. (1998). Prevention and intervention strategies for promoting resilience in disadvantaged children. *Social Service Review, 72*(3), 337–364.

Ward, L., Mallett, R., Heslop, P., & Simons, K. (2003). Transition planning: How well does it work for young people with learning disabilities and their families? *British Journal of Special Education, 30*(3), 132–137.

Appendix Table 10.8   Observation Schedule

Listening									
Questioning (closed, open?)									
Verbal/visual/activity/other-balance									
Use of self-disclosure, humor, irony, etc.									
Empathy?									
Enthusiasm, optimism, envisage goal state									
Calm/aroused balance?									
Developing trust-how?									
Caring/challenging balance?									
Encourage client to think-aloud/brainstorm									
Eliciting client question									
Informing (too much?)									

Appendix 10.8   continued

Explaining (simple, clear)									
Examples given?									
Suggesting, Proposing									
Agree/Disagree									
Build on client proposals									
Modeling									
Scaffolding (define) (too much?)									
Encouraging, Confidence-building (realistic?)									
Praising (appropritae?)									
Feedback-gentle, appropriate, friendly?									
Negotiation, Compromise									
Directing									
Checking understanding									
Small talk not for building trust									
No utterances									
Problem defining									
Resources/strengths/opportunities list									
Barriers/weaknesses/threats list									
Objective setting									
Action planning (with time scales)									
Prediction/rehearsal									
Review/monitor/evaluate action-debrief									
Update action plan									
Summarize progress & feed back (+/-)									
Consider where else skills useful									
Record progress									

11 Cultural and Educational Adaptation During Transition From Chinese to UK Universities

Yuefang Zhou, John Todman, Keith J. Topping, and Divya Jindal-Snape

CHINESE STUDENTS IN THE UK

It was estimated by the UK Council for International Student Affairs (UKCISA, n.d.) that in 2006–2007 almost 50,000 Chinese students were studying in the UK for a higher education (HE) award, the majority of whom were postgraduates. It is estimated that a substantial number of these Chinese postgraduate students were studying under the Sino–UK collaborative programs, involving formal links between UK and Chinese HE institutions. It is plausible that the experience of these students coming to study in a UK university from a UK partner university in China might well be different from those who come to the UK individually. One possible reason would be that they are usually better prepared in terms of having participated in adaptation programs prior to their arrival in the UK. It is also possible that students coming in large groups will exert some influence on teaching and learning, and raise the issue of whether UK tutors (and those in other host countries) will have to adapt more to the Chinese students. It is, therefore, timely to research the adaptation experience of Chinese postgraduate students coming to the UK, not only for the purpose of smoothing their transitional period and improving academic outcomes, but also for the purpose of encouraging UK and other host country staff to think about whether and how they also may need to adapt (Chalmers & Volet, 1997; Zhou, 2006; Zhou & Todman, 2008).

STUDIES ON INTERNATIONAL STUDENTS' ADAPTATION

In the area of international students' adaptation, a distinction has generally been made in the literature between psychological, sociocultural, and educational adaptation, and studies in these three areas have mostly been pursued separately. We suggest that a good strategy for understanding the adaptation experiences of international students is to explore their pre-departure expectations and subsequent experiences in these three areas holistically over a period of time. This would enable adaptation differences between students studying abroad in groups and those travelling individually to be investigated simultaneously across the three areas.

Two main strands of longitudinal investigation of student sojourners can be identified: predictive studies and monitoring studies. Predictive studies have found that pre-departure language competence is a strong predictor for all three (psychological, sociocultural, and educational) aspects of adaptation (e.g., Andrade, 2006; Yeh & Inose, 2003). For specifically educational (academic) post-arrival performance, motivation, and pre-departure expectations are among the other important predictor variables (e.g., Kennedy, 1999). Regarding changing patterns of adaptation, the general trend is that both psychological and sociocultural adaptation problems appear to be greatest in the early stages of transition and decrease over time (Ward & Kennedy, 1996). However, there seems little in the literature to suggest reliable patterns in students' educational adaptation, and longitudinal studies to investigate the process of educational adaptation of student sojourners seem urgent. In view of the large groups of Chinese students studying abroad under educational cooperation programs, it seems also important to investigate the extent to which the adaptation experiences of such students differ from those of students travelling individually.

Educational Adaptation and Mismatched Expectations

Although studies in the pattern of educational adaptation of international students are sparse, there are some studies that suggest that problems relating to intercultural classrooms are mainly due to mismatched cross-cultural educational expectations (e.g., Jin & Cortazzi, 1998; Jin & Cortazzi, 2006; Jin & Hill, 2001). As an example, independence of mind and critical evaluation are highly encouraged in UK education, but an assumed acceptance of authority is common in the Chinese educational tradition. These mismatched expectations are likely to result in dissatisfying and unpleasant classroom encounters (Ward, Bochner, & Furnham, 2001). Some recent research has pursued the problem of resolving mismatched expectations within a *cultural synergy* approach (to be discussed later). It remains necessary, however, to explore whether and how promoting shared perceptions relating to student problems may actually help smooth the adaptation process.

Cultural Synergy and Reciprocal Adaptation

Cortazzi and Jin's (1997, p. 88) discussion of "communication for learning across cultures" laid the ground for their proposal for a process of *cultural synergy* (Cortazzi & Jin, 1997; Cortazzi & Jin, 2002; Jin & Cortazzi, 1998), which is understood to require mutual efforts from both (UK) teachers and (Chinese) students to understand each other's culture and learn from each other, rather than simply expecting Chinese students to assimilate UK ways. In its concern with the acquisition of social and behavioral skills that differ among cultures (Ward et al., 2001), this view of two-way learning reflects the core theme of recent developments in the theory of culture learning.

Current views of culture learning imply a two-way reciprocal adaptation that stresses the mutual acquisition of social and behavioural skills by individuals from different cultures. In its attempt to go beyond mutual efforts to understand one another's cultures, to include necessary mutual behavioral adaptations that follow from the cross-cultural understandings, it may be viewed as an extension of the cultural synergy process. Since the idea of cultural synergy was advanced, much has changed in the intervening years in terms of increased intercultural awareness and readiness for accommodation from both teachers and students. It is, therefore, important to investigate whether and to what extent both parties have adjusted, and continue to adjust their teaching and learning strategies in pursuit of more satisfactory academic outcomes (Cadman, 2000).

In this chapter, we are presenting findings from a study conducted by Zhou (2006) to investigate these issues. The main research questions addressed in this study were as follows:

- What is the nature of Chinese students' psychological, sociocultural, and educational aspects of adaptation and how do patterns of adaptation within these three areas differ?
- How does the adaptation of Chinese students to UK styles of teaching and learning differ between those coming in groups and those coming individually?
- What is the effect on adaptation of student–teacher shared perceptions of students' problems?
- How far is adaptation a two-way reciprocal process in which both students and teachers adapt to one another?

METHOD

Participants

Student participants

These were 257 Chinese postgraduate students enrolled in masters courses at two Scottish Universities (names changed to University A and B), who completed one or more stages of a three-stage longitudinal questionnaire over a period of two years. They included students from two Chinese Universities (Wanli and Nanchang), the majority of whom came in groups under China–UK educational cooperation programs to study in the UK. The remainder came from a wide range of Chinese universities and travelled individually to study in a wide range of disciplines at the two UK universities. Participants were recruited either in China before departure for the UK (Stage I), soon after arrival in the UK (Stage II) or after being in the UK for about 6 months (Stage III). The students who came in groups from Nanchang came to study either Information Technology or Software Engineering at University A and those who came in groups from Wanli all came to study English for Professional Development at University B. Forty five of the students who came to the UK in groups under China–UK cooperation programs completed all three stages of the questionnaire. Other participants completed one or two stages according to availability.

Of the 45 students who came in groups and completed all three stages, 28 were further interviewed and 26 of those interviewed participated in focus group discussions. The questionnaire responses of 18 students who completed the Stage III questionnaire were matched with the responses of staff to an equivalent questionnaire component administered during a semi-structured interview. The staff responses were in reference to individual students for whom the staff member had educational responsibilities, such as teaching or supervision.

Staff participants

These were 26 staff members from the two universities who participated in a semi-structured interview with a questionnaire component. In addition to the 18 matched staff who responded with respect to individual students known to them, another 8 staff responded with respect to Chinese post-graduate students in general.

Instruments

Student questionnaire

Questionnaires, with items presented in both English and Chinese, were constructed for each of the three stages. The Stage I questionnaire included a question (Item 2) about difficulties anticipated when coming to the UK to study. This requested students to put ticks against all in a list of nine anticipated difficulties that applied to them. The list of difficulties, such as language problems, financial problems, difficulties in understanding lectures, and finding friends, was based on an examination of the literature. The Stage I questionnaire also included nine statements about aspects of differences between teaching and learning traditions and practices in China and the UK, such as: "Classroom discussion and debate are less encouraged in China than in UK universities." For the nine items (3–11) concerning differences between China/UK teaching and learning, responses were requested on a 6-point Likert scale ranging from 1 (*totally disagree*) to 6 (*totally agree*). Stage II and Stage III questionnaires were identical to the Stage I questionnaire except for necessary changes in tense.

Student interviews

A semi-structured interview schedule was developed to probe more deeply into students' positive and negative pre-departure expectations and post-arrival experiences in relation to general life, social life, and study life. Negative perceptions were explored both as difficulties anticipated and difficulties experienced.

Student focus group discussions

Four focus group discussions involving students who had been interviewed were conducted to get a more in-depth understanding of the participants' perspectives on the interview issues. This was done in order to take advantage of the greater depth of understanding that is assumed to emerge from the dynamics of the group interactions. Three of the discussion points in the discussion guideline were relevant to the issues addressed in this chapter. The first point began with a general discussion of culture shock, and invited examples from students' stay in the UK. The second was about their learning experiences in the UK and examples of educational adaptation stories. The third probed more deeply into similarities and differences in educational adaptation stories and coping strategies.

Staff interviews

Staff interviews were designed to elicit staff views on students' adaptation and their own adaptation to students. The interview schedule was semi-structured and included both quantitative and qualitative components. The quantitative component matched the Likert-type items on the student questionnaire, with staff being asked to indicate the extent of their agreement/disagreement with the nine statements. The qualitative component included the first two open-ended questions, which explored students' motivations and difficulties when studying in the UK, and elaborations on staff responses to the quantitative items.

Procedures

The procedures, which were part of a larger study, are described in detail in Zhou (2006).

Administrating the student questionnaire

The three-stage administration of the questionnaire took place over a period of 2 years as new students arrived or as contact was made with students who had been in the UK for some months. Forty five students completed questionnaires at all three stages. The remainder completed questionnaires at Stages II and/or III only.

Conducting student interviews

Among the students who completed a questionnaire at all three stages, those who agreed to participate in a follow-up interview were contacted by e-mail and a time and location was agreed. Interviews, each lasting about one hour, were conducted in Chinese by the first author. Within a broad interview schedule, considerable scope was allowed for participants to pursue themes of interest to themselves. In order to encourage openness, the interviews were not recorded. Notes were taken in Chinese during the interviews and were written up in English immediately afterwards.

Holding focus group discussions

Four focus group discussions were facilitated by the first author using the discussion points in the guideline and each session lasted about 45 minutes. The first author not only organized the process of the discussion, but also participated in it. This was because of evidence that when the facilitator shares some life experiences with the participants, in this case being an international student herself, the discussion is made more open when the facilitator actively participates (De Andrade, 2000). Discussions, which were in Chinese to encourage openness, were audio recorded, transcribed, and translated into English for data analysis.

Conducting staff interviews

Staff participants were shown the interview schedule ahead of time, so they were generally well prepared to respond to the questions. Each interview was audio recorded and notes of key points were taken during the interviews. With the help of the written notes, the audio recordings were transcribed as soon as possible after each interview.

Data Analysis

Quantitative questionnaire responses

Responses to Item 2 in student questionnaire were recorded as frequencies of each of the nine difficulties reported. Responses to Items 3 to 11 were recorded as degree of agreement ranging from 1 (*totally disagree*) to 6 (*totally agree*) with the statements describing differences between Chinese and UK teaching and learning traditions and practices. Scores on the 6-point agree/disagree scale were assigned to both students and matched staff. Mean scores were calculated for the three groups who responded to the nine questionnaire items. The groups were (a) staff discussing individual Chinese students; (b) the students under discussion (matched with staff); and (c) staff discussing Chinese students in general. Differences between staff and student pairs, and between the two staff groups, were tested and the correlation between paired staff and student responses was obtained.

Student interviews

The content of each interview was coded by the interviewer within categories and subcategories, following the development of a start-list of codes as described by Miles and Huberman (1994). Inter- and intra-coder reliabilities were checked and reached a satisfactory level (over 90%) according to Miles and Huberman's (1994) criteria, and a content analysis (for details see Zhou, 2006) was carried out. The two steps that are relevant to this account were: (a) counting the frequency of each code and; (b) comparing the frequencies between different categories (such as negative perceptions in relation to study life before departure and after arrival).

Focus group discussions

Some preliminary findings generated from student interviews as part of the larger study (Zhou, 2006) were used to provide a framework for the analysis of student focus group discussions. As part of the process of clustering and triangulation (Miles & Huberman, 1994), the focus group results were compared with the results from the student interviews, and the results from the staff interviews were subsequently compared with the results of the student interviews and the focus group/interview comparisons (for details, see Zhou, 2006).

Staff qualitative interview responses

Staff qualitative data included elaborations on the nine items that matched student questionnaire items and the first two open-ended questions regarding students' motivation and difficulties. As in the analysis of the focus group data, contents of the open-ended staff responses were clustered by topics, and characteristics of clusters were summarized, including some frequencies.

RESULTS

Student Questionnaire

Item 2: difficulties

The questionnaire data on expected and experienced difficulties at the three stages were analyzed separately for two groups of participants: students in groups completing all three stages of the questionnaire (Group G, $n = 45$) and students coming individually who completed the questionnaire at one or more stages (Group I, Stage I: $n = 46$; Stage II: $n = 18$; Stage III: $n = 46$).

So, some of the students in Group I were included in a comparison at only one stage, others were included in comparisons at two stages, but none were included at all three stages. For each of the three stages and for each of the nine difficulties listed in Item 2, the number of participants in the two groups who ticked that difficulty as applying to them was compared. In each case, the difference between groups in frequency of a perceived difficulty was evaluated using the Chi-Square test (for details, see Zhou & Todman, 2009).

There were two main findings. First, shortly after their arrival (Stage II), Group G was significantly ($p < .001$) more concerned about regional accents than Group I. Second, with regard to academic concerns, (reading and understanding lectures), Group G was more concerned ($p < .001$ and $p < .005$) at Stage I, and Group I was more concerned ($p < .05$ and $p < .01$) at Stage II.

As the size and composition of Group G did not change from stage to stage, it was possible to carry out a McNemar test of differences between any two stages (for details, see Zhou & Todman, in press). With regard to both of these potential difficulties concerning academic reading and

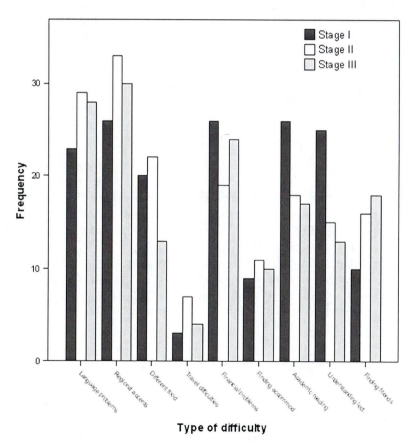

Type of difficulty

Figure 11.1   Frequency of perceived difficulties listed in questionnaire Item 2 for Group G (45 students coming in groups) over three stages.

understanding lectures, students in Group G were more worried about them (*ps* < .01) before leaving China (Stage I) than soon after arrival in the UK (Stage II). Figure 11.1 shows the changes in frequency of perceived difficulties for Group G over three stages.

Items 3 to 11: perceived differences between
Chinese and UK teaching and learning

A principal components factor analysis was carried out to extract factors from the nine questionnaire items. No consistently interpretable factors emerged following varimax rotation to simple structure. Reliability of a single scale comprising all nine items was then computed using Cronbach's coefficient alpha ($\alpha = 0.74$) for the group of 45 students who completed all three questionnaires.

A repeated measures ANOVA, followed by post hoc *t*-tests, was used to evaluate longitudinal effects using the data from the 45 students. The ANOVA revealed a significant difference among the three stages, $F(2,88) = 3.85$, $p < 0.05$. Follow-up *t*-tests suggested that only the difference between Stage I (in China: $M = 4.70$, $SD = 0.53$) and Stage II (soon after arrival: $M = 4.46$, $SD = 0.49$) was significant: $t (44) = 2.50$, $p < 0.05$. This suggests that students perceived fewer differences after arrival than they had expected, and that their immediate post-arrival perceptions did not undergo further change during the following 6 months.

Student and Staff Responses to the Quantitative Questionnaire Scale

For the matched pairs of students and staff talking about their own individual students, the mean scores on the nine quantitative items of the questionnaire were staff: $M = 4.38$ ($SD = 0.87$) and students: $M = 4.79$ ($SD = 0.63$). The difference between these means, which suggested that students may have expected greater China/UK differences than their tutors predicted was, however, not significant, $t(df = 17) = 1.70$, $p > .05$. The difference between the means of staff focusing on an individual student; $M = 4.38$ ($SD = 0.87$); and those focusing on Chinese students in general; $M = 4.99$ ($SD = 0.69$) was not significant either, $t(df = 24) = 1.64$, $p > .05$. In addition, the correlation between the views of the 18 matched students and staff was low and non-significant, $r(N = 18) = .11$, $p > .05$.

Student interviews

Data from the student interviews were recorded in the form of number of references made to positive and negative aspects of pre-departure expectations and post-arrival experiences in relation to general life, social life, and study life. Table 11.1 summarizes the findings for the differences in pre/post perceptions and positive/negative perceptions.

As can be seen in Table 11.1, in all domains (general, social, and study life), there tended to be more negative post-arrival experiences than pre-departure negative expectations ($p < 0.001$). Positive perceptions were more mixed and less statistically convincing. Positive perceptions regarding general life did not change significantly, whereas positive perceptions decreased after arrival with respect to social life ($p < 0.05$) and increased after arrival with respect to study life ($p < 0.01$). With regard to differences in the number of positive and negative perceptions, after arrival in the UK there were significantly more negative than positive perceptions in all domains (general life, $p < 0.001$; social life, $p < 0.001$; study life, $p < 0.05$). Before departure from China, however, there was only one significant difference, that being a greater number of positive than negative perceptions in the study domain ($p < 0.01$).

Student Focus Group Discussions

Manner of coming to the UK

It was confirmed from the focus group discussions that whether students came in groups or came individually would have different impacts on both students' adaptation and UK staff responses in dealing with such students. Table 11.2 summarizes the pros and cons of the manner of coming on students' adaptation.

The results suggested that students in the more protected environment that existed when they came in groups were more likely to adapt quickly and enjoyably to the new learning environment. A typical comment from a student who came in a group was:

> I understood that most of the teachers in my course are selected. They have very good experience of dealing with us Chinese students. They know our problems better than teachers in some other departments.

Other students in the same group continued on that topic.

> My supervisor has been working in China for six years and he can even speak Chinese. I have noticed that the teachers deliberately slowed down when they spoke English and they encouraged us to speak English in group discussions. I doubt that Chinese students who come individually will be so lucky to have this special treatment.

However, discussants also suggested that coming as groups of Chinese students and helping each other to deal with study problems was not necessarily seen as a positive impact on students; it was, in fact, sometimes seen more as an implicit negative impact, via the effect on the UK teachers, in that they may have remained unaware of their students' problems. One negative view about coming in groups was expressed as follows:

Table 11.1   Wilcoxon Tests of Differences Between Positive and Negative Aspects of Perceptions and Between Pre- and Post-Arrival Expectations and Experiences in Relation to General Life, Social Life and Study Life

Domain	Alternatives	Results of Wilcoxon test
Pre-departure vs. post-arrival perceptions		
General life	Positive perceptions	$T = 102, N = 20, p > .05$
	Negative perceptions	(post>pre) $T = 35.5, N = 26, p < .001$
Social life	Positive perceptions	(post>pre) $T = 3, N = 8, p < .05$
	Negative perceptions	(post>pre) $T = 11, N = 20, p < .001$
Study life	Positive perceptions	(post>pre) $T = 30, N = 19, p < .01$
	Negative perceptions	(post>pre) $T = 6, N = 25, p < .001$
Positive vs. negative perceptions		
General life	Pre-departure	$T = 52, N = 18, p > .05$
	Post-arrival	(neg>pos) $T = 23, N = 21, p < .001$
Social life	Pre-departure	$T = 17.5, N = 11, p > .05$
	Post-arrival	(neg>pos) $T = 0, N = 18, p < .001$
Study life	Pre-departure	(pos>neg) $T = 27, N = 17, p < .01$
	Post-arrival	(neg>pos) $T = 78.5, N = 24, p < .05$

I don't think coming individually is too bad. One of my friends in China is a boy. He was very lazy in his studies and my English and some other performances were much better than his when we were in China. Now, after nearly one year of studying in the UK, I am so envious of his excellent English. I am also surprised that his ability to deal with some other study problems is so good. I came with groups of Chinese students and he was one of the few Chinese students in the 'name' Department.

Nonetheless, in terms of the overall impact of the manner of coming on UK staff, it was confirmed that UK teachers did make some adjustments to accommodate these students, especially when they comprised a big group of Chinese students on the course. There were two reasons for UK staff adjustments in their teaching and support strategies that emerged in the discussions. First, they were responding to the university's mission to provide better services to "customers," as Chinese students now form a large

Table 11.2   Focus Group Pros and Cons of Students Coming in Groups or Individually

	Coming in groups	Coming individually
Pros	• Help each other within groups • UK teachers take special care • Initial adaptation likely to be smoother	• Learn English more quickly • Learn about a different culture
Cons	• Prone to speak Chinese and practice less in English • Fewer chances to learn about a different culture	• Initial adaptation likely to be more difficult

proportion of international students in UK universities in general. Second, they were attempting to meet the challenge of improving teaching quality and learning outcomes, for example, by selection of experienced teaching staff. Chinese students' views were mixed with respect to how they responded to these UK staff efforts to help Chinese students aid their transition. Students appreciated the efforts that UK staff made in order to help them adapt; however, they were generally dissatisfied with the quality of the support, especially in terms of its effectiveness. As several participants expressed in a focus group discussion:

> We know that the university has been trying to be good to us. We have regular meetings with teachers every term organized by the university. I am the student representative. I gathered views from my classmates and reported the problems at the meetings. The last meeting was several months ago. Many students complained that we had too many classes every week and we couldn't get enough supervision. I reported and we didn't hear anything from them so far. Finally we asked. We were told that they were concerned about our problems and were working to improve the situation. But it was not going to be us who would benefit from any improvements; it would be the new students who would be the real beneficiaries.

> It is not very reasonable, is it? We hope we can benefit from the improvements.

> We appreciate what they did for us. You know, our teachers are good to us and they are ready to help. But they actually don't know very well about our problems. We usually turn back to our classmates to solve some problems.

> . . . I suppose the teachers don't see many of our problems because we have dealt with most of them already within our groups.

Mismatch of course design and recruitment

Another new topic that emerged from focus group discussions was that students commonly complained that the university lacked serious consideration of the match between some aspects of the course design and students' educational background. For example, illustrations drawn from European countries were not considered very relevant to the Chinese students' experience and knowledge background.

Staff Interviews

UK staff adaptation to Chinese students

The staff interviews confirmed that UK staff were affected by and responded to teaching Chinese students. Most of the UK staff adjusted their teaching strategies in response to Chinese students both at an individual level and at the departmental and university levels, as one staff interviewee said:

> *I did pay special attention to my teaching. I use less jargon and I slow down my English. I am very careful to get myself involved in their group discussion in order to help them. You know, sometimes it is hopeless; they all speak Chinese in their groups.*

A different view also emerged from staff data, to the effect that UK universities should be careful about how much adjustment should be made for Chinese students. For example, a lecturer in Applied Computing strongly advocated that some core issues in UK teaching and learning should not be flexible for anyone:

> *I agree that UK tutors and supervisors should be aware of the culture difference when teaching Chinese students and in some sense we need to adjust our teaching strategies to achieve better academic outcomes. However, UK tutors and supervisors should always stick to the rules and regulations about some core issues in teaching and learning, such as in dealing with the issue of plagiarism.*

Mismatch of course design and recruitment

The finding from students' focus group discussions that the UK universities lacked serious consideration of the suitability of some courses for Chinese students was confirmed from staff interviews. As one of the lecturers in English for Professional Development said:

> *Chinese students on the course have some problems that are related to the course design. They are required to relate what they have learned to*

their working context. It is very hard for them as they don't have any working experiences. I think on the whole the University has picked up the wrong modules for them.

Tailor-made programs

A new theme that emerged in the staff interviews was the issue of whether UK-based masters degrees or tailor-made programs would be more appropriate for collaborative programs involving Chinese students. It was admitted that both Chinese students and UK staff were struggling to deal with the mismatch of educational expectations. A lecturer in information technology described the issue in the following terms:

The Masters degree . . . requires independent thinking, problem-solving and analytical skills. The current module does not build in enough time to train them (Chinese students). There is also a vacuum of context here. The organizations and businesses we talked about are western companies and British organizations, which they don't have a lot of knowledge about. They have a lot of knowledge about the organizations in China, which we don't know about. From the UK university point of view, we need to decide what the final product is that we are going to sell to Chinese students. Is it a UK-based Masters degree or a special programme tailored to Chinese students?

DISCUSSION

The results are discussed in relation to the four research questions that were posed in this study.

- What is the nature of Chinese students' psychological, sociocultural, and educational aspects of adaptation and how do patterns of adaptation within these three areas differ?

Regarding the longitudinal data for Group G, there was a reduction in the frequency of perceived academic difficulties (academic reading and understanding lectures) from Stage I to Stage II. When comparing the adaptation of students coming together (Group G) and those coming independently (Group I), systematic pre-departure preparation and Chinese peer group support after arrival may have contributed to reduced academic concerns after arrival in the UK for students coming in a group. Considering the overall patterns of change in Figure 11.1, it is important to note that the frequency of difficulties relating to general life, social life, and study life each changed over time, and that the pattern of changes differed among the three aspects of students' adaptation. At Stage I, academic problems loomed large but reduced to such an extent at Stages II and III that they were overtaken by some of the general life issues (e.g., different food and financial problems) and even by social problems (e.g., finding friends) at Stage III. This pattern of change across the three domains reflects the more general relatedness of changes in affect (A), behavior (B), and cognition (C) expressed in the ABC model in the social psychological literature (Zhou, Jindal-Snape, Topping, & Todman, 2008), and makes it unlikely that educational adaptation can be considered in isolation from general life and social aspects of students' adaptation. Adaptation to study life was, however, distinctive in another respect.

It emerged from the interview data that the frequency of negative experiences was greater than students had expected with regard to all three domains (general life, social life, and study life). However, it was only for study life that the frequency of positive experiences was also greater than they had anticipated. This balance between positive experiences (enjoyments) and negative experiences (challenges) in the area of study life may have contributed to the reduction over time in the importance of academic problems; there were always positive academic experiences to alleviate the impact of negative academic experiences.

- How does the adaptation of Chinese students to UK styles of teaching and learning differ between those coming in groups and those coming individually?

Shortly after arrival in the UK, the Group G students perceived the differences between Chinese and UK teaching and learning traditions and practices to be fewer than they had expected before departure, which may have been related to the provision of systematic pre-departure preparation for groups. Another possibility is that the differences may have been softened by a willingness of their tutors to meet them half-way in the adaptation process.

The fact that students coming in groups experienced fewer differences in teaching and learning in general than they had anticipated may have contributed to the fact that they also experienced fewer academic difficulties after arrival than they had anticipated. Indeed, the most intriguing result concerning perceived difficulties was the reversal of the difference between Group G and Group I from Stage I to Stage II with respect to study difficulties (academic reading and understanding lectures). A "group" hypothesis focusing on the supportive aspects of being in a group of Chinese peers seems plausible (Lin, 2006). Students in Group G might be less motivated to study in the UK (they just went with the flow) and therefore expected academic difficulties. However, they benefited from group support after arrival. Students in Group I, on the other hand, may have been more academically motivated (having sought out a course for themselves), which might have resulted in their being more academically confident before departure. After arrival, however, they may have found the unfamiliar academic demands hard to deal with initially, due to their relative isolation and lack of preparation. This is a clear example of an interaction between manner of coming and the stage at which problems present, suggesting that different solutions are likely to be required. For students in groups, pre-departure familiarization with the substantive content of their intended courses may be helpful, together with a post-arrival emphasis on making effective use of their tutors instead of relying on help from their peers. For students coming individually, however, the greatest benefit may derive from pre-departure and post-arrival familiarization with teaching/learning differences.

- What is the effect on adaptation of student–teacher shared perceptions of students' problems?

The absence of a significant difference between means of staff focusing on a matched student and those focusing on Chinese students in general is consistent with the finding from the qualitative data that staff were often unaware of the problems of their individual students. It appeared that, when Chinese students came in groups, they tended to rely on helping one another to deal with their study problems, which may have had a negative impact on the UK teachers, in that they were more likely to remain unaware of their students' problems. It was also found that there was very little agreement between the staff views and the matched student views on the nature of the expected differences between China and the UK. This suggested that discrepancies remained between teacher and student views about student adaptations (for details, see Zhou & Todman, 2008). In view of the lack of staff awareness of their students' problems and the low level of shared perception between students and staff, we may have to accept that much remains to be done in terms of cultural synergy before there is substantial scope for resolving students' problems based on common understandings.

- How far is adaptation a two-way reciprocal process in which both students and teachers adapt to one another?

Findings from student focus group discussions and staff interviews were consistent with the situation discussed in the literature by Ward et al. (2001), that, as international students became a major source of revenue for a lot of western universities and institutions, staff members had to respond to the university's mission to provide good customer services. The evidence from the data was also consistent with two-way consequences implied in discussions of cultural synergy (Cortazzi & Jin, 2002; Jin & Cortazzi, 1998). Findings from staff interviews suggested that they also gained new professional insights into intercultural teaching and learning when working with international students. In this sense, it can be seen as a reciprocal adaptation process, in that both parties had gains and enjoyments.

Regarding the issue of who makes the greater adaptation, findings from student group discussions suggested that students realized that the whole-sale adoption of western values and approaches (assimilation) was not the preferred solution for them; and UK staff members suggested that some core aspects (e.g., attitude toward plagiarism) of the UK system were non-negotiable. Our results suggest that HE institutions in the UK need to find ways to adapt to international student requirements that do not challenge their core academic beliefs. Marcy (2004) suggests that ideas involving quite profound institutional transformation will be required to meet the needs of an increasingly diverse student body.

Our data suggested that there might be potential problems with some China–UK educational cooperation programs. For example, some UK contexts used in teaching were unfamiliar and inapplicable to the Chinese situation. There was further discussion around the desirability of adopting standard UK-based masters degree courses, contrasted with the development of tailor-made programs for international students. Evaluative research is urgently needed in this area and attempts are indeed beginning to be made to examine the appropriateness and effectiveness of knowledge transfer and knowledge sharing within educational cooperation programs (e.g., Peelo & Luxon, 2007; Richard, 2007).

LIMITATIONS AND FUTURE RESEARCH

The student sample in the study primarily comprised two groups of Chinese students from two areas of China coming to two Scottish universities. Therefore, in view of the sample characteristics, the findings relating to students' educational adaptation experiences need to be interpreted with caution. In addition, differences between coming in groups and coming individually must be treated with circumspection because the manner of coming may be confounded with other variables such as specific universities in China and subjects being studied in the UK. Apart from sample limitations, some ethical issues relating to the reluctance of some staff to expose the problems of their individual students limited the number of staff/student matches that could be achieved.

In response to the sample limitation, future research should aim to achieve a more even balance between students coming individually and students coming in groups so that the two groups of students' adaptation experiences can be better compared. On a broader scale, joint research needs to be undertaken across universities to evaluate their cooperation programs and to explore suitable modules and courses for large groups of Chinese students coming to study in the UK. Finally, research is needed to clarify what kinds of preparation, at which stages, are most effective; and there is also a need to learn more about the conditions that encourage cultural synergy and effective reciprocal adaptation.

CONCLUSION

This chapter focussed on students who were not only making transitions from one educational institution to another, but were also making a transition from one country to another along with all the associated changes of language, life style, etc. As suggested elsewhere in the transition literature, the results highlighted that educational adaptation cannot be considered in isolation from general life and social aspects of transition. Similar to other transitional studies, it was found that familiarization with teaching/learning differences and peers aided the transition process. Further, for successful transition the emphasis should not only be on the teachers being aware of the students' needs and students making an effort to adapt, but also on the HE institutions needing more strategic planning to meet the needs of an increasingly diverse student body.

Note: The research reported in this chapter was carried out as part of the first author's 2006 Ph.D. thesis in the School of Education, Social Work and Community Education, University of Dundee. The authors thank all the research participants.

REFERENCES

Andrade, M. S. (2006). International students in English-speaking universities. *Journal of Research in International Education, 5*(2), 131–154.

Cadman, K. (2000). 'Voices in the air': Evaluations of the learning experiences of international postgraduates and their supervisors. *Teaching in Higher Education, 5,* 475–491.

Chalmers, D., & Volet, S. (1997). Common misconceptions about students from South-East Asia studying in Australia. *Higher Education Research & Development, 16*(1), 87–99.

Cortazzi, M., & Jin, L. (1997). Communication for learning across cultures. In D. McNamara & R. Harris (Eds.), *Overseas students in higher education* (pp. 76–90). London: Routledge.

Cortazzi, M., & Jin, L. (2002). Cultures of learning: The social construction of educational identities. In D. C. S. Li (Ed.), *Discourses in search of members: In honour of Ron Scollon* (pp. 49–77). New York: University Press of America.

De Andrade, L. L. (2000). Negotiating from the inside: Constructing racial and ethnic identity in qualitative research. *Journal of Contemporary Ethnography, 29,* 268–290.

Jin, L., & Cortazzi, M. (1998). Expectations and questions in intercultural classrooms. *Intercultural Communication Studies, 7*(2), 37–62.

Jin, L., & Cortazzi, M. (2006). Changing practices in Chinese cultures of learning. *Language, Culture and Curriculum, 19*(1), 5–20.

Jin, L., & Hill, H. (2001). Students' expectations of learning key skills and knowledge. *International Journal of Language and Communication Disorders, 36* (Suppl.), 333–338.

Kennedy, A. (1999). *Singaporean sojourners: Meeting the demands of cross-cultural transition.* Unpublished doctoral thesis, National University of Singapore.

Lin, C. (2006). Culture shock and social support: An investigation of a Chinese student organization on a US campus. *Journal of Intercultural Communication Research*, 35(2), 117–137.

Marcy, M. B. (2004). When diversity and dollars collide: Challenges for higher education. *Innovative Higher Education*, 28, 205–218.

Miles, M. B., & Huberman, A. M. (1994). *Qualitative data analysis* (2nd ed.). Thousand Oaks, CA: Sage.

Peelo, M., & Luxon, T. (2007). Designing embedded courses to support international students' cultural and academic adjustment in the UK. *Journal of Further and Higher Education*, 31, 65–76.

Richard, L. (2007). Knowledge transfer in international education collaboration programme: The China perspective. *Journal of Technology Management in China*, 2, 84–97.

UKCISA. (n.d.). *Higher education statistics*. Retrieved May 6, 2009, from http://www.ukcosa.org.uk/about/statistics_he.php.

Ward, C., Bochner, S., & Furnham, A. (2001). *The psychology of culture shock* (2nd ed.). Hove, UK: Routledge.

Ward, C., & Kennedy, A. (1996). Crossing cultures: The relationship between psychological and sociocultural dimensions of cross-cultural adjustment. In J. Pandey, D. Sinha, & D. P. S. Bhawuk (Eds.), *Asian contributions to cross-cultural psychology* (pp. 289–306). New Delhi: Sage.

Yeh, C. J., & Inose, M. (2003). International students' reported English fluency, social support satisfaction, and social connectedness as predictors of acculturative stress. *Counselling Psychology Quarterly*, 16(1), 15–28.

Zhou, Y. (2006). *Processes of cultural pedagogical shock and adaptation of Chinese postgraduate students in the UK*. Unpublished doctoral dissertation, University of Dundee, Dundee, Scotland.

Zhou, Y., Jindal-Snape, D., Topping, K. J., & Todman, J. (2008). Theoretical models of culture shock and adaptation in international students in higher education. *Studies in Higher Education*, 33, 63–75.

Zhou, Y., & Todman, J. (2008). Chinese students in the UK: A two-way reciprocal adaptation. *Journal of International & Intercultural Communication*, 1(3), 221–243.

Zhou, Y., & Todman, J. (2009). Patterns of adaptation of Chinese students in the United Kingdom. *Journal of Studies in International Education*, 4 online first, doi:10.1177/1028315308317937. Retrieved on 22nd September 2009 from http://jsi.sagepub.com/cgi/content/abstract/10283153083179937vl.

12 Transition From Secondary School to Employment in Japan for Students With Disabilities

Jun Yaeda

Transition from school to work is a challenge for everybody, especially for students with disabilities. A smooth transition avoids unnecessary institutionalization, it makes students more independent, and it improves the quality of life of students with disabilities and their parents (Hughes, Copeland, Fowler, & Church-Pupke, 2002; Yaeda, Shibata, & Umenaga, 2000).

This chapter describes the concept, service provision, and the current research and practice of transition from school to work for secondary students with disabilities in Japan. Two transition case illustrations, one for an inclusive education setting and the other for a special school setting, are presented. It is suggested that a sequential individual plan for education, training, transition, employment, and community living can help special needs education, vocational rehabilitation, and social work staff to work in a joined up manner. Then, the traditional Japanese concept of the value of "WA," the harmony, is introduced as an unspoken collaboration for interdisciplinary teamwork by special needs education coordinators, vocational rehabilitation counselors, job coaches, work support coordinators, and social workers in Japan.

INTRODUCTION

There are about 7.24 million people with physical, intellectual, or psychiatric disabilities in Japan (Ministry of Health, Labour and Welfare, 2008a), which is about 5.7% of the 127 million Japanese population (Ministry of Internal Affairs and Communications, 2009). Of the 7.24 million people with disabilities in Japan, 5.3% (387,000) are children and youth with disabilities. Of those 387,000 children and youth, 25% (98,000) are individuals with physical disabilities, 32% (125,000) are individuals with intellectual disabilities and 42% (164,000) are individuals with psychiatric disabilities under the age of 20 (Ministry of Health, Labour and Welfare, 2008a).

About 2% of all Japanese students in compulsory education have some kind of disability. There are about 220,000 students with disabilities as of 2007 in Japan. Of those, 26% (58,000) students with disabilities are in 1,026 special needs schools, 51% (113,000) are in 29,647 special needs classes, and 20% (45,000) are in regular classes. The remaining 3% are probably hospitalized.

In 2008, more than 76,000 students with disabilities were in secondary schools in Japan. This includes 26,044 students in the 3-year junior high schools, and 50,369 students in 3-year high schools. Figure 12.1 shows the estimated percentage of transition from school to higher education, employment, and welfare facilities based on the descriptive statistics provided by the Ministry of Internal Affairs and Communications (2009); the Ministry of Education, Culture, Sports, Science and Technology (2009); and the Ministry of Health, Labour and Welfare (2008b). After they graduated 3% went to college, 24% went to work, and 63% went to welfare facilities. According to a survey of welfare institutions of 2006, an average of 5% of the 20,000 individuals with physical, intellectual, or psychiatric disabilities who have been living in the rehabilitation or welfare institutions moved out because they obtained employment (Ministry of Health, Labour and Welfare, 2006a). The average transition rate from welfare institutions and/or work support facilities to work varies from 1–2% every year, with the national average being 1.3% (Ministry of Health, Labour and Welfare, 2008b). The data indicates that once you are in the welfare facilities, the chance of getting employment is very low.

When compared to regular high school graduates, the difference becomes clear. Figure 12.2 shows the estimated percentage of transition from school to higher education and employment of students without disabilities as a comparison. The ratio of those going to colleges and universities is 53% in the general population, as compared to 3% in the case of students with a disability (Ministry of Education, Culture, Sports, Science and Technology, 2009). Those who are not in college, universities, or work, which would account for about 27%, may be described as the population of 0.64 million

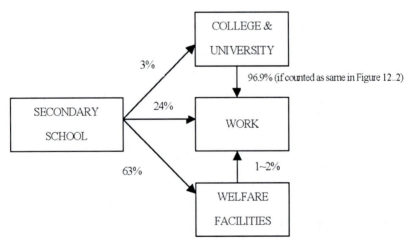

Figure 12.1 From school to where? (Students with disabilities.)

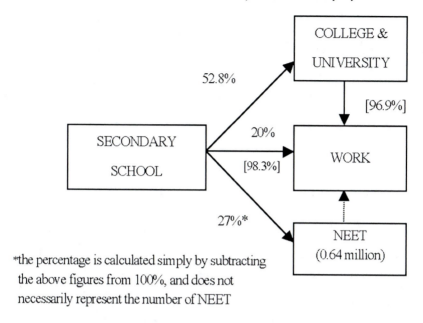

Figure 12.2 From school to where? (Students without disabilities.)

NEET (Not in Education, Employment, or Training) as estimated in 2006 (Ministry of Health, Labour and Welfare, 2006b).

As can be seen in the Figure 12.2, about 20% of regular high school graduates do not move on to higher education, but rather get a job immediately. According to the national survey conducted both by the Ministry of Health, Labour and Welfare, and the Ministry of Education, Culture, Sports, Science and Technology (2007a), some 20% went to work after graduating from high schools, and 98.3% got jobs. As a comparison, some 52.8% went to college and university after graduating from high schools, and 96.9% of them got jobs as of April 1, 2008. Whether you are a high school graduate or a college graduate, the employment success rate is quite high. Apparently, education is a key for transition to employment. However, this is not true when a social-economic crisis hits the labor market significantly. Even though every child and young person with a disability has the right to a good education at a special needs school or at a regular school, the chance of getting a job upon graduation is very limited.

According to Tanaka, Hosokawa, and Inagaki (2003), more than 80% of students with intellectual and developmental disabilities live with their parents, and have no jobs. About 10% of individuals with intellectual disabilities are institutionalized and the number of such welfare institutions keeps growing in Japan. This could mean that there is a definite need for good quality institutions where their freedom and privacy are more respected. However, as stated earlier, the fact is that once they move into welfare institutions in Japan, only 1–2% of them get a job and move out, while the rest stay there (Ministry of Health, Labour and Welfare, 2008b), being dependent and unproductive, not because they want to but because they are expected to play that dependent role. Many families are unhappy about this, but do not complain because it is rather a dead end situation for them too. They would be happier, of course, if their children got a chance to go to college, got a decent job, and lived independently in the community. The question is how, and the answer could be, to let them transit directly from school to work, not to a welfare institution.

TRANSITION—CONCEPT AND PRACTICE

Every school child with disability should have an equal chance of getting a decent job after graduation. The school to work transition for students with disabilities is considered to be a key aspect of interdisciplinary collaboration by rehabilitation professionals (Yaeda, 2008; Yaeda et al., 2000).

The transition conceptualization is simple: (1) the sooner you start the transition planning, the better the outcome is; (2) the more focused on what they like, the better the job matches; and (3) the better the job matches, the longer they keep the jobs. The transition practice is not complicated or difficult. What you do basically is: (1) to give them a chance to try; (2) to be creative as to how you can teach the essential vocational skills; and (3) to let them find their own ways to do the job.

Transitions take place throughout one's life. A good transition will bring a better life. Since school to work transition occurs at an early stage of life, it is important to be successful earlier. Once you start working, it is a matter of how you retain the job, feel happy about the job, and keep yourself healthy on the job. While at school, students with disabilities must learn the meaning of work and the quality of working life (QWL). The best way for them to learn the realistic meaning of work is to get paid work experience within the community.

The following are two case illustrations of school to work transition in Japan. The first case is the transition from regular school to work, and the second case is the transition from special needs school to work.

Ken's Case: Transition from Regular School to Work

Ken (name changed) had autism and had not been successful in finding a decent job for 5 years after he graduated from a regular high school. He was 23 years old and had been to the vocational rehabilitation centers, unemployment offices, but had no luck. No jobs were available for him anywhere, and apparently the vocational counselors were giving up on him. One time he was able to get a job interview, but the employer said no to him without giving him a reason. Ken has a language proficiency certificate that proves he can write and read some sophisticated Japanese words. However, the employer could not find a place for him to use his particular, specific skill.

Ken and his mother visited me, with a referral through the Education Counseling Center at the University of Tsukuba. He was very quiet and looked serious. After listening to what he wished to do, what he likes most, and what he does best, I told him and his mother that he is able, not disabled. What I did first was to simply ask him to do a little office chore for me. I had a ton of business cards that had not been sorted out alphabetically and they were scattered all over my desk, disorganized. First, he did not make a move, so I showed him a way to pile up those business cards alphabetically by names. Most Japanese characters represent one word that has two or three different ways of reading or pronouncing it. So, you must know that first, and you must guess what sounds appropriate as a Japanese name. Ken worked hard, patiently, seemingly enjoying the task for 20 minutes, and successfully accomplished the sorting task with 95% accuracy. There were names which I could not have read correctly. So, his success rate was pretty high. I complimented him and he smiled slightly for the first time in our meeting. Next I asked him whether he would like a cup of fresh coffee for a break. I ground coffee beans and poured hot water on it carefully through a paper filter into his cup. He looked curious about this rather ritualistic, sophisticated, artistic task. His face brightened up again, so I asked him if he would like to make another cup of coffee for us. Ken nodded and started his very first drip-coffee job. The result was one fine fresh coffee. Good enough for the first-time learner. If Ken had got a job right after his graduation from high school, with a little help from his teacher, a career guidance school counselor, or a transition coordinator, he would not have had to come to my office.

Knowing what Ken could achieve, I referred him to a job coach who could give him work support service on the job. Ken now works as an office clerk at a non-profit organization, earns above minimum wage, and occasionally enjoys making a cup of coffee for his colleagues.

Ken's case was of a transition of a student with autism from a regular school to a work setting with support from a job coach. I did not do anything new. All I did was to search his interests that would match with his vocational ability and to let him try some specific tasks he would enjoy. I then referred him to a job coach who placed him in a work setting and supported him on the job as long as was necessary.

Ellie's Case: Transition from Special Needs School to Work

This is an example where a transition coordinator was involved from the beginning within a secondary special needs school. Ellie (name changed) was 17, diagnosed as having a moderate intellectual disability. She went to a special needs school and hoped to work as a care worker in an elderly care house. Ellie's class teacher made an Individual Transition Plan (ITP) with assistance from the vocational counselor. The career goal in the ITP was for Ellie to become a care work assistant upon graduation. The team members in the ITP included Ellie and her parents, Ellie's class teacher, a job coach, the potential employer and a vocational counselor.

After getting real work experience at a care house for the elderly, Ellie expressed her feeling that helping others made her proud. Her parents encouraged her every day, and let her know that they respected her career choice. When Ellie was discouraged by her work and hesitant to go to work, the job coach would come and pick her up. It was also the parents' role to remind her how helpful she has been, trying to raise her sense of self-efficacy.

The vocational counselor taught Ellie the self-monitoring strategy on and off the job. Although her main job was to wash the toilet, bathroom, and to do the laundry, which she complained about occasionally, Ellie was able to manage her feelings. The support from the job coach was gradually faded out from the job site, but he came back periodically to monitor her progress and to help resolve interpersonal problems Ellie had encountered. The employer liked her job performance and her work attitude, and so did the other employees. The job coach did not have to encourage support from her co-workers, as that atmosphere of mutual support was already there.

After graduation, Ellie was employed as an assistant at the same care house with a job coach helping her occasionally on the job. With ongoing support from her job coach, Ellie enjoys her work and supports other students like her, by getting them the same field work experience she has had at the care house.

Job Retention: A Key Factor for Successful Transition

The previous two cases are the successful examples of transition from school to work. Using supported employment technique (Gold, 1980; Mcloughlin, Garner, & Callahan, 1987; Wehman & Moon, 1988; Wehman, Sale, & Parent, 1992), both Ken and Ellie were successfully employed. The supported employment technique works, if someone like a transition coordinator can connect the client to the next step by referring to a job coach. Thus, it becomes important that a transition coordinator is responsible for assessing the vocational interests and needs of the students before making referrals to vocational counselor and/or a job coach. A transition coordinator must keep watching the client's progress, because the job is not over just by connecting two service agencies, but to keep monitoring the progress as long as necessary in order to retain the acquired job.

Job retention thus becomes a key aspect of the successful transition. But it may not always be the specific job skills which make it possible to retain a job. Rather, it may be the basic daily living skills or social skills which are important to obtain and retain the job (Horiie, 2008). Suzuki, Yaeda, and

Kikuchi (2009) evaluated working behavior of 127 individuals with intellectual disabilities and found that daily living skills, conceptual skills, self-direction skills were the major factors contributing to their job retention, rather than the specific job skills. This is one of the reasons why a transition coordinator must keep monitoring the transition progress because successful transition to work is not achieved if you cannot keep your job.

PUBLIC POLICY AND LEGISLATION

A combination of a qualified transition coordinator in a school setting and a job coach in a work setting makes a good team in special needs education and vocational rehabilitation (Yaeda, 2003, 2008). Their working status must be secured by legislation, and their expected roles and functions must be specified clearly in the ITP. The current service delivery system for special needs education and vocational rehabilitation in Japan do exist, but it can be better provided if school to work transition is articulated in the two key legislations: (1) School Education Act; and (2) Employment Promotion Law for People with Disabilities.

School Education Act

The School Education Act, which includes special needs education, was amended in 2007 and changed the term from "special education" to "special needs education," and also changed the term from "special school" to "special needs school." Formerly known as "Schools for the Blind," "Schools for the Deaf," and "Schools for the Intellectually Disabled, the Physically Disabled and the Health Impaired", they are now just "Special Needs Schools," not limited to one particular type of disability, but accepting several types of disabilities. Special needs education includes resource rooms and special classes in regular schools.

The special needs schools are expected to function as a hub of the community resources, and to coordinate various human service agencies such as social welfare facilities, hospital, clinics, and vocational rehabilitation agencies. Recently, more and more students with developmental disabilities are in special needs schools as well as in regular schools so that special needs education coordinators are supposed to function as the key person for inclusive education (Ministry of Education, Culture, Sports, Science and Technology, 2006; Sato, 2008).

According to the national study conducted by the Ministry of Education, Culture, Sports, Science and Technology (2007a), there are about 680,000 students with developmental disabilities such as Learning Disabilities (LD), Attention Deficit/Hyperactivity Disorder (ADHD), High-Functioning Autism. They make up 6.3% of all students in regular schools (Ministry of Education, Culture, Sports, Science and Technology, 2002). As a new piece of legislation, the Developmental Disabilities Support Act was enacted in 2007 and the School Education Act also was amended in the same year to meet the needs of those multiple types of disabilities. The law requires a special needs school to make the Individual Education Plan (IEP) that would meet each student's educational needs. The Individual Transition Plan (ITP) is to be included in the IEP. Each special needs school must have a special needs education coordinator whose major roles are: (a) to support or supervise the school teachers through in-service training; (b) to provide professional consultation and relevant information on special needs education; and (c) to collaborate with medical, social, and vocational agencies.

Employment Promotion Law for Persons with Disabilities

The other law, the Employment Promotion Law for Persons with Disabilities, is a Japanese vocational rehabilitation law. Each of the 47 prefectures in Japan has a Local Vocational Centre for People with Disabilities, and more than 400 Vocational Counselors for Persons with Disabilities are currently working as vocational rehabilitation professionals. These counselors have bachelors and higher degrees in subjects such as education, social work, counseling psychology and rehabilitation. They must pass the national examination set by the Ministry of Health, Labour and Welfare before beginning their career as vocational counselor for persons with disabilities.

Employment Services are provided by these counselors who make an Individual Vocational Rehabilitation Program (IVRP). On average, there are five to six such counselors in each of the Local Vocational Centers. They coordinate community vocational rehabilitation services through job coaches and re-work supporters. This was supported by research. According to the national survey for vocational rehabilitation professionals in Japan, almost 70% respondents expected that the central role of the vocational rehabilitation professional was to function as a coordinator (Yaeda, 2003).

The role of a job coach, the key player for supported employment, has been expanded since 1990 in Japan. The Employment Promotion for Persons with Disabilities Act Amendments of 2006 has selected the term "Work Adjustment Supporter" instead of "Job Coach." Now, more than 1,000 work adjustment supporters or the job coaches have been trained in Japan, and 4,000 more will be trained in the next 4 years. Some of them are social workers, and some of them are school teachers. They can get a certificate by attending in-service, short-term training programs. Job coach plays an important role, not only in the work place, but also in school.

System Integration for School to Work Transition

The School Education Act and the Employment Promotion Law are operated separately by the different ministries. Often the so-called "wall" of bureaucratic system would hinder a smooth school to work transition. While the School Education Act is under the jurisdiction of the Ministry of Education, Culture, Sports, Science and Technology, the Employment Promotion Law for Persons with Disabilities is under the jurisdiction of the Ministry of Health, Labour and Welfare. Generally speaking, teachers and vocational counselors do not work together on a daily basis. Special needs school teachers do not know much about vocational rehabilitation, and vocational rehabilitation counselors in Japan do not work at schools. The knowledge gap between the two cannot be ignored. This gap can be filled by collaborative teaching in pre-service and in-service training programs. For example, Inter-Professional Education (IPE) has been in effect recently across many Japanese universities which has interdisciplinary professional educational programs in human services.

It is this author's belief that those two pieces of legislations are better combined into one, or they should have a concrete common transition service provision in the future. Then both IEP and IVRP must have shared objectives for the best practice of school to work transition. Although there have been some educational and vocational initiatives for school to work transition for students with disabilities in Japan (Ministry of Education, Culture, Sports, Science and Technology, 2007a; Ministry of Health, Labour and Welfare, 2008c), the employment rate still remains low. Education and training of special needs education coordinators just started in several universities in Japan, but their roles, functions, and proficiencies are yet to be defined by empirical research. It has not been clear as to how a school principal will select a qualified special needs education coordinator. Research needs to be done regarding the qualification and accreditation issues as well.

Individual Plans: Education, Transition, Employment and Community Living

Individual plans are the key tool to connect separate areas of human services. These plans are interrelated and share some objectives and strategies. Figure 12.3 shows a conceptual framework for the integrated individual plans.

The ITP has two phases: (1) three years before the graduation, and (2) three years after the graduation from secondary special needs schools (National Association of Special School Principals, 2002, 2004; Tokyo Research Council for School to Work Promotion for Students with Disabilities, 2003).

Figure 12.4 illustrates these two types of ITP, which are planned by a special needs school teacher or a career guidance counselor/teacher at special needs school. Both of the two forms basically include short- and long-term goals and specific support plans for the fields of: (1) education, (2) social welfare, (3) community living, (4) medical services, and (5) labor. Contact persons and the time-limited service periods for each of the five fields must be specified in detail and they vary from school to school.

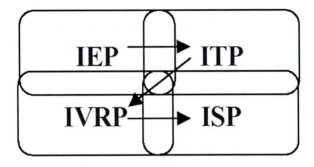

IEP: Individual Education Plan
ITP: Individual Transition Plan
IVRP: Individual Vocational Rehabilitation Plan
ISP: Individual Support Plan

Figure 12.3   Integrated individual plans.

It is required that special needs education teachers must make individual transition plans from both educational and vocational aspects. They are the key players in the transition process because they know their students best. It is their responsibility to correctly identify the vocational skills that match with the student's interests and strengths, and refer to a job coach and a vocational rehabilitation counselor in a timely manner. It is rather obvious that the earlier they intervene, the better the outcome is, and the more key persons are involved, the more efficient is the transition.

Once ITP is made, then it is connected to the Individual Vocational Rehabilitation Plan (IVRP) written by a vocational rehabilitation counselor. Furthermore, ITP and IVRP can be connected to the Individual Support Plan (ISP), which is another new individual plan specified in the Services and Supports for Persons with Disabilities Act of 2006. This law promotes their independence in the community living through work support such as "transition support for employment" and "support for continuous employment" (Ministry of Health, Labour and Welfare, 2006c). The ISP is written by a social worker who is in a position of service management practice in welfare service business operator for persons with disabilities.

The previously-mentioned individual plans for education, transition, employment, and community living should work when they are planned on a continuous basis, based on their lifespan development. However, the plan is just a plan. Making such a plan in itself does not solve anything.

In reality such plans may not even be made. For example, national data shows that only 3.6% of special needs high schools had made IEP (Ministry

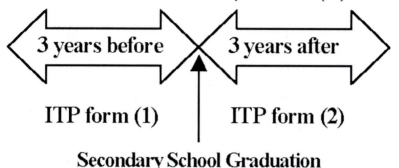

Figure 12.4   Two types of ITP forms.

of Education, Culture, Sports, Science and Technology, 2007b). What we need is to have a qualified professional who implements the plan with a great deal of flexibility and well-modified new strategies and techniques. The plan is like an action plan as to what you wish to achieve, by when, by applying which evidence-based approach for whom. You must specify who is involved in the plan implementation and what you expect them to achieve as a team.

It has been a career guidance teacher's role to support a student in finding a job, but many teachers simply do not have enough time to do the job development or vocational training. Then, it becomes a vocational counselor's role to connect various professionals such as a special needs education coordinator, a job coach, and a work support coordinator.

Another professional might be work support coordinator, although the training program has just started at several universities in Japan. Since social workers play the role of a job coach, they could call themselves "Vocational Rehabilitation Worker" or "Work Support Social Worker" as a collaborator between the field of social work and vocational rehabilitation (Yaeda, 2009, p. 42). In 2009, every school of social work that prepares future certified social workers through an accredited university program must offer a new elective course, called "Work Support Services." Professional development of the work support coordinators has just begun in Japan.

At one time, the Ministries of Health, Labour and Welfare were separate ministries in Japan. Now it is an integrated ministry for both social work and rehabilitation. Next step may be an integrated system for special needs education, social work, and vocational rehabilitation.

Despite the fact that many professionals are involved in transitions in Japan, there are no professionals dealing exclusively with transition. Although the need for training such *transition service coordinators* or *transition coordinators* has been explicit (China, 2008; Hara, 2004; Tanaka & Yaeda, 2008; Yaeda, 2008; Yaeda et al., 2000), the roles of such transition service coordinators as a full-time profession dealing with transition service exclusively have not been empirically examined in Japan. A full-time-equivalent professional dealing exclusively with transition coordination is necessary if we are to assure the quality services for school to work transition of students with disabilities at both special schools and regular schools in Japan.

As previous research shows one of the four major roles of vocational rehabilitation professional is the "Transition Support," including: (a) "to provide transition service from school to work"; (b) "to provide support for social adaptation of a particular client"; and (c) "to provide psychological counseling for a particular client facing specific problems" (Yaeda, 2003, p. 38).

The roles of special needs education coordinator and career guidance teachers or counselors at special needs schools may be similar in terms of coordination and transition. According to a recent national study, China (2008) has identified five primary duties of career guidance counselors in 303 schools for students with intellectual disabilities in Japan. A total of 36 job duties of career guidance counselors was factor analyzed that derived the following five job roles: (1) assessment; (2) information dissemination; (3) liaison; (4) job search and matching; and (5) spearheading programs. Some of the duties relevant to transition included: (a) "to consult with the specific employers as to how they can deal with disabling condition of students with disabilities"; (b) "to act as an intermediary between teachers and referral professionals and agencies to solve support needs specified in the Individual Transition Plan"; (c) "to support work adjustment of the individual periodically"; (d) "to initiate and conduct job development activities"; and (e) "to lead and organize each teacher's role in work support of the student" (China, 2008, p. 6).

China also found that the job stress of career guidance counselors who have full responsibility was significantly lower than those who have a partial responsibility shared by more than one counselor. The result indicates that a shared responsibility by various school staff may not necessarily contribute to decreasing the job stress. Rather he or she may be better off working individually to avoid unnecessary stress. What we can learn from the study is the importance of clarifying the role expectations among the staff members having the same job titles. If the mutual role expectation is vague, it could lead to stress.

Although Japanese are supposed to be good at the "unspoken collaboration" or the harmonized "WA" spirit, it may not be true at all times or at all places. Lee, Yaeda, and Okuno (2008) have studied factors related to the coordination of vocational rehabilitation service providers through multiple regression analysis. They found that one of the major variables predicting the degree of coordination was the "agency attitudes" toward coordination. The attitude is unspoken as well, and it is hard to measure. Where there is a positive attitude toward coordination within the service agency, good teamwork seems to be present.

The next section touches a little bit on this teamwork issue by introducing the traditional Japanese spirit of "WA," the harmony.

THE SPIRIT OF "WA," THE HARMONY

Traditionally, Japanese value the concept of "WA," which means harmony. When you add another word to it, for example, "HEI," meaning plain or plateau, then it becomes "HEI-WA," meaning peace.

"WA" has been at the very heart of Japanese culture. "WA" works where work must be done by a group of people peacefully and systematically, only if you realize its value. Whether you are a medical doctor, a nurse, a therapist, a counselor, a social worker, or a teacher, "WA" connects you with other people. When you are in an interdisciplinary rehabilitation team, you are not supposed to break the unspoken atmosphere of "WA" spirit. This unspoken collaboration is the heart of "WA," that Japanese are meant to be naturally good at.

The bottom line is that the people expect each other to behave peacefully and efficiently in order to keep a nice harmony. Every team member is supposed to read between the lines, or understand a hidden meaning to it, avoid an unnecessary direct interface, and act accordingly. Self-centeredness is not allowed most of the time under the "WA" spirit.

Since Japan has such a long, social value of WA, the spirit of harmony, the collaboration and coordination among educational, vocational, medical, and social services seems natural in modern society. However, this is not something that is verifiable. It is abstract and difficult to explain. Its meaning may differ between young and old. However, if there is a certain kind of Japanese style for teamwork, whether it is business, sports, or human services, one thing for sure is that the WA spirit is indispensable to teamwork in Japanese culture.

CONCLUSION: WORK AS REHABILITATION

The employment rate heavily depends on the global economic status and/ or the company's hiring policies. Every day large numbers of competent employees lose their jobs, and people with disabilities tend to be made redundant easily from the competitive labor market. Disability cannot be an excuse for making people redundant. Why do they lose their jobs then? While poor interpersonal skills, lack of self control, and poor time management skills are often considered to be the fundamental reasons, it is found that many workers with disabilities tend to leave their jobs due to interpersonal problems. Unless there is job retention over the long term, a true school to work transition is not achieved. This is why job coaches need to monitor their clients' progress and intervene as long as they need support, why vocational counselors need to coordinate not only the vocational rehabilitation services but also community rehabilitation services, why social workers or work support coordinators must learn how they can help persons with disabilities, and why a special needs education coordinator must function as a true coordinator who can connect education to employment and community living. All of the transition coordinators must have the ability and skills to offer the comprehensive services from a lifespan developmental perspective.

WA, the spirit of Japan, will not work if we just keep counting on somebody else in the name of unspoken "coordination," "collaboration," or "integration," which anyway is merely an ideal state. Successful transition from school to work for students with disabilities in secondary schools has yet to come, but the future looks bright if both the conceptually rigid practical collaboration as well as the evidence-based scientific collaboration is achieved in Japan. For example, Tokunaga (2008) introduced how various professionals can utilize the International Classification on Functioning, Disability, and Health (ICF) as a tool for collaboration when making an IEP for a particular child with disability. However, there is more work to be done in the field of lifespan development and rehabilitation in Japan, especially in terms of research. Empirical studies focusing on the effectiveness of various individual plans that connect education, work, and community living are encouraged in the future.

REFERENCES

China, A. (2008). Chiteki shogai yogo gakko ni okeru shinro shido kyoyu no yakuwari to futankan no kanren: Shinro shido kyoyu no ikou kodineta teki yakuwari no kanosei no kento [A survey on the relationship between the job scope and the perceived sense of burden of care guidance counselor in school for the intellectually disabled: Potential as transition coordinator of career guidance counselor]. *Shokugyo Rihabiliteshon [Vocational Rehabilitation]*, 22(1), 2–13.

Gold, M. W. (1980). *Try another way: Training manual*. Champaign, IL: Research Press.

Hara, T. (2004). Iko shien: Kobetsu iko shien keikaku no genjo to kadai [Transition Support: Current issue of Individual Transition Plan]. *Hattatsu Shogai Kenkyu [Japanese Journal of Developmental Disabilities]*, 25(4), 217–224.

Horiie, Y. (2008). Shogaisha no shuro to kyoiku: Ippan koko wo sotsugyo shita chiteki shogaisha no jirei wo chushin ni [Work and education of people with disabilities: A case of intellectual disability who graduated from a general high school]. In K. Yamanouchi (Ed.), *Kyoiku kara Shokugyo eno Toranjishon [Transition from School to Work]* (pp. 178–197). Tokyo: Toshindo Publishing.

Hughes, C., Copeland, S., Fowler, S., & Church-Pupke, P. (2002). Quality of Life. In K. Storey, P. Bates, & D. Hunter (Eds.), *The road ahead: Transition to adult life for persons with disabilities* (pp. 157–171). Augustine, FL: Training Resource Network.

Lee, M., Yaeda, J., & Okuno, E. (2008). Chiteki shogaisha no shokugyou rihabiliteshon kanren jigyosha no renkei kanren yoin [Factors related to the coordination of vocational rehabilitation service providers for individuals with intellectual disabilities]. *Shokugyo Rihabiliteshon [Vocational Rehabilitation]*, 21(2), 2–9.

Mcloughlin, C. S., Garner, J. B., & Callahan, M. (1987). *Getting employed, staying employed*. Baltimore: Paul H. Brookes.

Ministry of Education, Culture, Sports, Science and Technology. (2002). *Heisei 14 nendo Gakko Kyoiku Kihon Chosa [A Survey Report on Basic Education]*.

Retrieved April 25, 2009, from http://www.mext.go.jp//b_menu/toukei/001/003/index03.html.

Ministry of Education, Culture, Sports, Science and Technology. (2006). *Gakko Kyoikuhoto no Ichibu wo Kaisei suru Horitsuan ni Taisuru Futai Ketsugi [A Partical School Education Act Amendments: An Incidental Resolution].* Retrieved April 25, 2009, from http://www.mext.go.jp/b_menu/hakusho/nc/06072108/002.html.

Ministry of Education, Culture, Sports, Science and Technology. (2007a). *Tokubetsu Shien Kyoiku no Genjo [Survey on the Current Status of Special Needs Education System] (September 1, 2008).* Retrieved April 25, 2009, from http://www.mext.go.jp/a_menu/shotou/tokubetu/002.html.

Ministry of Education, Culture, Sports, Science and Technology. (2007b). *Tokubetsu Shien Kyoiku no Suishin ni tsuite (tsuchi) [Promoting Special Needs Education]* Retrieved April 25, 2009, from http://www.mext.go.jp/b_menu/hakusho/nc/07050191.html.

Ministry of Education, Culture, Sports, Science and Technology. (2009). *Gakko Kihon Chosa [A Survey Report on Basic Education].* Retrieved April 25, 2009, from http://www.mext.go.jp/b_menu/toukei/001/08121201/001.html.

Ministry of Health, Labour and Welfare. (2006a). *Heisei 18 nen Shakai Fukushi Shisetsuto Chosa Kekka no Gaikyo [Survey of Social Welfare Institutions of 2006].* Retrieved April 25, 2009, from http://www.mhlw.go.jp/toukei/saikin/hw/fukushi/06/index.html.

Ministry of Health, Labour and Welfare. (2006b). *Heisei 18 nendo ban Rodo Keizai no Bunseki [White Paper on the Labour Economy 2006].* Retrieved April 25, 2009, from http://www.mhlw.go.jp/wp/hakusyo/roudou/06/index/html.

Ministry of Health, Labour and Welfare. (2006c). *Shogaisha Jiritsu Shienho. [Services and Supports for Persons with Disabilities Act of 2006].* Retrieved April 25, 2009, from http://www.mhlw.go.jp/topics/2005/02/tp0214-1c.html.

Ministry of Health, Labour and Welfare. (2008a). *Shougaisha Hakusho [White Paper on People with Disability].* Retrieved April 25, 2009, from http://www8.cao.go.jp/shougai.whitepaper/h20hakusho/zenbun/index.html.

Ministry of Health, Labour and Welfare. (2008b). *Shakai Hosho Shingi Kai Shogaisha Bukai Dai 33 Kai [Disability Committee of the 33th Council on Social Security for People with Disabilities].* Retrieved April 25, 2009, from http://www-bm.mhlw.go.jp/shingi/2008/06/s0609-6.html.

Ministry of Health, Labour and Welfare. (2008c). *Heisei 20 nendo hattatsu shogaisha shien sesaku no gaiyo [A Summary of Service System on Developmental Disabilities in 2008].* Retrieved April 25, 2009, from http://www.mhlw.go.jp/bunya/shougaihoken/hattatsu/gaiyo.html.

Ministry of Internal Affairs and Communications. (2009). *Jinko Suikei Geppo [Monthly Census Population]. Statistics Bureau, Director-General for Policy Planning & Statistical Research and Training Institute, Japan.* Retrieved April 25, 2009, from http://www.stat.go.jp/data/junsui/pdf/200904.pdf.

National Association of Special School Principals. (2002). *Kobetsu Iko Shien Keikaku: Shugyo Shien ni Kansuru Chosa Kenkyu Hokokusho Bijuaru Ban, Zenkoku Tokushu Gakko Cho Kai [Individual Transition Support Plan: Visual Version of the Report on Work Support Coordinated by Educational and Vocational Agencies].* Tokyo: Kyoiku Shinsha.

National Association of Special School Principals. (2004). *Kobetsu no Kyoiku Shien Keikaku, Zenkoku Tokushu Gakko Cho Kai: Chukan Matome [Individual Education Plan for Special Schools: Visual Version of the Interim Report].* Tokyo: Kyoiku Shinsha.

Sato, S. (2008). *Tsujo Gakkyu no Tokubetsu Shien [Special Needs Education in Regular Class].* Tokyo: Nihon Bunka Kagaku.

Suzuki, Y., Yaeda, J., & Kikuchi, E. (2009). Chiteki shogaisha no shokuba teichaku no tame no shien yoin [Factors indicating necessary support for job retention of individuals with intellectual disabilities]. *Shokugyo Rihabiliteshon [Vocational Rehabilitation]*, 22(2), 13–20.

Tanaka, A., Hosokawa, T., & Inagaki, M. (2003). Chiteki shogai yogo gakko sotsugyosei no shinro to shido taisei: Yogo gakko kara chiiki seikatsu e no iko no sogai yoin to shien saku ni kansuru chosa kekka kara [Career guidance practice for students with intellectual disabilities at special schools: From a survey on factors and service strategies for transition from special school to community living]. *Nihon Tokushu Kyoiku Gakkai Dai 41 Kai Taikai Ronbunshu.* Tohoku Daigaku. 2003 nen 9 gatsu 20–22 nichi [In the *Proceedings of the 41st Conference on Japan Special Education Academy*, 391–391, September 20–22, Tohoku University].

Tanaka, A., & Yaeda, J. (2008). Hattatsu shogai no aru seito ni okeru koto gakko kara shuro e no iko shien no tenbo: Beikoku no ITP to waga kuni no kobetsu iko shien keikaku no kadai kara [Perspectives on transition support from secondary school to work for students with developmental disabilities: A comparison between ITP in the U.S. and ITP in Japan]. *Nihon Hattatsu Shogai Gakkai [Japanese Journal on Developmental Disabilities]*, 30(1), 9–18.

Tokunaga, A. (2008). The attempt of the practical application of International Classification of Functioning, Disability, and Health (ICF) as a tool for collaboration among various professionals: A perspective on its applicability to "individualized educational support plan." *Bulletin of the National Institute of Special Needs Education, 9*, 1–25.

Tokyo Research Council for School to Work Promotion for Students with Disabilities. (2003). *Tokyo to* chiteki shogai yogo gakko shugyo sokushin kenkyu kyogikai. *Kobetsu Iko Shien Keikaku Q & A Kiso Hen. [Individual Transition Plan Q & A (Basics)]*. Tokyo: Kyoiku Shinsha.

Wehman, P., & Moon, M. S. (1988). *Vocational rehabilitation and supported employment.* Baltimore: Paul H. Brookes.

Wehman, P., Sale, P., & Parent, W. (1992). *Supported employment: Strategies for integration of workers with disabilities.* Boston: Andover Medical.

Yaeda, J. (2003). Shokugyo rihabiliteshon jujisha ni kitai sareru yakuwari to senmonsei [Expected roles and proficiencies of vocational rehabilitation professionals]. *Shokugyo Rihabiliteshon [Vocational Rehabilitation]*, 16, 33–42.

Yaeda, J. (2008). Shogai fukushi ni okeru senmonshoku no yosei. [Professional development in the field of disability social work]. In E. Okuno & T. Yuki (Eds.), *Seikatsu Shien no Shogaisha Fukushi [Disability Social Work for Life Support]* (pp. 150–165). Tokyo: Akashi Shoten.

Yaeda, J. (2009). Shokugyo Rihabiliteshon. [Vocational rehabilitation]. In S. Sawamura & E. Okuno (Eds.), *Rihabiliteshon Renkei Ron [Comprehensive Rehabilitation]: Theory and Practice for Universal Society* (pp. 40–45). Tokyo: Miwa Shoten.

Yaeda, J., Shibata, J., & Umenaga, Y. (2000). Gakko kara shokuba e no iko: Rihabiliteshon sabis renkei no kagi [From school to work transition: A key to rehabilitation collaboration]. *Shokugyo Rihabiliteshon [Vocational Rehabilitation]*, 12, 32–39.

Part V
Conclusions

13 Moving On
Integrating the Lessons Learnt and the Way Ahead

Divya Jindal-Snape

This chapter summarizes the ideas, research, and theoretical underpinnings from the preceding chapters. It looks at any emerging trends, interventions, and theories from different types of transitions. This chapter concludes this book by considering the way forward for academics, researchers, practitioners, and policy makers. However, it is important to say that some of these ideas have come directly from the authors of the chapters; some will be my interpretation based on my own experience of research and practice which might be very different from the author/s' original thoughts. The readers will perhaps come up with some other interpretations based on their own experiences and context.

You will also find that there are some contradictions evident in the arguments presented in different chapters; however these are perhaps reflective of the context of that country, policy, and more importantly the needs of the children and young people they were, or are, working with. Where relevant, I will highlight these as we consider the different parts.

TRANSITIONS

In the previous chapters, the authors have pointed to various conceptualizations of educational transitions in the literature. Some have highlighted that other authors have conceptualized transition as a single event at the end of, or the beginning of, one educational stage, while others have viewed it as an ongoing process. In Chapter 9, Pietarinen, Soini, and Pyhältö, have conceptualized transition as vertical (from one stage to another) and horizontal transition (within the same stage but the constant adaptation and adjustment with peers and teachers). Adeyemo (Chapter 3) cited Wesley (2001) in defining transition as a change from one style, state, or from one place to another. It has been suggested that transition involves a change in relationships, teaching style, environment, space, context for learning, etc. (Fabian & Dunlop, 2005). In Chapter 11, Zhou, Todman, Topping, and Jindal-Snape conceptualize transition as a process of pedagogical, psychological, and cultural adaptation. Transitional periods have been seen as both an exciting and a challenging time.

THEORETICAL PERSPECTIVES

The book set out to discuss some theoretical perspectives, namely, resilience, self-esteem, and self-efficacy, and emotional intelligence (Chapters 2, 3). Jindal-Snape and Miller (Chapter 2) have explained the social and psychological processes experienced by individuals through the theories of self-esteem and resilience. They suggest that a two-dimensional theory of self-esteem which looks at the students' experiences and interactions in the light of self-competence and self-worth (Mruk, 1999) provides insights into understanding the transition process. They report that research suggests that resilience during adverse situations is due to the internal attributes of the individual and protective factors in the family and the wider community (Luthar, 2006) and that self-esteem has been seen as a personal characteristic of individuals who survive, or even thrive, in the face of adversity.

Akos (Chapter 8) has also considered resilience and has reported that transition leads to a break in social networks, and that high levels of social skills and strong peer relationships can work as protective factors and keep students more resilient to the challenges of transition. Akos noted that according to Newman, Lohman, Newman, Myers, and Smith (2000) students perceive peers as both a challenge and a support system during transition. This is similar to Newman and Blackburn (2002) who suggest that the same factors can be risk and protective factors (Chapter 2). Mayer, Amendum, and Vernon-Feagans (Chapter 6) have suggested that close teacher–child relationships may serve as a protective factor for students who exhibit high levels of externalizing problem behaviors in the transition to primary school. As will be seen later, almost all authors in this book have emphasized the importance of good relations with peers and teachers for successful transition.

Adeyemo (Chapter 3) suggests that individuals need psychological skills and resources that will help them with adaptations, adjustments, and understanding of self required to navigate the transition process. For this he used an emotional intelligence intervention and conducted an experimental study to assess its impact on school to university transitions. His findings suggest that this intervention was successful, and also that self-efficacy was one of the core aspects of emotional intelligence intervention. Pietarinen et al. (Chapter 9) have emphasized the construction of well being as a learning process and that it regulates new learning and is a crucial asset of resilience. This suggests a link between emotional intelligence and resilience.

Other theoretical perspectives that emerged throughout the book are well-being, attachment theory, self-regulation, ecological systems theory, maturational model, interactionist model, motivation, and social interaction. Some of these were hinted at and some were described in detail. The links between some of these theories and frameworks are tangible and some are elusive. For example, resilience theory (Luthar, 2006) and ecological systems theory (Bronfenbrenner, 1979, 1992) both emphasize the importance of focusing on all significant others in the child's environment who play a part in the transition process. Chapter 2 details the link between resilience and self-esteem, and Chapter 3 does the same with emotional intelligence and self-efficacy.

In preschool to primary school transition (Chapters 4, 5, 6), as in other stages of transition (Chapter 8), researchers have used the ecological systems model proposed by Bronfenbrenner (1979, 1992) to demonstrate the multi-faceted dimensions that play a part during transitions. Bronfenbrenner conceptualized the ecological systems as systems ranging from those closest to the individual to those most remote, that is, microsystem, mesosystem, exosystem, macrosystem, with the addition of the chronosystem model later. See Chapter 4 for details of a case study where this model has been used as a framework to present data from Scottish parents.

PRESCHOOL TO PRIMARY TRANSITION

Three chapters focused on educational transitions in the context of Scotland, the US, and New Zealand, as well as on the research evidence from around the world. Hannah, Gorton, and Jindal-Snape (Chapter 4) discuss maturationist and interactionist models of readiness to school. They present the perspectives of a group of Scottish parents regarding their and their child's experience of transitions. Peters (Chapter 5) presents data from two studies and her doctoral work in the context of New Zealand. She effectively uses metaphors to describe a pupil's school journey. Mayer, Amendum, and Vernon-Feagans (Chapter 6) discuss readiness to learn and review the data in the American context focusing on the characteristics of key players in the transition process.

As can be seen in these chapters, there is an ongoing debate regarding school readiness. In some countries, there is continuing focus on optimal school starting age. Research has been inconclusive about the appropriateness of age as a predictor for readiness to start school (Ford & Gledhill, 2002; Stipek, 2002). Elsewhere the focus seems to have moved to readiness to learn as well as social and emotional readiness. The overarching debate is whether it is about the child being ready or is it about the schools being ready to work with every child as an individual recognizing his/her unique differences and building on his/her strengths (interactionist model; see Chapters 4, 5). Mayer et al. (Chapter 6) suggest that readiness is at levels beyond the child, and includes the community, school, and family. They cite Vernon-Feagans, Odom, Panscofar, and Kainz (2008) who conceptualize readiness as the interaction and fit between the child and his/her family, and the readiness of the school to teach that child.

There seem to be interesting tensions emerging from the educational systems in different countries. In Scotland, similar support and resources are provided to preschoolers and primary school children irrespective of the socioeconomic background of their parents or ethnicity. However, this might be different in countries where free, state education is not the norm. Of course even in Scotland there are possibilities of differences in preschool provision depending on whether the parents send their child to a private partnership nursery or state nursery or provide care at home. Regardless of the country, authors have emphasized that smooth transition depends on the quality of preschool experience. Therefore, it is important to ensure that all children get good quality preschool provision either through formal preschool systems or through a supportive family and community. Importance of communication between teachers from preschool and primary school, other professionals such as counselors and teachers (see also Chapter 12 in the post-school context), between teachers and parents, teachers and students (see also Chapter 11 in post-school context), and students and students has been emphasized by Hannah et al., Peters, and Mayer et al. (see also Chapter 7, 8, 9 in primary–secondary context). According to Pietarinen et al. (Chapter 9), pupils saw the processing of social conflicts in pupil–pupil and teacher–pupil relationships as an important prerequisite for learning and well-being in schools. As can be seen, the importance of good communication has been documented across all stages of educational transition.

Hannah et al. emphasize the importance of involving parents in the transition process (see also Peters in Chapter 5 and Mayer et al. in Chapter 6). It is argued that it is not only the child who is experiencing a transition; the parents are making a transition as well. The data suggested that parents require support themselves but they also want information so that they can explain the process to the child at home. Parents felt 'useless' if they could not support their child during the transition process.

Hannah et al. reported that parents think that a good relationship between the primary school teacher and their child was very important, and they wanted this to start developing before the child started primary school. They suggested that instead of one long visit to the primary school prior to transition, it would be better if the child visited the school several times for a shorter duration to enable him/her to form a relationship with the teacher and also with his/her peers. In this context, they found that the pictures that the school had provided of important people (including the class teacher) and places (e.g., dining room) in the school were very useful as the child could familiarize him/herself with them over the summer prior to entering school. Chapter 4 also cited Fabian (2000) where home artifacts were used to provide emotional support to the child during transition. Peters (Chapter 5) gave examples of a reciprocal nature, where children took their kindergarten portfolios to share with their primary school teachers and peers. Teachers found these helpful in getting to know the child and his/her strengths.

Hannah et al. and Mayer et al. also discussed the importance of peer relationships during transitions. Research in the past has been inconclusive about the impact of children moving together from the same preschool setting to the same primary school (Ledger, Smith, & Rich, 2000; Margetts, 2002). Hannah et al. report that although parents perceived it was important that the child started school with some of their friends, it did not seem to have any quantifiable relationship with whether the transition was successful or not. Mayer et al. report that children who enter school with friends tend to make better gains in their academic performance and that peer rejection can lead to a negative attitude toward school. The importance of moving up with familiar peers has also been noted in other educational contexts (see Chapters 7, 11). Most importantly in all cases it has been noted that making new friends is an important concern of all children and young people when moving up (e.g., Chapters 4, 7, 11).

All three chapters in this part emphasize the importance of good communication between preschool and primary school teachers. Hannah et al. found that although it is expected that communication would be best between a primary school and its feeder nursery school, the reality was that the parents of children who thought that there was good communication between nursery and primary school came from different nurseries (including the feeder nursery of course). This was the same for parents who thought the communication was not good. It has to be remembered that these are parents' perceptions and that staff perceptions might be different. Elsewhere also, this communication between staff from different schools and other professionals has been seen as important (see, for example, Chapters 7, 8, 12).

Parent to parent relationships were reported to be important by Hannah et al. This was not only parents experiencing transition supporting each other but also parents with older children supporting parents whose first child was going to school. This is an important finding as parents and the community are a valuable resource that is underutilized and perhaps underrated. Parents can support each other emotionally but also through answering simple practical queries.

Peters (Chapter 5) examined school transitions as complex journeys where differences between the cultures of the preschool and primary school setting can mean that a child making a transition is crossing the border between two cultures. This implies that the child has to learn new rules based on the teachers' expectations and his/her own role in the new context, and he/she has to learn to 'do school.' She cites research that suggested that children who know how to 'do school' are at an advantage at school and in learning the content of schooling. This disadvantages children who might not know how to 'do school' or where the understanding is so different that they have to unlearn what they learned at home or in a preschool setting. Parents in Hannah et al. (Chapter 4) suggested that children should be given a chance to practice activities and rules that are new to them in a simulated setting, for example, learning how to place an order for school lunch before they need to do so (in the local authority of that school the norm was for children to attend primary school for half days during the first three weeks, therefore they did not stay for school lunch at the beginning).

Peters reports on the revised school curriculum in New Zealand, which was the outcome of stakeholder consultations, and resulted in a shorter core school curriculum with more freedom to schools to organize learning and teaching that is meaningful and beneficial to their pupils. This is similar to Scotland where 'A Curriculum for Excellence' has been introduced and aims to provide more freedom to schools in teaching and assessment (Chapter 4). In New Zealand, key competencies that align with the strands of the early childhood curriculum have been introduced. These are thinking; using language, symbols and texts; managing self; relating to others; and participating and contributing. It is acknowledged that these will develop over time; therefore it is hoped that post-transition more emphasis will be placed on building relationships between teacher–pupil, pupil–pupil, and teacher–parent. Peter believes this moves the focus from content only to developing key competencies where learners and teachers co-construct knowledge and learning. She presents an example of how learning stories were used to assess key competencies (see Chapter 5).

In terms of transitions, acknowledging children's prior knowledge is seen to be important. Peters cited Thomson (2002) that children bring *virtual backpacks* filled with knowledge, experiences, and dispositions, and that it is important for the teacher to open these backpacks to understand the child's strengths and potential. She reported a project where teachers used children's early childhood portfolios as a tool for opening these virtual backpacks. This is a good example of developing belonging, and fostering empowerment among the children making transition to school.

Mayer et al. introduced the dimension of socioeconomic status and report that effective transition practices are particularly important for children and families in poverty, and that they were found to moderate the effect of poverty on individual child outcomes including academic achievement (Schulting, Malone, & Dodge, 2005). According to Schulting et al. (2005) the transition practice that had the most impact on children's academic achievement was the opportunity for parents and children to visit the primary school classroom prior to transition. Also, school transition practices had a positive effect on parent involvement in schools. They suggested the necessity to offer more transition practices in schools serving low-income families.

Mayer et al. emphasize that a successful transition to primary school is important for children's early literacy development. They cite Ramey and Ramey (1999) that children who received support from parents, teachers, and school systems during the transition to primary school performed better on standardized literacy measures and that children who experience ineffective transitions to primary school were at a greater risk of experiencing difficulty in school, especially in literacy (Coyner, Reynolds, & Ou, 2003). This is supported elsewhere in terms of students' attainment at secondary school (e.g., Chapter 7).

PRIMARY TO SECONDARY TRANSITION

In this part, perspectives have been presented in the context of England, the US, and Finland. Galton has explored data and trends over 30 years in England. There is evidence of improvement in practice over the years. Finland has also introduced a comprehensive basic education curriculum to address the issue of academic and curricular aspects of transitions. In the US, pupils at this stage face two transitions, to the middle school and high school. There is evidence of curricular progression. It seems that policy and practice in terms of curricular progression has received close attention and that the educational systems have been changed to address any issues related to this.

Galton (Chapter 7), Akos (Chapter 8), and Pietarinen et al. (Chapter 9) have highlighted transition practices and activities in England, the US, and Finland respectively. These include reciprocal visits by pupils, secondary school staff visiting primary school, induction days, bridging activities, etc. Some examples of good practice and recommendations for practice have been listed later in this chapter.

Galton also listed pupils' pre- and post-transition concerns identified in the literature over the last three decades. These included personal adjusting with other pupils especially ones older than them, coping with different subjects, getting lost, adjusting to several teachers, making and retaining friendships and concerns related to new school's rules and systems. Prior to transition the most concerns were related to friendships (see also Chapters 4, 5, 6), followed by concerns about the size of school and getting lost, and third most frequently cited were concerns about harder work and coping with homework. Interestingly he reports that the latter were balanced out by identification of increased opportunities and better facilities. He reports that he found that post-transition, organizational and move-related concerns were most frequently mentioned but this time they were positive. Although at a different stage of transition, this is similar to Zhou et al. (Chapter 11) in that there are differences in expectations related to everyday life situations prior to transition which positively change post-transition. The research reviewed by Galton also suggested that concerns about peer relationships and work were still frequently cited, closely followed by concerns about various teachers. However, the nature of concern regarding work moved from ability to cope, to disappointment about the repetition of activities they had undertaken in primary school. This suggests that post-transition the concerns are to do with relationships with peers and teachers. This is similar to the ideas presented by Akos (Chapter 8) in a US, and Pietarinen et al. (Chapter 9) in a Finnish context.

Transition literature and chapters in this book have reported that a conflictual relationship with the teacher can lead to discomfort, externalizing behavior, and possible disengagement with school (Chapters 6, 8, 9). Research has suggested that pupils who are able to build good relationships with their teachers are better able to deal with transitions, and it also has a positive impact on their attainment and well-being. Perhaps in this context it is important to note that Zhou et al. reported that when Chinese postgraduate students came to study at Scottish universities, they were not the only ones who had to learn to adapt to the new educational system and pedagogical approach; the Scottish staff also had to adapt and understand Chinese students' needs to ensure that the transition was smooth. Perhaps when the transition and difference are so obvious, teachers are more aware of the need for them to adapt as well? Is there a lesson to be learnt here for all teachers?

Similar to Peters (Chapter 5) and Mayer et al. (Chapter 6), Akos has also discussed 'school's readiness,' that is, the school's capacity to respond to the students' needs. He has also discussed that transition becomes challenging for young children when leaving primary or elementary school as they feel a sense of loss at leaving teachers with whom they had secure attachments and also because they were used to the family like environment. They find it difficult to adjust to the bigger school (middle school in the case of the US with transition at the age of 10) and the less personal and more academic environment. This is similar to research in Scotland (e.g., Jindal-Snape & Foggie, 2008) and also at other educational stages (see Chapters 4, 5). Akos has pointed that this might lead to a decline in motivation, achievement, and attitudes toward school (see also Anderman, Maehr, & Midgley, 1999; Gutman & Midgley, 2000), and that this might be due to poor 'person environment fit' (see Eccles et al., 1993; Vernon-Feagans et al., 2008; see also Chapter 6).

An interesting concept discussed by Pietarinen et al. is about vertical and horizontal transitions. If we look at transitions from this point of view, even though a vertical transition might happen once when moving from one educational stage to another or even yearly in the case of gradual progression of curriculum, horizontal transition is an ongoing process as the pupil makes sense of his/her social environment and adjusts according to sometimes unpredictable changes. As mentioned earlier, Galton, Akos, and Pietarinen et al. have all reported that schools and teachers were getting good at managing vertical transition, for example through continuity in the curriculum. This has been a dimension that has been much debated and researched.

However, although some work has been done to address horizontal transitions, for example through buddy systems, meeting the teachers prior to transition, etc., this dimension needs further attention. The problem here comes due to transition being seen by some as a one off event rather than a process where children and young people have to make sense of everyday changes and relationships. Galton has written that the evidence over the last three decades in England suggests that school efforts are still focused on short term concerns of pupils and that the schools need to think longer term. To explain this he has used the example of Nicholson's (1987) work-role transition phases from the field of occupational psychology. These four phases are preparation, encounters, adjustment, and stabilization. Galton (Chapter 7) has explained how these phases are linked with school transitions and emphasizes that schools should work on bringing about adjustment and stability post-transition.

It has been interesting to note that in most countries not only pupils but also their parents are concerned more with the social and emotional aspects of transition than the academic aspects (Jindal-Snape & Foggie, 2008; also see Chapter 11 in this book). There was some contradiction, however, in terms of the evidence provided by Akos (Chapter 8) as parents from some ethnic groups in the US (especially those experiencing poverty) during transition to middle school seemed to show concerns regarding the impact of transition on academic attainment. This is similar to the research presented by Mayer and colleagues (Chapter 6) in the US but in the context of pre-school to primary school transitions and an aspect that might be worth exploring further with parents from various ethnic backgrounds.

Galton, Akos, and Pietarinen et al. have pointed to the interaction between curricular/academic aspects and emotional intelligence, well-being, self-esteem, etc. In other words, if the pupils were attaining well academically that could have an impact on their self-esteem and vice versa (see Chapter 2). This is similar to other stages of educational transitions (see Chapter 3). Pietarinen and colleagues raise an interesting dimension related to this. They have suggested that it is possible that for a pupil one aspect (e.g., good relations with peers) might be positive and the other negative (e.g., conflictual relations with the teacher) at the same time. In those circumstances, there is a conflict for a pupil and successful transition might depend on the relative strengths of the positive and negative factors (see Figure 9.1). There are elements of resilience and self-regulation at play in this context (see Chapter 2).

There is another interesting tension between continuity and discontinuity of curriculum that Galton has raised. According to him, it is important that there is enough continuity for a pupil to make that transition easily; however it should also have enough discontinuity to let the pupil feel that he/she has progressed sufficiently to enjoy a sense of achievement. This is similar to the argument presented by Jindal-Snape and Miller in Chapter 2, that the idea is not to remove the risk factors completely, but to make them manageable (see Rutter, 1987).

This also reminds the reader that transition is not always a negative experience. There are several aspects of transitions, especially at this educational stage that pupils find really positive, namely, increased choice of subjects, increased choice of meals, opportunity to make new friends, working with a range of teachers, etc. (see also Jindal-Snape & Foggie, 2008). As Akos has pointed out, it is also the period when a pupil is asserting himself/herself as an individual and exploring his/her own preferences and identity. The element of choice provides exciting opportunities for some pupils.

Other important ideas discussed in this part are of the 'active learning agency' (i.e., a capacity for intentional and responsible management of new learning), 'active participation' and/or 'feeling in control.' All three chapters have highlighted the importance of involving the pupils in the transition process (see also Chapter 10). This perhaps also leads to increase in motivation to learn and self-esteem. Galton has also emphasized that schools need to listen to the voices of the pupils. Perhaps one positive aspect of the research cited in these chapters is that the researchers have tried to listen to the voices of children, as compared to the research conducted on the transition to primary stage where only a few researchers have managed to capture the voices of very young children (e.g., Dockett & Perry, 2004).

Again, the three chapters and studies reviewed by them emphasize the importance of involving the parents in the transition process (see also Chapters 4, 6). This is important, especially if we see transitions in the context of Bronfenbrenner's (1979, 1992) ecological model and recognize the role of child–home interaction. Galton has reported that in some secondary schools in England, parents' meetings were held one year prior to the transition (although he felt this was more to do with attracting new students to their schools rather than good practice related to transitions).

Pietarinen et al. have emphasized that practitioners and researchers need to have a reciprocal dialogue to understand the entirety of basic education and school as a learning environment (see Chapter 5 for example of teachers and researchers as co-researchers). They report on the implementation of undivided basic education (UBE) in Finland which focuses on a constructivist view of learning which involves an active and collaborative nature of learning. They believe that facilitation of active learning agency requires that teachers have identified challenges and resources they have within their school community to promote vertical and horizontal coherence making. This is similar to Peters's (Chapter 5) idea of opening children's *virtual backpacks*.

SECONDARY TO POST-SCHOOL TRANSITION

The three chapters in this part have focused on different types of transitions. Zhou et al. (Chapter 11) focused on a double transition experienced by Chinese students when moving to a different country (Scotland) and a different educational system plus a different educational stage. Topping and Foggie (Chapter 10) have focused on transition of individuals seen to be vulnerable in the Scottish context, and Yaeda (Chapter 12) has focused on young people with disabilities and the employment situation in the context of Japan.

Zhou et al.'s data indicated the 'reciprocal adaptation' of the students and teachers to make transition easy for the students. There seems to be an interactionist model operating in Zhou's chapter, however, this adaptation seems to have not been due to a planned approach. It seems to have developed as a natural and organic process due to the interaction between the Chinese students and Scottish staff. However, this 'reciprocal adaptation' or readiness to adapt on the part of teachers and students can be a very important factor in making the transition process smooth for all.

In Zhou et al. an important aspect which was having an impact on transition was the language skill of the learners. Although this is in the context of somebody specifically coming from a different country, it might be relevant in the context of children and young people born and brought up in that country but from bilingual families or where English (or the language used in academic studies) is not a language used at home, irrespective of the education stage. This concurs to some extent with the research reported in Chapters 6 and 8 in an American context.

One of the important aspects of the Zhou et al. chapter is that they conceptualize transition as pedagogical, psychological, and cultural adaptation. This has implications for other within-the-country transitions. Researchers and policy makers have extensively looked at pedagogical adaptation, and in recent years the focus on psychological adaptation has increased (as can be seen in the previous chapters, e.g., Chapters 2, 3, 8). Interestingly when one thinks of students going overseas, we very quickly consider cultural adaptation; the reality is that even within the same country a child or young person has to go through 'cultural adaptation' as the organizational cultures can be very different as one moves from one stage to another (see also Chapter 5), as well as there being differences between the home and school cultures.

Another very relevant idea, which has found support in other transitions literature, is that of the ABC (Affective, Behavior, Cognitive) model (Zhou, Jindal-Snape, Topping, & Todman, 2008) and that during transition academic concerns become secondary and social concerns occupy the minds of the individuals making the transition (see the previous section). This chapter also emphasizes the multi-stage longitudinal conceptualization of transition and follows the students over a length of time before and after their move to Scotland. This can then indicate how individuals' transition experiences (positive and negative) change over time.

Zhou et al. also emphasized how expectations prior to moving up, and the reality after moving up, can be different and lead to either discomfort or pleasant experiences. This is something that has been identified in other literature during other stages of transitions (e.g., see Delamont, 1991; Jindal-Snape et al., 2006; Jindal-Snape & Foggie, 2008 about 'horror stories'). Although it should be noted that in Zhou et al. it was not what the students might have heard from others. It was based on their own perception of life and study in the UK, sometimes based on the information packs and videos provided by the universities prior to leaving China.

Similar to the parents' views in Hannah et al. (Chapter 4, preschool to primary transition) and Akos (Chapter 8, primary to middle school and high school transitions), Zhou et al. also found that students who moved to the UK as part of a group found transition to be easier than the ones who came individually. However, it was also found that there were pros and cons of coming in groups and individually. Coming as a group helped in adaptation to life in the UK, psychologically and culturally; however, the ones who came individually became better at language acquisition and also might have been better placed to seek support from staff.

Topping and Foggie, and Yaeda, focused on the professionals' role in successful post-school transition in Chapters 10 and 12. Topping and Foggie focused on a project which was systematically put in place to make sure the transition to training or college, employment, and independent living for young people who were at the risk of exclusion was smooth. The idea behind this project was that the young people would move from being 'passive recipients' to 'active learners.' They believed that as individuals became independent and 'active learners' there will be enhanced self-awareness, self-efficacy, self-regulation and resilience on the part of learners.

In Topping and Foggie's chapter, the professionals were from different professional backgrounds, such as social work, community education, careers services, higher education, and voluntary sectors. This is similar to the situation in Japan where professionals from different background are involved in the transition process. However, the main difference is that unlike in the Japanese context, in the Scottish context one individual was assigned the responsibility for working with the individual during transition. It is also important to note that guidance teachers and in some cases, such as in Scotland, community link workers and educational psychologists have worked with class teachers and head teachers to facilitate transitions at other stages of educational transitions.

Topping and Foggie report that the key workers in their study perceived that more than two thirds of the young people had developed or maintained adequate independence skills, but found that key workers were not using interactive behaviors that could promote independence skills in the young people. Not surprisingly this was different from the perception of key workers who thought they were using independence promoting behavior in their interactions with the young people. Also, they report that the key workers did not seem to have any exit strategies in place. This raises the question that despite their perception of relevant transferable skills being developed or maintained, either the transition key workers perceived that these young people could not function without them or they themselves were not ready to let go. As Topping and Foggie suggest this could be due to people behaving differently when being observed. However, it could equally be due to lack of appropriate training in this area. They have suggested that pre-service and continuing professional development (CPD) training should be provided to transition key workers. This is similar to Yaeda's view regarding the need for adequate training provision in Japan.

In his chapter, Yaeda has argued for a more systematic and planned approach to transition in Japan. This, perhaps, is something that everybody will agree with and has been highlighted in other chapters in this book (e.g., Chapters 4, 5, 6, 7, 8, 9). Again similar to other authors (Akos, Chapter 8), Yaeda has argued for transition planning to start at an early stage and for it to continue well after the child or young person has moved on; in Japan it is happening as early as three years prior to and three years after transition from secondary school. This suggests aspects of horizontal transition (Chapter 9) as well as a focus on transition as a process.

Yaeda has also emphasized the importance of collaboration amongst professionals, which in the Japanese context of 'WA' might be an unspoken collaboration. Other authors have also indicated the need for good collaboration and effective communication amongst professionals and this has been across other educational contexts as well (e.g., Chapters 4, 5, 6, 7).

Topping and Foggie, Zhou et al., and Yaeda, all have, explicitly or implicitly, emphasized the importance of certain skills and qualities on the part of professionals involved in transition. These can be summarized as readiness to change and adapt, developing trust, listening, patience, confidence building, enthusiasm, optimism, interest in the learner, empathy, awareness of the learners' needs and context, etc. These again are applicable at all stages of transition.

TRENDS ACROSS ALL STAGES OF EDUCATIONAL TRANSITIONS

It is clear from the previous parts that certain aspects are not only common to one educational stage or country, they are found across all stages, countries, and contexts. To summarize, amongst others, the key aspects that were discussed earlier are:

   i. Most authors in this book have conceptualized transition as a process rather than a one-off event, with ongoing adaptations on the part of the child/young person.
  ii. It is important that children/young people are actively involved in the transition planning and preparation, and should feel in control.
 iii. Although research regarding the impact of peers moving up to the same educational setting is inconclusive, there is enough evidence to suggest that peers from one setting should be given an opportunity to move together into the new setting.
  iv. Transition has an impact not only on the child/young person but also his/her family. Families experience joys and anxieties during their child's transitions. They should also be provided support so that not only are they able to deal with the transition themselves but also so that they can be actively involved in making the transition smooth for the child.

    v. The community can also play a significant part in transitions and readiness to learn.

   vi. Professionals play an important role in supporting children and parents during transitions. However, it is possible that their own needs, especially training needs, have not been identified.

  vii. Curricular continuity is important. Some countries have changed their curriculum and educational systems radically to achieve this. However, it is important to have some discontinuity with the child/young person feeling a sense of progression and achievement.

 viii. For some individuals choices and changes can be overwhelming, however others might excel in that situation.

   ix. Research suggests that there can be a dip in academic attainment during transitions and that effective transition practice can support academic achievement.

    x. Individuals experiencing transitions are sometimes more focused on social and emotional aspects of transitions, especially in the short term.

   xi. Supportive teachers and schools make the transition experience positive for learners.

  xii. Communication between teachers from different schools, other professionals such as counselors and teachers, between teachers and parents, teachers and students, and students and students is very important and can play a big part in determining whether a transition is smooth or not.

 xiii. The theoretical conceptualizations are similar, with the most frequently cited ones being resilience, self-esteem, self-efficacy, emotional intelligence, well-being, attachment theory, self-regulation, ecological systems theory, maturational model, interactions model, motivation, and social interaction.

 xiv. The change in the school/university/work place culture, size of school/university/work place and number of teachers/other professionals, concerns about ability to do higher level academic work, lack of familiarity, and difference in systems and structures can all lead to concerns during transitions. Adequate information and exposure to these prior to transition can alleviate some concerns.

  xv. Some individuals experience differences in expectations prior to transitions and the reality post-transition. These can be both positive and negative. It is important to provide accurate information to bridge the gap between expectations and reality.

 xvi. The debate about readiness has moved from the child/young person to the readiness of the educational and employing organizations' to adapt to the individual's unique needs.

xvii. Systematic and planned transition, which starts several months prior to the transition and carries on for several months post-transition, has been emphasized.

xviii. Most countries have been responsive to the impact of transitions and this is reflected in their educational policy and systems. However, the emphasis has mainly been on the continuity of the curriculum and there is a need to take more account of the psychological and social aspects of transition.

xix. There has been an improvement in transitions practice across all settings and countries. However, more work is required to improve the transition activities and programs. In some contexts, there was evidence of identified and trained transitions personnel. However, this was not always the case.

xx. There has been an increase in research on educational transitions. However, some areas need further research and it is important to involve practitioners in research.

IMPLICATIONS FOR PRACTICE

In terms of transition planning and preparation, all chapters in the book have emphasized the importance of good quality transition activities and programs. According to some it should start several months (approximately 6 months) prior to transition and carry on for some months post-transition (perhaps another 6 months), and some even over some years. According to others, as transition is a dynamic process with changing roles and relationships between the individual and peers, and individual and teachers/professionals, it is important to focus on transition activities throughout the educational life span. The important thing to consider is the need of an individual and providing support as long as required.

A holistic approach to education is required to ensure emphasis is not on academic goals alone, and that holistic educational goals are considered. This will help with the development of well-being and transition. It is important for stakeholders to conceptualize 'readiness' to learn or to move on within an ecological framework. This will lead to a more holistic overview of factors related to transition and consideration of how significant others in that individual's environment can facilitate smooth transitions.

There has been evidence that even within the same country and the same city, children and young people experience differences in school/organizational culture. It seems that professionals are more aware of the need for reciprocal cultural adaptation when they are with students who have come from overseas. It is important that professionals realize that organizational cultures that the individual is used to can be very different and more attempts should be made to understand what the individual has brought in his/her *virtual backpack*. This will not only help the individual feel accepted and valued; it will also help the professionals recognize the individual's strengths and help understand him/her better. However, for this to happen, professionals will require flexibility and space in the curriculum.

Several examples of good transition practice across the world and suggestions of what can be done have been presented in the book. Some of these are:

   i. Galton (Chapter 7) discussed five bridges of transition and bridging units as part of local pyramids which are meaningful to children/ young people and staff in their own context. He gives the example of 'who killed the chef' and how teachers were able to plan progression in the activities children undertook in primary and secondary schools.

   ii. Induction days, whether a day long or over several shorter sessions, were found to be useful in different contexts and educational stages. Galton cites a child who suggested that it is a good idea to organize activities where children can work in small groups, such as being given a map to work together and treasure hunt different parts of the school.

   iii. Parental involvement was important not only during their own child's transition but also to support other parents whose children might be making a transition. This can be facilitated by face to face meetings but also through online web forums where parents can discuss any concerns and get simple practical queries answered.

   iv. Artifacts or portfolios from the previous educational setting to the new one were used for emotional support of the individual as well as providing the professionals with an indication of the individual's strengths and interests to build upon.

   v. Using information packs that are meaningful not only to the parents/ carers but also the child/young person, for example, through photographs of significant others and places in the new context.

   vi. Sharing pedagogy across schools and other educational contexts can be one way forward. This could also involve team teaching and sharing of ideas, practice and resources.

   vii. Akos (Chapter 8) suggested that it is useful to prepare and document transition plans, and review and monitor them periodically.

   viii. Another suggestion was to create transition teams in the district and the school to enable the development and implementation of a systematic transition program.

   ix. Several authors suggested involving the child as an active learner and participant in the transition process through learning stories and other creative means.

   x. Examples were provided of teachers and other practitioners working with researchers and undertaking action research to improve their practice related to transitions.

   xi. Akos identified that it was important that educational transitions are in line with developmental transitions of an individual.

xii. It is evident from several chapters that it is important to undertake staff training needs assessment in the context of transitions.

xiii. It is suggested that we research, evaluate, and document transition program effectiveness on an ongoing basis.

xiv. Adeyemo (Chapter 3) has detailed an emotional intelligence intervention and how it can be used to facilitate effective transitions.

xv. It is suggested that prior to transition, children/young people are involved in simulated role-play, drama, storytelling to provide opportunities to express their transition concerns and tackle them in a secure and familiar environment (Jindal-Snape, Vettraino, Lowson, & McDuff, under review).

xvi. Having named transitional professionals was seen to be effective.

xvii. Information passed from one stage to another should not only be about academic attainment. It should also include personal and social factors that might have an impact on the individual during transitions.

xviii. Secure attachments opportunities should be provided through buddy system or guidance and counseling staff, especially for individuals who might not have supportive networks at home or in the community.

Further examples and details of the previously-mentioned examples are available in Chapters 2 to 12.

IMPLICATIONS FOR FUTURE RESEARCH

Research related to transition from preschool to primary school has mainly focused on the perspective of professionals and parents with limited research on children's perspectives (e.g., Dockett & Perry, 2004; Fabian, 2000). Future research needs to focus on listening to the voices of children. The nature and ethics of such research has to be carefully thought through. Innovative ways of collecting data will have to be considered, perhaps using the Mosaic Approach (Clark & Moss, 2001, 2008), which uses different ways of collecting data such as giving children disposable cameras, through stories, etc. Again there are issues about securing informed consent from children in the age group of 3 to 6 years. However, none of these are insurmountable issues and researchers really need to engage with very young children to gather their perspectives to not only understand their unique experiences but also to ensure that they are active participants in determining transition practice and programs.

Longitudinal studies across one stage of transition have been undertaken (e.g., Jindal-Snape & Foggie, 2008; Zhou et al., 2008). However, to the best of this author's knowledge, no longitudinal studies across different educational transitions have been published. The chapters in this book and the research they have reviewed suggest that if the child is experiencing problems prior to transition, transition would be more difficult or there is a higher risk of things going wrong. However, nobody has any evidence to say what happens when one transition goes wrong or is difficult and what, if any, is the impact on other transitions. If a child experiences discomfort when staring primary school, would that experience teach him/her and the parents how to negotiate the future transitions or would it set them up for further problems? There is some evidence that things settle for most pupils a few months after a transition, however it is not clear what the trend is for those who are unable to cope with that transition for a long time. What can we do as professionals or parents to support the child/young person through those transitional problems? Do problems encountered during one transition trigger the need for more structured and planned work with that individual during any future transitions?

There is an emphasis on passing information from one professional to another in a different setting—and let's say this is done, for example, between the preschool staff and primary teacher. What about the communication between the teachers who work with the same child in the first and last year of primary school—do they communicate about past transitional issues and its possible impact on future transition? And for that matter, should they? The same applies to professionals working in the first year and last year of secondary school. In this context it might be even more challenging as several teachers work with one child/young person. None of these questions can be answered without longitudinal research. However, how feasible is longitudinal research across an entire educational lifespan of an individual? Who will fund it? Who will conduct it? Is it too ambitious? Nonetheless, it is really crucial to get the entire picture. The answers to all those contradictory questions are important for us to understand educational transition better.

In Chapter 3 Adeyemo presents empirical data to show that emotional intelligence is an important psychosocial process during transition. Other research has also looked at self-efficacy (Eccles & Midgely, 1989). However, rigorous research needs to be conducted to investigate the role of resilience and the two-dimensional theory of self-esteem and how they are affected during the transitions process or have an effect on successful adaptation during transitions. Also, it is important to research the development of self-esteem in young children and its role in the early years transitions.

Akos has reported findings from his previous research (Akos & Galassi, 2004) that suggest that during transitions, ethnicity and gender of the pupil play a part. The findings suggest that whether they externalize or internalize their stress is gender related. Mayer et al. have also referred to gender and ethnicity in their chapter. However, as very few studies across the world have looked at the gender and ethnicity of the child/young person and the ethnicity of parents when understanding their perceptions of transitions, future research should explore this.

As mentioned earlier it is not clear whether all professionals are getting adequate training and support in the context of transitions. It is important to conduct a training needs assessment and to identify how these professionals can be supported.

IMPLICATIONS FOR POLICY

Several countries, such as the US and Finland, have aligned their educational system and curriculum to the individual's developmental stages and needs within the context. New Zealand has moved to competencies, giving an opportunity to celebrate and build on the diverse strengths of the learners. Similarly, e.g., in Scotland, there is an emphasis on the involvement of parents in their child's education and the life of school through the Scottish Schools (Parental Involvement) Act 2006 (Scottish Government, 2006). It is important to learn from each other's educational policies to see how they might be applicable to our own context.

In Chapters 10 and 12 a case has been made that key transition personnel working with young people with disabilities should be provided appropriate transition related training. This does raise an important question at other stages and in other contexts. In these two chapters, when individuals had identified support needs, transition planning was put in place and either one or a range of transition professionals worked with that individual. As these were identified professionals a case has been made for adequate training for them. What about numerous teachers and professionals involved in transitions at all stages of educational transition? They might be involved not because they are the 'transition experts or professionals' but because they happen to be the class teacher of the first or last year of primary or secondary school. We need to question whether the early years and initial teacher training programs provide adequate training related to transitions work. What about higher education professionals or employers? Are we making a fuss about nothing as most individuals successfully manage transitions? Or are we identifying that there is a need for better transition related training for all professionals? We know that in terms of management in organizations, several training programs and indeed higher degrees focus on managing organizational change. Is this what we are looking for in education related programs? Some teacher training programs do provide this as a component of training. However, what is required is a more discreet element of this in the prequalifying and CPD training. It is imperative for the educational policy across the world to consider these issues and identify how these can be implemented in their own context.

The policy emphasis on curricular continuity is evident. More focus is required on other aspects of educational life, especially those that have an impact on psychological and cultural adaptation.

Chapter 6 reports on Head Start research in the US, which looked at what provision can be put in place, especially prior to formal schooling, to support families and communities (especially the ones in poverty), to provide a child with rich experiences that can support his/her learning and readiness to learn in a formal context. This remains an important area to investigate further. Similar consideration should be given to children/young people who have other support needs due to disabilities or from bilingual families.

In this chapter, I have made an attempt to capture some snapshots of the journey I went through when reading the other chapters. This is, by no means, a complete picture. There are several gems in the previous chapters that I have not had the space to highlight here. Hopefully for the readers who started their journey with this chapter, there is enough information to signpost them to all the exciting places they can go to in this book. For the readers who came to this at the end, I hope this chapter provides confirmation to some of their own thoughts. Either way, hopefully this book has given you some new insights into transition-related theory, research, practice, and policy (as applied to different educational stages and in different countries), which will help you think of ways in which you can apply these to your own context and make a positive difference to the quality of transition experience of the individuals you work with.

REFERENCES

Akos, P., & Galassi, J. (2004). Gender and race as factors in psychosocial adjustment to middle and high school. *The Journal of Educational Research, 98*(2), 102–108.

Anderman, E., Maehr, M., & Midgley, C. (1999). Declining motivation after the transition to middle school: Schools can make a difference. *Journal of Research and Development in Education, 32,* 131–147.

Bronfenbrenner, U. (1979). *The ecology of human development. Experiments by nature and design.* Cambridge, MA: Harvard University Press.

Bronfenbrenner, U. (1992). Ecological systems theory. In R. Vasta (Ed.), *Six theories of child development* (pp. 187–249). London and Philadelphia: Jessica Kingsley Publishers.

Clark, A., & Moss, P. (2001). *Listening to young children: The Mosaic Approach.* London, UK: National Children's Bureau Enterprises Ltd.

Clark, A., & Moss, P. (2008). *Spaces to play: More listening to young children using the Mosaic Approach.* London, UK: National Children's Bureau Enterprises Ltd.

Coyner, L., Reynolds, A., & Ou, S. (2003). The effect of early childhood interventions on subsequent special education services: Findings from the Chicago Child–Parent Centers. *Education Evaluation and Policy Analysis, 25*(1), 75–95.

Delamont, S. (1991). The hit list and other horror stories. *Sociological Review, 39*(2), 238–59.

Dockett, S., & Perry, B. (2004). Starting school: Perspectives of Australian children, parents and educators. *Journal of Early Childhood Research, 2*(2), 171–189.

Eccles, J. S., & Midgley, C. (1989). Stage-environment fit: Developmentally appropriate classrooms for young adolescents. In C. Ames & R. Ames (Eds.), *Research on motivation in education: Goals and cognitions,* Vol. 3 (pp. 139–186). New York: Academic Press.

Eccles, J. S., Wigfield, A., Midgley, C., Reuman, D., Mac Iver, D. J., & Feldlaufer, H. (1993). Negative effects of traditional middle schools on students' motivation. *The Elementary School Journal, 93*, 1553–1574.

Fabian, H. (2000). Small steps to starting school. *International Journal of Early Years Education, 8*(2), 141–153.

Fabian, H., & Dunlop, A. (2005). The importance of play in the transition to school. In J. R. Moyles (Ed.), *The excellence of play, 2nd ed*, (228–241). Berkshire: Open University.

Ford, J., & Gledhill, T. (2002). Does season of birth matter? The relationship between age within the school year (season of birth) and educational difficulties among a representative general population of children and adolescents (aged 5–15) in Great Britain. *Research in Education, 68*, 41–47.

Gutman, L. M., & Midgley, C. (2000). The role of protective factors in supporting the academic achievement of poor African American students during the middle school transition. *Journal of Youth and Adolescence, 29*(2), 223–248.

Jindal-Snape, D., Douglas, W., Topping, K. J., Kerr, C., & Smith, E. F. (2006). Autistic spectrum disorders and primary–secondary transition. *International Journal of Special Education, 21*(2), 18–31. Retrieved April 24, 2009, from http://www.internationalsped.com/documents/03Jindalsnape.doc.

Jindal-Snape, D., & Foggie, J. (2008). A holistic approach to primary–secondary transitions. *Improving Schools, 11*, 5–18.

Jindal-Snape, D., Vettraino, E., Lowson, A., & McDuff, W. (under review). Using drama to facilitate primary–secondary transition. *Education 3–13*.

Ledger, E., Smith, A. B., & Rich, P. (2000). Friendship over the transition from early childhood centre to school. *International Journal of Early Years Education, 8*(1), 57–69.

Luthar, S. S. (2006). Resilience in development: A synthesis of research across five decades. In D. Cicchetti & D. J. Cohen (Eds.), *Developmental psychopathology: Risk, disorder, and adaptation* (pp. 739–795). New York: Wiley.

Margetts, K. (2002). Transition to school: Complexity and diversity. *European Early Childhood Education Research Journal, 10*(2), 103–114.

Mruk, C. (1999). *Self-esteem: Research, theory and practice*. London: Free Association Books.

Newman, B. M., Lohman, B. J., Newman, P. R., Myers, M. C., & Smith, V. L. (2000). Experiences of urban youth navigating the transition to ninth grade. *Youth & Society, 31*(4), 387–416.

Newman, T., & Blackburn, S. (2002). *Transitions in the lives of children and young people: Resilience factors*. Edinburgh: Scottish Executive Education Department.

Nicholson, N. (1987). The transition cycle: A conceptual framework for the analysis of change and human resources management. *Research in Personnel and Human Resources Management, 5*, 167–222.

Ramey, S. L., & Ramey, C. T. (1999). *Going to school*. New York: Goddard Press.

Rutter, M. (1987). Psychosocial resilience and protective mechanisms. *American Journal of Orthopsychiatry, 57*, 316–31.

Schulting, A. B., Malone, P. S., & Dodge, K. A. (2005). The effect of school-based kindergarten transition policies and practices on child academic outcomes. *Developmental Psychology, 41*, 860–871.

Scottish Government. (2006). *Scottish schools (Parental Involvement) Act 2006 asp8*. Retrieved March 13, 2009, from http://www.opsi.gov.uk/legislation/scotland/acts2006/pdf/asp_20060008_en.pdf.

Stipek, D. (2002). At what age should children enter kindergarten? A question for policy makers and parents [Electronic version]. *Society for Research in Child Development Social Policy Report, 16*(2), 3–17.

Thomson, P. (2002). *Schooling the rustbelt kids: Making the difference in changing times*. Sydney: Allen & Unwin.

Vernon-Feagans, L., Odom, E., Panscofar, N., & Kainz, K. (2008). Comments on Farkas and Hibel: A transactional/ecological model of readiness and inequality. In A. Booth & A. C. Crouter (Eds.), *Disparities in school readiness* (pp. 61–78). New York: Lawrence Erlbaum Associates.

Wesley, P. (2001). *Smooth moves to kindergarten*. Chapel Hill: Chapel Hill Training Outreach Project Incorporated.

Zhou, Y., Jindal-Snape, D., Topping, K. J., & Todman, J. (2008). Theoretical models of culture shock and adaptation in international students in higher education. *Studies in Higher Education, 33*, 63–75.

Contributors

Dr. Divya Jindal-Snape is a senior lecturer in the School of Education, Social Work and Community Education at the University of Dundee, UK. She has experience of working in primary and secondary schools, and higher education in different countries. Her research interests lie in the field of educational transitions and inclusion. A significant proportion of her work has been with children and young people with additional support needs, especially children and young people with visual impairment, autism, learning difficulties, and emotional and behavioral needs. This has also involved developing social interaction through drama techniques and other forms of creative arts education. http://www.dundee.ac.uk/eswce/staff/djindalsnape.php

School of Education, Social Work and Community Education,
University of Dundee,
Nethergate, Dundee DD1 4HN, UK
Telephone: +44-1382 381472
Fax: +44-1382 381511
d.jindalsnape@dundee.ac.uk

Dr. David A. Adeyemo is a senior lecturer in the Department of Guidance and Counselling, Faculty of Education, University of Ibadan, Ibadan, Nigeria. He holds a bachelor of arts in education from the University of Ife, and a master of education and a doctor of philosophy in counseling psychology from the University of Ibadan, Nigeria. He has published extensively in local and international journals with several chapters in books. He has close to 60 publications to his credit. His current area of research interest is on the application of emotional intelligence to educational and career development issues

Department of Guidance and Counselling,
University of Ibadan, Ibadan, Nigeria
drdaadeyemo@yahoo.co.uk

Dr. Patrick Akos is an associate professor of school counseling in the School of Education at the University of North Carolina at Chapel Hill. He is a former college, elementary, and middle school counselor and was recognized in 2004 as the American School Counselor Association's Counselor Educator of the Year. Dr. Akos's research focuses on the transition into and out of middle school and Strengths-Based School Counseling. Currently, his research continues on how school personnel can promote successful transitions and how school counselors can intervene and advocate for optimal development of early adolescents. More information can be located at: http://www.unc.edu/depts/ed/med_sch_counseling/faculty.html.

Box #3500—SOE,
School of Education,
University of North Carolina,
Chapel Hill, NC 27599, USA
Telephone: +1 (919) 843-4758
pta@unc.edu

Dr. Steve J. Amendum is an assistant professor of literacy education at North Carolina State University. He teaches courses on literacy research and methods in the elementary education undergraduate and masters programs. His research focuses on early literacy intervention for struggling learners, literacy issues for multilingual learners, and classroom-based literacy instruction reform efforts. As a former K–2 multiage teacher and literacy coach, Dr. Amendum's research interests are grounded in classroom experiences and exchanges with students and teachers in diverse classroom and school settings.

Department of Elementary Education,
College of Education,
North Carolina State University,
317K Poe Hall, CB 7801,
Raleigh, NC 27695-7801, USA
Telephone: +1 (919) 513-2809
Fax: +1 (919) 513-0919
steve_amendum@ncsu.edu

Jocelyn Foggie was a research assistant in the School of Education, Social Work and Community Education at the University of Dundee, Scotland. She now works for the Fairbridge charity (http://www.fairbridge.org.uk) supporting young people to develop their confidence, motivation, and personal and social skills.

Fairbridge in Dundee,
1b Kemback Street,

Dundee, DD4 6ET, UK
Telephone: +44-1382 451500.
ifoggie@hotmail.com

Professor Maurice Galton is a former professor and Dean of Education at the University of Leicester. He is now Senior Research Fellow in the Centre for Commonwealth Education at the University of Cambridge. He is best known for his studies of teaching in the primary and lower secondary school, including his latest research on the use of group work and his work on transition.

Faculty of Education,
University of Cambridge,
184 Hills Road,
Cambridge CB2 8PQ, UK
Telephone: +44-1223 767512
mg266@cam.ac.uk

Heather Gorton has worked as an educational psychologist for 14 years in three different local authorities in the UK. Currently she works for Edinburgh City Council and has a particular interest in early years work. She is generic psychologist to two stand alone nurseries, a child and family center and chairs a service working group in this area. Moving from an English to a Scottish context she has become interested in the increased flexibility that there is in school starting age in Scotland. She hopes to find out more about the impact of this through her study toward a professional doctorate in educational psychology at the University of Dundee.

5 Corrennie Drive,
Edinburgh, EH10 6EQ, UK
Telephone: +44-131 447 0974
gortons@blueyonder.co.uk

Dr. Elizabeth Hannah is a chartered educational psychologist. Currently, she is employed as a teaching fellow at the University of Dundee and as a Depute Principal Educational Psychologist in a local authority psychological service in Scotland. Her research interests include autism spectrum disorder, educational transitions, education in the early years, researching the views of children, and promoting mental health and wellbeing.

School of Education, Social Work and Community Education,
University of Dundee,
Nethergate, Dundee, DD1 4HN, UK
Telephone: +44-1382 381400
e.hannah@dundee.ac.uk

Dr. Kelley L. Mayer is an assistant professor of early childhood education in the Department of Teacher Education at the College of Charleston. Dr. Mayer teaches courses on early childhood development, early literacy, and research methods. Her research focuses on teacher–child relationships and children's writing in preschool and the primary grades. Before completing her doctoral work she taught kindergarten for 5 years in a public school setting just outside of Washington, D.C.

Department of Teacher Education,
School of Education, Health, and Human Performance,
College of Charleston,
66 George Street, Charleston, SC 29424, USA
Telephone: +1 (843) 953-7372
Fax: +1 (843) 953-8109
mayerk@cofc.edu

Dr. David J. Miller taught in state schools in the UK and abroad before embarking on a career in higher education. He has since worked in teacher education in Aberdeen and is now senior lecturer in education at the University of Dundee. His interests centre on self-perceptions, classroom interactions, and the use of games in learning.

School of Education, Social Work and Community Education,
University of Dundee,
Nethergate, Dundee DD1 4HN, UK
Telephone: +44-1382 381400
d.j.miller@dundee.ac.uk

Dr. Sally Peters is a senior lecturer at the University of Waikato, New Zealand. She has a background in early childhood education and a particular interest in children's development from 0–8 years. Her membership of the reference group for Te Marautanga o Aotearoa/New Zealand Curriculum Project, and her PhD work on transition to school, led to a number of research projects working collaboratively with teachers to explore pedagogy that is designed to develop 'key competencies' and learning dispositions over time, and to investigate ways to enhance 'border crossing' between home, early childhood education, and school. Her current projects include a review of literature on starting school in New Zealand, and research exploring young children's working theories and the ways in which they make sense of their world.

Department of Human Development and Counselling,
University of Waikato,
Private Bag 3105,

Hamilton 3240, New Zealand
Telephone: + 64 7 856 2889 ex 8386
speters@waikato.ac.nz

Dr. Janne Pietarinen is a senior researcher in the Faculty of Education at the University of Joensuu. His research interests include learning, agency, and well-being in basic education and educational transitions in youths' life course.

Faculty of Education,
P.O.BOX 111 (Tulliportinkatu 1),
University of Joensuu, FIN-80101, Finland
Telephone: +358 50 465 0642
janne.pietarinen@joensuu.fi

Dr. Kirsi Pyhältö is a pedagogical university lecturer in higher education at the Centre for Research and Development in Higher Education, Helsinki University. Her research interests include postgraduate education, learning and professional development in higher education, and agency and well-being in basic education.

Centre for Research and Development of Higher Education (YTY),
Faculty of Behavioural Sciences,
P.O.BOX 9 (Siltavuorenpenger 20),
University of Helsinki, FIN-00014, Finland
Telephone: +358 50 41 50132
kirsi.pyhalto@helsinki.fi

Dr. Tiina Soini is a senior researcher in the Department of Teacher Education, in the University of Tampere. Her research interests include learning, agency, and well-being in basic education, and transfer of learning and professional development in higher education, especially in doctoral training.

Department of Teacher Education,
Faculty of Education,
University of Tampere, FIN-33014, Finland
Telephone: +358 50 350 1188
tiina.soini@uta.fi

Professor John Todman was emeritus professor of applied cognitive psychology in the School of Psychology at the University of Dundee, where he lectured on individual differences and research methods for 30 years. He published extensively in the areas of computer-aided communication, computer anxiety, education, and social psychology.

Professor Keith J. Topping is professor of educational and social research in the School of Education at the University of Dundee, where he mainly researches peer learning. He has published over 130 peer reviewed journal papers, 40 chapters, and 17 books. His work has been translated into 11 languages. Further details at www.dundee.ac.uk/eswce/staff/kjtoppong.php.

School of Education, Social Work and Community Education,
University of Dundee,
Nethergate, Dundee DD1 4HN, UK
Telephone: +44-1382 383000
k.j.topping@dundee.ac.uk

Dr. Lynne Vernon-Feagans is the William C. Friday Distinguished Professor of Human Development and Psychological Studies in the School of Education and coordinator of the doctoral program in Early Childhood, Intervention and Literacy in the School of Education at the University of North Carolina at Chapel Hill. Dr. Vernon-Feagans is principal investigator of a 10-year program project from NICHD that is examining the risk and protective factors for a birth cohort of 1,300 children who live in poor rural areas of this country. Dr Vernon-Feagans is also the co-principal investigator of the National Research Center on Rural Education Support, which was established by a grant from the US Department of Education to work toward improved teaching, learning, and student achievement in rural schools nationwide. She is the author of numerous books as well as the author of over 100 articles and chapters on children at risk.

The University of North Carolina at Chapel Hill,
School of Education,
CB# 3500, Peabody Hall,
Chapel Hill, NC 27599-3500, USA
Telephone: +1 (919) 843-5623
Fax: +1 (919) 843-1533
lynnevf@email.unc.edu

Dr. Jun Yaeda is an associate professor of the Graduate School of Comprehensive Human Sciences, University of Tsukuba in Japan. He has published extensively in the area of vocational rehabilitation. Currently he is the chair of the international division and an editorial board member of Japan Society of Vocational Rehabilitation, and the president of Japan Rehabilitation Counseling Association.

Masters & Doctoral Rehabilitation Program Lifespan,
Developmental Science,
Graduate School of Comprehensive Human Sciences,

University of Tsukuba,
3-29-1 Bunkyo, Otsuka, Tokyo 112-0012, Japan
Telephone: +81-90-4091-8014
jyaeda@human.tsukuba.ac.jp

Dr. Yuefang Zhou is a Chinese national with extensive experience of second-language teaching in China. She was awarded an MSc with distinction in applied research methods in 2003 and a PhD on "Processes of cultural pedagogical shock and adaptation of Chinese postgraduate students in the UK" in 2006, both by the University of Dundee. She is currently working in the Bute Medical School, University of St. Andrews.

Bute Medical School,
University of St. Andrews,
St. Andrews, Fife, KY16 9TS, UK
Telephone: +44-1334 462018
yz10@st-andrews.ac.uk

Index